My Musical World

A Lifetime in Music

[Handwritten inscription: To Doug, With best wishes and I hope you enjoy "My Musical World" Yours faithfully, J Fox]

John Fox, ARCM

Eloquent Books

Copyright 2009
All rights reserved — John Fox, ARCM

No part of this book may be reproduced or transmitted in any form or by any means, graphic, electronic, or mechanical, including photocopying, recording, taping, or by any information storage retrieval system, without the permission, in writing, from the publisher.

Eloquent Books
An imprint of Strategic Book Group
P.O. Box 333
Durham CT 06422
www.StrategicBookGroup.com

ISBN: 978-1-60860-302-2

Printed in the United States of America

This book is dedicated to my dear sister Judy who during the early years helped me so much right up to the time of her passing in 2007. I miss her very much.

Contents

Acknowledgments vii
Chapter 1—The Beginnings. 1
Chapter 2—Those Dangerous Teen Years. 9
Chapter 3—First Love 13
Chapter 4—Life in the RAF Playing Piano 15
Chapter 5—Atomic Bomb—War Over! 21
Chapter 6—Making Up for Lost Time! 25
Chapter 7—Successful College Days 29
Chapter 8—Sally Barnes—Marriage to Jackie—Big Bands 33
Chapter 9—About Religion and Songwriting 41
Chapter 10—Serious Composing and Arranging 43
Chapter 11—Teaching and My Trip to Krakow 63
Chapter 12—BBC Orchestras and Solo Piano. 67
Chapter 13—Grand Hotel Eastbourne and Dangerous Journeys. 73
Chapter 14—BBC Radio Orchestra and Female Vocalist, Joy Devon 79
Chapter 15—Arranging 85
Chapter 16—BBC Recording of "George Gershwin" 87
Chapter 17—Jackie and Joy. 91
Chapter 18—A Dangerous Mission! 97
Chapter 19—The Loss of Jackie and Taly. 101
Chapter 20—The Loss of Mum and a Vision 105
Chapter 21—Marriage to Joy and a Wonderful U.S. Contract 129
Chapter 22—The French Grand Piano and Something Rather Fishy! 135
Chapter 23—The Royal Bath "Classy Gig" and a Comedy Situation! . . . 139
Chapter 24—Memories of Tigger and Benjie 143
Chapter 25—Rain Fantasia—Selections and Television 147
Chapter 26—My Special Joy, Music in East Germany and Richard's
   Baton Case. 153
Chapter 27—Prostate Problem and Loss of Pets 163

Chapter 28—The Loss of Lee 167
Chapter 29—Puerto Pollensa and "Sad Occasions" 171
Chapter 30—Robert Farnon Society and a Popular French Songwriter .. 175
Chapter 31—English Folk Songs and English Pastoral Music 181
Chapter 32—The BBC Producers 183
Chapter 33—A Dangerous Week in Belfast 187
Chapter 34—Joy's Migraines and a Fantastic Concert 191
Chapter 35—Good News—Then Bad News 195
Chapter 36—Composing for Piano—Bill—and All Saints Church 199
Chapter 37—The Tragic Death of Maureen 203
Chapter 38—Jamie—Sophie—and Our Neighbours 205
Chapter 39—Redundancy of the BBC Orchestras—Librarians and
  Copyists 207
Chapter 40—Farewell to Maida Vale 3 213
Chapter 41—Musicals Here and in the United States 215
Chapter 42—The 100-Year-Old Concert Pianist and Marion 221
Chapter 43—Changes in the Turn of the Century 241
Chapter 44—Another John Fox Connected with Harold Turner's
  Niece! 245
Chapter 45—Philip Lane and Gavin Sutherland 247
Chapter 46—Country Talk 249
Chapter 47—"Comedy Situations" 253
Chapter 48—Classical Arrangements and Holiday Disaster! 257
Chapter 49—The Saddest Occasion—The Loss of Joy 261
Chapter 50—The Light Blue Estate Car—The Colour of Joy's Eyes ... 271
Chapter 51—"Love of Joy"—My Promised Suite for Full Orchestra ... 293
Chapter 52—Loneliness—Perpetua—Spongebob Squarepants! 297
Chapter 53—"A Surrey Rhapsody" 303
Chapter 54—Marriage to Perpetua 307
Chapter 55—Conductors and Special Musicians 315
Chapter 56—Classical Composer 319
Chapter 57—English Composers, American Jazz and Musical 325
Chapter 58—Hugh's Courage and Jam Sessions 331
Chapter 59—Concert for Princess Diana 335
Chapter 60—Friends and Artists 339
Chapter 61—Wishes and Hopes 347
Chapter 62—Is Light Music Going into Oblivion? 351
Chapter 63—Fond Memories of the Past 353
Chapter 64—The Sad Death of Judy 355
Chapter 65—Carol Fantasia with a Mishap 359
Chapter 66—Peps, the Zimbabwean Crisis and the Archbishop of
  Canterbury 363
Chapter 67—Notes of South Africa 367
Chapter 68—Grand Finale 373

Acknowledgments

The writing of my memoirs has been a wonderful journey, at times joyful and full of laughter as I recalled days of happiness and the many comedic situations throughout my life and at times very painful when memories I would rather forget were brought to the surface. But it was essential if I was to tell my life story not just as a composer, arranger and conductor who had been given a gift to share with millions of people the world over but as a man who has faced adversity in his personal life.

However without the help and support of several friends and family, I could not have made this musical and personal journey. Firstly, my deep, deep and heartfelt thanks go to Perpetua, my wife, who first suggested I should write this book and whose unfailing love, constant help, patience and encouragement has been a Godsend throughout the whole project. It goes without saying that what she has endured during this time living with a composer and his artistic temperament has been indeed truly remarkable.

Of course, writing this book has taken me some time and I had the invaluable help from three of Pepsi's close friends. Pauline Machache, a charming lovely lady, took on the mammoth task of typing most of my handwritten notes from hundreds of pages or transcribing the tapes from my Dictaphone. Selina Ruguwa also helped with the typing, working very hard and accurately. These two extremely likeable young ladies were tolerant of my scribbles and remained charming throughout the long hours they sat in my office. Fiddes Mususa, a well-educated and affable young man, was also very patient and would type away furiously as I dictated to him. My warmest thanks go to Pauline, Selina and Fiddes for tackling this arduous and essential task.

I thank my close friend Brian Allgar whose sound advice was so welcome and for his editing, which helped enormously with the final copy. He would often call me from Paris where he lives with his charming Parisian wife Francoise to discuss factual points or to offer some constructive words of wisdom. Special thanks go to my good friend Sam who is very 'punny'! He helped Pepsi and me with the computer when we didn't know what to do and helped tremendously with all our technical hiccups. Without fail, he came over from Sutton whenever we sent out an SOS. Also I could not forget young Bronte who finished typing the last few chapters of my book.

I am also immensely grateful to Tina Abbey who interviewed me relentlessly over several months to ensure nothing of my life was left untold and for helping me to write my story in an interesting and engaging manner. I honestly don't know what I would have done without her patience and determination during the writing of this autobiography. We also had lots of laughs, enjoying many puns, which come so naturally to me when talking! This certainly helped during our long telephone conversations. Finally, I am indebted to my second wife, Joy Devon, who died in 2004 of cancer. She had the ability to bring the best out in me and during the mid-years of my career, she was a pillar of support taking on all administration duties and encouraging me to try out new areas. This gave me the confidence to expand my musical abilities and ultimately reach audiences all over the world. Joy always seemed to have plenty of good ideas and I doubt I would have achieved the high level of success if she had not been there for me as my partner in music and as my soul mate. This only leaves me to say, although my mother, father and sisters are no longer with me, without doubt I owe them the biggest thanks of all. Their love, encouragement and unfailing support in my early years and throughout their own lives have been a major influence both on me and on my music.

1

The Beginnings

It was a strange beginning because the path to my musical career nearly had me packed off to an asylum. All I can say is I was born with music in my soul and from an early age I needed to express my strong musical feelings, which I felt I had no more control over than my breathing. I would sit in our warm kitchen and listen to all kinds of music on our small battery radio and whenever the batteries wore out, I was distraught, crying endlessly until my father said, "We had better replace the batteries then!"

I tried to imitate the orchestral instruments I heard on the radio, making one hell of a noise as I mimicked sounds from screeching high violins to the deep boom of brass and percussion. I would run about the house throwing my arms around wildly, vocalizing all these sounds at the top of my voice. My three sisters, totally vexed would ask me, "*What on earth* are you doing? *Why* are you doing that?" My family was quite convinced I was totally mad and fortunately our immediate next door neighbour was deaf!

My poor mum and dad were so worried about their only son, they eventually sought help from the educational services. I remember this very well-spoken, educated gentleman coming to the house to see me. Luckily, he recognized my talent straight away, happily telling my family that one day I would become a great musician. It was such a relief for my parents, who set about organizing piano lessons with a local woman called Mrs. Hammond, a very soft-spoken and good-natured teacher. Her husband was a violinmaker who, in a fashion, also played the violin and often Mrs. Hammond would arrange for me to accompany him on the piano. I do believe my love of strings came from this very early influence. We had an old piano at home in our front room that I could practice on and it wasn't long before I became Mrs. Hammond's favourite pupil.

I was born on April 30, 1924 in our home in Clarence Road, Sutton Surrey. It was a small semi-detached house built in the early 1900s and it is still standing today. There was a very small front garden with a door that opened on to the stairs, a front room, a kitchen, a scullery, a dining room, and three bedrooms. My father kept our front room locked and we only used it on special occasions until I began piano lessons when he would allow me in the room to practice. Also, because of my obsession with the radio, he would let me listen to it in the front room so I didn't continually disturb the whole family!

Despite the fact we were very poor in those days, apart from the bedrooms, which were freezing so we would have to sleep with hot water bottles, our house was warm in the winter and our mother always cooked a lovely hearty meal every day. We didn't have a bathroom, only an outside loo and we had chamber pots under the bed at night. Every Friday night was our bath time with my mother boiling the water in very large heavy saucepans on a gas stove to fill an old tub in the scullery.

To me there seemed to be two types of people living in Sutton, with the less well off living towards the bottom of the town and the better off at the top. We lived very happily at the bottom part of Sutton with our local pub, The Robin Hood, just up the road. It remains largely the same today as how I remember it all those years ago and the seats where once my father and mother sat are still there, too! Since those early days, it seems the rest of Sutton has now changed remarkably with new buildings, supermarkets and a "walkabout" high street. There is a fine old local church, St. Nicholas, where I attended Sunday school throughout the year and where as a family we went at Christmas, Easter and other important religious dates. All my three sisters were married at this church and much later on, I married my first wife, Jacqueline, there, too. There were two music shops in Sutton, one was Landaus, which sold sixpenny copies of popular songs, and the other was Deweys, which was at the top of the high street. Deweys was more aristocratic, and they sold music such as Chappells for one shilling a copy.

We were a happy family and I loved my mother and father very much. I had three elder sisters, Florence, Maude and Lucy; I was the youngest and only boy in the family, named Thomas John. It was a tradition that went back generations because my grandfather and my father were also named Thomas John Fox. Originally the family name was John Thomas Fox, but for obvious reasons, but I am not sure when, the names were switched. Strange as it seems, later in life all four of us changed our names! My sisters were named after our aunts on my father's side and as they didn't get on with them particularly well, they decided in their early teens to choose their own names! So Florence became Lee, Maude became Maureen and Lucy became Judy (after Judy Garland the famous film star) and from an early age Judy always called me Jack; later she was instrumental in helping me with my music career. She was a real daredevil and when I was still very small, Dad made a small pushchair with a rope to guide the two front wheels. I loved sitting in this pushchair and one day Judy pushed me up a very steep hill in Robin Hood Lane. At the top of that hill, she turned the pushchair round and pushed me at quite a force and let it go. I was petrified but I somehow guided that pushchair down the hill at a tremendous pace and fell off at the bottom! Luckily for me, there weren't many cars about in those bygone days, and apart from a few childish pranks in my early years, Judy was always there for me.

Another incident that sticks in my mind as a young child is the R101 air disaster. There was this big noise thundering out of the sky and the whole family rushed out to the garden looking skywards and saw this huge airship flying very, very low. It was the R101 airship going on its maiden voyage from Croydon airport to Karachi, then part of British India. The airship was massive and the passengers were waving happily at us from their windows. It was so close that it felt as if we could almost shake hands with them! The next day, on the fifth October, 1930, that great airship crashed into a hillside north of Paris after encountering strong winds. Engulfed by flames, forty-eight out of the fifty-four people on board were killed. At the tender age of six, the sheer size and the scale of this ill-starred airship was striking and often I would recall this tragedy many years later when I wrote various pieces of music depicting the theme of disasters.

My father was strict but fair and never once smacked us. To me, he was a lovely generous caring dad. He was born into a big family within the sound of Bow Bells in London and although he spoke with a cockney accent, he always behaved like a gentleman and I never once heard him swear, which has influenced me greatly throughout my life. He sweated blood for us working shifts at the Gas Works as a gas stoker in Wandsworth South London. He would cycle the long road there and back while often at night he would keep us awake with an awful hacking cough that came from working in such an unhealthy environment. He had an allotment so we could have fresh vegetables for our meals and often entered local competitions where he won many prizes.

My mother, Laura Wyatt, also came from a large family. She was one of ten children and before she married my father, lived in a bungalow at Carshalton near to where the St. Helier Hospital is today. We always referred to it as the 'bungalow up the lane'! She was a wonderful mother and wife who looked after us all very well. She was warm and kind and I never once heard her shout. In those days, schoolchildren went home for lunch and I remember how lovely it was to have a decent meal during the day. My mum was a great cook and the fresh vegetables tasted like vegetables, so unlike those we have today. She had a great sense of humour and we were always pulling her leg. One of my lasting impressions from my childhood is the fact she was always there for me and how well-loved she was by everyone who knew her, which remained the same throughout her life.

There was a time when she had serious trouble with her teeth and had to have the whole lot taken out! It's difficult to explain just how worried we were as she had them taken out over a short period of two days and we thought we would lose her. Her gums bled and bled for many days, and she would sit in a chair with this bucket by her side to catch the blood pouring out of her mouth. Then all her teeth were plugged and gradually, the bleeding stopped. What courage our lovely mum had as we never heard her complain.

We used to go on holidays, and I still have old photographs of my family in Brighton where we would stay. I am particularly fond of one showing me when I was about six months old sitting on my mother's lap. Sometimes we went to Bognor Regis and stayed at the same boarding house, year in, year out. I would spend the days on the beach and loved the sea so much. My early love of the sea inspired the many compositions I wrote about the sea many years later with large orchestras and when writing this music the old memories from my childhood holidays would came flooding back.

The Fox family is said to be distantly related to Lady Hamilton (Emma), who was of course a very close friend of Lord Horatio Nelson. The great Nelson's column still stands proudly today facing south over Trafalgar Square, London. My grandfather and my father tried to follow this family connection up, but unfortunately the solicitor's fees became too prohibitive and the whole case was dropped. Apparently, some property in Shaftsbury Avenue, London, belonged to Lady Hamilton and a person called Fox. Evidently Lady Hamilton was not only beautiful but very musical. Maybe someone in the family will one day take up this connection once again and finally discover where my inherited musical talent came from!

When I was eight years old, something happened that became the turning point in my life and would help mould my future as a musician. I believe it was the moment my musical career really began. It was my birthday and I did a very silly thing. I did a leapfrog over a high post, fell and fractured my right arm. I remember trying to be brave, because I was with Jim Sargent, the boy who lived next door to our little house in Clarence Road Sutton, and I didn't want him to see me cry. So I shouted for him to go home because I was in such pain! Of course, when he left, I cried my eyes out! Someone ran off to fetch a doctor and our local GP, Dr. Ritchie, eventually arrived with another doctor and put me under anaesthetic to set my arm. The last thing I remember hearing was our lovely yellow canary bird singing from its cage. It sang beautifully, which totally relaxed me and when I woke up that canary was still singing!

Because this happened on my birthday, my eldest sister, Lee, and her boyfriend, Harry, promised to take me to a live big band concert. It was to see Geraldo and his orchestra, with Dorothy Carless singing. Geraldo was a famous name in those days with his highly successful and popular band and Concert Orchestra. The concert was held at the Granada Tooting in South London, and it was very exciting for me because Geraldo's orchestra was my favourite and Dorothy Carless, his female vocalist, was pure magic to my ears. My mother was concerned about me going but I insisted as I knew nothing was going to keep me away from the opportunity to see Geraldo live.

At the end of the evening, Lee took me round to the Stage Door and we waited for him to appear so I could ask him for his autograph. I was very excited when he arrived and especially when he spoke to me asking about my arm and said I was a very brave boy.

Even at that age, I had the ability to hear that Dorothy Carless's diction and style were fantastic. Carol Carr was her young sister and both of them sang in similar styles. Later on Carless sang for different well-known orchestras, including that of the famous young Robert Farnon who was a composer, conductor and arranger, considered by his peers to be the 'finest arranger' in the world. Both of these superb female singers were very attractive blondes and my favourite was always Dorothy.

In my early school days, my sister Judy and I used to read 'The Magnet' (I called her Lu after her real name Lucy) which was a magazine about a fictitious private boys' school in Kent called 'Greyfriars.' Frank Richards, who seemed to be a wizard at this type of story, wrote these wonderful tales. They featured great characters like Billy Bunter the Fat Boy ('I say you fellows!') together with The Famous Five: Harry Wharton, Bob Cherry, Frank Nugent, Johnny Bull and Singh (an Indian boy). Mr. Quelch was their form master, with two characters, Loder and Lock, in the sixth form and a boy named Wingate as the head prefect. I also remember a teacher character called Mr. Prout of the sixth form and the headmaster, Dr. Locke.

We so enjoyed reading this magazine that Lu and I used to fight over who got to read it first! These magical stories helped me so much in my future career in terms of the meaning of words and good English. They also taught me not to 'split on anyone,' not to 'tell tales out of school' (and 'promise not to tell').

Every year at Christmas, the Greyfriars Annual came out, and my parents would give it to me as a present. To this day, I still have many of them somewhere in the loft of my house including quite a number of 'Magnet' magazines and the monthly smaller and thicker books called 'Schoolboys Own.' I loved these stories as a youngster, and I shall never forget them.

At our little house we used to have family parties, and in those days we had a big family with lots of aunts, uncles, and grandparents. On these happy occasions, I played the piano and everyone would have a singsong. They would sing their hearts out with their favourite old time songs drinking many glasses of beer with my dear mum drinking Guinness. Bless her!

Often people would cry at my father's rendering of "If Those Lips Could Only Speak." I am sure this early influence encouraged my later love and enjoyment of accompanying singers and instrumentalists.

My school days at Sutton West were quite good and mostly uneventful. Math and English were my strong subjects (as well as music of course!) But it was only later in life I found out you have to be good at these two subjects, especially math, to be a professional composer and arranger.

In the classroom, I sat at the back with a boy named Paste who had regular fits. It is extremely frightening for such a young person to witness a fit, and somehow the intensity of the emotion of such an episode helped me as a musician to recapture and relate those experiences through my music in many of my compositions.

The music teacher, Mr. Wood, sometimes sat down to play the piano asking the class to name the melody he was playing. I was always the first to put my hand up with the correct answer. In the end, Mr. Wood told me not to tell anyone in that classroom what music he was playing on the piano because he knew I would always have the right answer! I was often first in exams at school and I seem to recall the boy sitting next to me came second! Isn't copying for the copyists?

2

Those Dangerous Teen Years

I was fifteen years old when the Second World War broke out. Unlike many people who heard the news on the radio that war had been declared and then wondered how their lives would be affected, for me the reality of war was immediate. That very morning there were German and English fighter planes already fighting high in the skies only four miles away from Sutton. This was because of Croydon Airport, which over the first weekend in September 1939 saw its transformation in the space of forty-eight hours from a civil airport into a military aerodrome. It became a base for fighter squadrons and with Lufthansa flying regularly from Croydon before the outbreak of war; the airport was well-known to the Germans who made it top of their list as a target in the London Blitz. To witness this dogfight first-hand on the outbreak of war was a very frightening experience for me.

At this time, I loved experimenting at the keyboard and I was already composing piano pieces as I enjoyed most types of music including classical, light, popular songs and of course jazz. In later years, I realized how important it was being so versatile. It certainly helped me to become a comprehensive and universal composer.

A couple of years before the war, I joined the ATC (Air Training Corps) a sort of pre-RAF (Royal Air Force) young men's association that prepared you for the event of "calling up." In the ATC, I met an accordionist, a saxophonist and a drummer and suggested we form a band. So we did and called it the ATC Dance Band. In the evenings, we would rehearse at my little house until 10.30 at night when my mum would cook us scrambled eggs for supper. This band was my solace during the harrowing days and nights of the war coupled with long, boring days as an office boy.

A couple of days after that first morning of war, I wrote a very dramatic piece of music to depict the fighter planes over Croydon. Sadly, I lost the manuscript many years ago and I can no longer remember it. However, this piece was instrumental in helping me to realize that as a composer, I had the ability through my music to produce sounds that portray events, emotions and feelings.

From February 1939 to the outbreak of war, the government supplied everyone with an Anderson Shelter kit made of galvanized corrugated steel panels. In our little garden, my father dug a hole and made steps down into this air raid bunker. When the air sirens started, which was usually during the evenings, we would dash to this shelter and all pile into it and try to get some sleep on the bunk beds. How I hated it! There were so many of us and I found it difficult to sleep. When I could not stand it any longer and often even before the 'all clear' sounded, I would look over at Judy and wink whispering, "Let's go back to the house." We would creep out while everyone else was still asleep, scrambling back to our beds in the house. It certainly was hazardous and probably very silly of us but somehow we just wanted to get back to our own beds.

How terribly troubled I felt as soon as that piercing sound, first high, then low, blasted the air followed by the drone of enemy planes that often carried on through the night, sometimes until four in the morning. How sweet the sound when we heard the 'all clear.' It was a very dangerous time and it had a huge effect on me because I was frightened I would be killed. Only later did I understand how these terrifying experiences became my catalyst for the composition of some of my more sublime pieces. Many years later, I would furiously scribble out my music as I relived those events and recalled the roller coaster of emotions I had experienced.

Of course, it wasn't bad the whole time and it was during this period I had the fortune to meet a drummer called Willy Hawker, who was a sheet metal worker for my sister Lee's husband, Harry. As we both had pianos, if air raids allowed, we would get together every Tuesday and Friday evening either at my home or his. These meetings were extremely enjoyable and we called them 'jam sessions.'

Before the war began, my youngest sister Judy helped me to find a job as an office boy at a theatre agency located in the prestigious area of Park Lane, London. A middle-aged woman called Mrs. Tudor Owen, who was quite attractive but had rather sharp features, ran the office. She was often harsh at times and would shout at me, "Come on, why haven't you done this or that?" or "Why haven't you finished yet?"

Once or twice a week in the late afternoon, a good looking gentleman in a top hat carrying a lovely bunch of flowers would visit Mrs. Tudor Owen. I could not believe it when I realized this gentleman caller was none other than the prominent Jack Strachey who composed the very popular song 'These Foolish Things.' I loved his type of music and was in total awe of him. He always called out in a cheery way, "Hello there, Jack!" How thrilled I was!

Mrs. Owen also had a secretary who was a very pretty brunette about thirty years old, whom I fancied I was very much in love with! She made what seemed very long days more enjoyable and even taught me to 'touch type.' Lunchtimes were my favourite times when I sat on a bench in Hyde Park to eat my sandwiches and feed the pigeons. Anyone who does not know much about pigeons might believe they are just boring birds. But nothing is further from the truth. Not only do they have many kinds of different plumage and colourings, but they have different character, too. I loved those Hyde Park pigeons; they were a pure delight and before long, I could easily tell each individual one apart. Sometimes twelve or more lovely pigeons would hang on to me, all fluttering and cooing. Mrs. Poppins, eat your heart out!

I would travel to London either by Green Line Coach or by train to Victoria and occasionally by underground from Morden. But once the air raids began, it was impossible to use the trains if I wanted to get to work on time. So my father bought me a bicycle. As you can imagine, it was quite perilous to cycle to London at this time and it was also a very long way from Sutton to Park Lane. It was fine cycling to work in the mornings because it was all downhill, but coming home was another matter. Puffing everyday up Tooting Hill and then uphill to Sutton made me realize just how low central London lies.

The air raids were intense and I saw many distressing scenes, rubble and destruction. My worst memory is of a red, double-decker London bus in a big hole caused by a German bomb. I shall never forget the screams, seeing the blood everywhere, people dying and bits of bodies lying about.

It became so dangerous that my parents became increasingly unhappy about me working in the centre of London. In the end, for the sake of my own safety, they insisted I leave. I did not mind leaving the job at all but I did miss my fascinating pigeons and that lovely secretary!

After that, I worked for my brother-in-law Harry who hated music and smoked like a chimney. But then everyone seemed to smoke in those days—including me! Once again, I was an office boy and although I worked with my sister who ran the office at Spraysine Ltd., I didn't enjoy the work very much. I asked to be transferred to the workshop carrying sheets of metal that cut my hands to pieces. I tried to find gloves to wear because as you can imagine this type of work was disastrous for a young pianist's hands. What kept me cheerful was going home to my music every night and playing in my band. I also began to teach the piano at this stage, which included teaching my aunt Evelyn and her son Roy who subsequently immigrated to Toronto, Canada.

Like the office work, I didn't really enjoy teaching; I knew in my heart my real calling was to create music because that's when I felt at my happiest, but I was young and in desperate need of an income. Still, this was about to change as I was called up in the RAF.

3
First Love

During one of my 'jam sessions' with Willy Hawker, the drummer, when I was about sixteen years old, I met my first love, Hilda Whitehead. She was the same age as me and we were both very shy. It was ages before I had the courage to ask her for a date but luckily for me she said, "Yes!" enthusiastically and I took her to the movies. I was very taken with her as she was a gorgeous girl with lovely blue eyes and beautiful fair hair. I don't think we saw very much of the movie! It was teenage love, so young and innocent.

Later on, I composed a piece of piano music especially with her in mind. One's first love is always very special because everyone remembers his or her first love and that's exactly what I called the piece, 'First Love.' Later in my life, I orchestrated this composition, and it was played many times in many countries throughout the world.

It was Hilda, as well as Judy, who walked me to Sutton station when I was first called up to the RAF and she knitted me lovely pullovers and scarves, which she sent to our camp. While I was away, she would regularly visit my mother, walking round to the back door and straight into the house, which only special people were allowed to do. She loved my mum and dad.

While I was quite infatuated with Hilda, I was having such a good time in the RAF entertaining, I didn't write home or to Hilda. My mum and dad were very worried about not receiving letters from me so my eldest sister, Lee, sent a telegram to the RAF's camp officer. I was nearly put on a charge for negligence to my family! I don't think anyone could ever have felt as ashamed of this episode as I did.

When I was on leave about a year later, I met Hilda and wanted to pick up where we had left off before I went away. But she wouldn't have any of it and I couldn't blame her. I had neglected her badly. She was a girl of principles and obviously knew I had changed a lot during that time, too. She later married a businessman much older than her and some years later, when I lived in St. James Road, Sutton, I met her pushing a pram containing two lovely babies. I felt sad because she seemed to have aged quite a lot but she still had those wonderful blue eyes and lovely fair hair. We chatted awhile, then Hilda went on her way and I never saw her again. But I did find out later that shortly after our meeting, her husband died.

It was long after this teenage episode in my life that I recorded this particular piece of music for my publishers, Sonoton Music. I still have the LP, which was released in 1977 on a record called *Twilight Love* when I was conducting sessions in Germany with the John Fox Strings and Voices.

What is more, when I selected this LP to play recently, I discovered I had written a dedication on the sleeve—but not to Hilda. It says, "To Joy, remembering the lovely times when we made this LP in Germany. Love, John xxx."

Yes, Hilda was my 'first love' in those heady teenage days when I was discovering life and everything was new, innocent and exciting, but I couldn't have known then that my first *real* love would be Joy, my second wife.

4

Life in the RAF Playing Piano

I felt very sad to leave home because for me it was such a big wrench. I certainly wasn't like so many other young lads who were firing up to go to war! I suspect being the youngest and only boy in the family, especially with three elder sisters looking after me, I was rather spoiled at times. At the age of eighteen, the fateful day came when I had to leave to join the RAF. I left our house and walking up the road towards the station I saw my mum standing at the gate for a long time waving and waving until I was out of sight.

My mother was the most loving mum in the world and in later years, I often arranged to have her name mentioned by well-known presenters on the radio such as Bob Monkhouse, Pete Murray, David Jacobs and Steve Race. They would play the lovely song called 'Laura' in her honour, which I arranged and conducted. So that morning was tough for me seeing my mum there waiting for me to turn the corner. I hate goodbyes because for me it's like someone has taken my soul away. Sadness is a very special feeling of loss and much later in my life, I composed many *Emotions and Sad* pieces that were played throughout the world as Library Music. I shall talk later about this special kind of composing.

On the way to the Weeton RAF Station near Blackpool, by chance I met a young man on the railway platform. We were both very miserable because we thought we would never ever get out of the forces. He said, "What do you do?" I replied, "I'm a musician—I play the piano. What do you do?"

"I'm a tap dancer," he replied.

Discovering we shared the common love of music, we became immediate friends. Dancing was his whole life as music is mine and after we had settled in the RAF camp at Weeton, we formed a partnership with me playing the piano and him tap dancing. There were many pianos in public places in those days, and we loved entertaining in the clubs and pubs. There was one particular pub that had a lovely grand piano right in the middle of a rather large bar. The manager of this pub asked my friend to dance on top of this grand piano, and it brought the house down! I shall never forget that evening many, many years ago, and in my opinion, he was another Fred Astaire! Sadly, after a few months, this brilliant tap dancer got posted to another RAF station and we never met again.

Training in the air force was certainly not my cup of tea and marching about a mile to the cookhouse wasn't much fun either, especially with a military band blaring at quite a fast tempo to keep you marching quickly! Then there was trying to get through assault courses struggling under wire fences, jumping over streams and falling in! The sergeant would be screaming at me, "Come on, Fox! Get on with it, Fox!"

There was one particular time involving a rifle. We were learning how to shoot and for some reason, I couldn't make the thing work. I pointed the gun straight at the Sergeant in charge and pulling the trigger shouted, "Look Sarge! It won't work!" I've never seen anyone move away so quickly. He came back to me fuming and put me on a charge! Much later in my musical life recalling the funny incidents in those far-off days, I wrote many musical comedy situations and slapstick effects.

While at the camp, we were all issued bicycles and there were times when my friends and I cycled from Weeton to a pub where the boss liked my piano playing. He would often send drinks over to me and even paid me a small fee for entertaining the customers.

One night, a beautiful young blonde came up to me while I was playing some romantic songs. She told me she adored my playing and she flirted quite outrageously, even buying me a drink! I was enjoying myself very much and I promised to see her when the pub closed. At the end of the evening, I packed my music up and crept out the back way to meet my glamorous date as arranged. Unfortunately for me, there was no blonde waiting and before I had time to think, a large chap loomed out of the shadows and shouted, "So you're the one!" and punching me hard on the jaw, knocked me out.

Down I went with my music flying all over the place like confetti. Luckily my friends who had come with me sorted the situation out and we cycled back to the camp. Being slightly cocky, I said, "If that's a punch on the jaw, it was nothing," and laughed about it, that is, until the next morning when I couldn't open my mouth to talk. I was livid! So my good friends and I went back to the pub for the next night or two to look out for this chap but he didn't appear again—probably because he didn't want to risk bringing his pretty girlfriend back or perhaps he was worried I might give him a black eye for knocking me out!

After training I was posted to another base at Sandtoft. There was a lovely grand piano in the officers' mess and I would sit down to play it. Little did I know one evening the air commander (Group Captain) in charge was in the mess listening to my playing. He came over and asked my name, commanding me to go to his private office the next day. Of course, I went to see him with all the paraphernalia of saluting and feeling slightly nervous wondering what I had done. I need not have worried; he simply said, "Fox, I like your piano playing, and this camp is short of good musicians such as yourself, so I want you to play at the airmen's mess, sergeants' mess and officers' mess. I shall now relieve you of your other duties."

I couldn't believe my luck. It had never crossed my mind that I was so talented the Group Captain would think it was essential to ensure I was exempt from military duty. I became what was known as 'screened.' My new role meant I got to know many of the aircrews, including pilots, radio operators and rear gunners who flew Lancaster Bombers on air raids to Germany. I made many friends with those aircrews and how desperately sad I felt when some of the crews didn't return to base. It was always a heart-breaking experience, and I never got used to it.

It wasn't long before the Group Captain asked me to advertise and form a band to entertain in the three messes. I soon found an accordionist, a tenor saxophone player with a walrus moustache, a guitarist and a drummer. I wrote many arrangements for the band and got them to rehearse and rehearse until their playing improved. Because we would often play until quite late in the evening, we were given a Nissen hut all to ourselves, and our commanding officer gave the five of us chits so we could lie in bed in the mornings! What a treat!

The commanding officer also allowed us to run our own dances in the village. Any money that we made we shared among us after paying for someone in the ticket office and for the services of a Master of

Ceremonies (MC). If I remember rightly, this was an RAF officer who was very good at doing this essential job.

Roughly five miles from camp was a small village called Crowle, where we would often play in the dance hall when the RAF camp didn't need us. We certainly enjoyed those events because with most of the male population away fighting, there were plenty of young pretty girls about, giving us lots of attention! We would hire a car to pull a trailer containing the drum kit, double bass, saxophone and a guitar, and the driver would take us to the dance hall and pick us up again at the end of the evening at 12:30 a.m.

One particular night, a pretty girl delayed me, and the driver, becoming impatient, went back to camp. That night I had to trudge all of the five miles back to base! I didn't do that again!

Many of the dances we organized ourselves and we generally enjoyed a full house. When we returned to the Nissen hut at the end of the evening, I would empty the money bag in the middle of the room onto a blanket to share the proceeds among the members of the band. Sometimes we made about five pounds each in a night and sometimes even ten pounds, which was quite a lot of money in those days!

It was very dangerous at times when there were air raids at our base station but we all managed to keep our chins up; although it may sound strange, over a period of time one became less bothered and more accepting of living in such hazardous conditions.

Whenever I could, I would send my mother some money and told her to enjoy herself. I wanted her to spend it on some nice things, have a good time with my dear father and share it with friends.

Also, while I was at Sandtoft, my mother visited me on several occasions, staying for two or three weeks at a time. She enjoyed being able to spend some time with me and to get away from the constant dreadful bombing in London, which affected Sutton so badly. Everyone loved her and she would often accompany the band to hear us playing at various venues. I would always play the lovely song 'Laura' in her honour. My relationship with my mother was very special and I would feel very miserable when she returned home.

A small incident during my time at Sandtoft had a big impact on my musical career. One day, I was playing in the officer's mess when a pilot officer came over to ask if he could have a go on this lovely grand piano, so I stood aside to let him play. I can remember as if it were yesterday because this handsome, fair-haired pilot astounded me by magnificently playing the whole of *The Warsaw Concerto* by Richard Addinsell without music! The particular wartime piece in question came from a very popular British film called *Dangerous Moonlight,* which most people knew and loved. It made me suddenly realize what little experience I had playing difficult pieces. I felt very jealous of the wonderful rendering of this difficult concerto, and I swore to myself that when the war was over, I would try my hardest to study music very seriously.

Going home on leave was very exciting for me, seeing my lovely parents again, my sister Lee, my friends and our family pets, Nigger the cat and Bonzo the dog. Later in my life, I was commissioned to compose music called *Animal Lovers* and those two pets together with all the lovely dogs and cats I have owned ever since, have often been the source of my inspiration.

I didn't see my other sisters, Maureen and Judy, very often because they had also been called up. Lee wasn't called up because her husband, Harry, ran his own company making important aircraft parts for the war and she was the company director. Unfortunately, Lee's house in Cheam, Surrey was bombed to the ground and they lost all their belongings, which was very hard for my sister.

Luckily, both she and her husband would often drive down to a village called Clandon near to Guildford to be in a safe place away from the constant bombing. When I went to see the ruins of her lovely house the next morning, I could hardly believe what I saw. I left feeling very distressed as I knew it was only by luck my sister and her husband had not been in the house at the time. They certainly had their Guardian Angel looking after them that night.

Travelling to London on the train was eventful as it was always full of service men and women either travelling home to loved ones or going back to base. One particular morning in the very early hours, I was on the underground tube at Charing Cross and on the platforms there were hundreds of people singing their hearts out! The underground was a safe shelter from the constant bombing and these people were keeping their spirits up by singing. It was quite a scene. As I stepped over the crowd to catch the train for Morden, there was even an accordionist playing lovely well-known tunes, old and new. Of course, they all sang songs such as 'There'll always be an England' and 'The White Cliffs of Dover' and naturally I was proud to be English! I am happy to say I still am to this very day.

5

Atomic Bomb—War Over!

When the war in Europe ended in 1945, I was still playing at the same RAF station. What joyful news it was, but everyone went a little mad on that special VE (Victory in Europe) day including me! I got terribly drunk with a friend of mine and didn't turn up for the celebration in the Navy, Army, Air Force Institute (NAAFI) base's canteen. I was too ill, so the group had to play without a pianist. How dreadfully ashamed I felt the next day and the boys didn't speak to me for ages and ages. Of course, I couldn't blame them and it certainly taught me a big lesson, because since that day well over sixty years ago, I have never been late again for any sessions whether composing, arranging, conducting or playing the piano.

At this stage the Japanese and the South Sea Islands were still at war, so many in the RAF were transferred from the Air Force to the Fleet Air Arm and I was posted to HMS Condor in Scotland, close to Arbroath and Dundee. I made good friends in Dundee and had a great time there. In particular I remember a family I became very friendly with one Christmas and New Year. I met this amicable Scot playing the piano in a pub and we got chatting. He told me he had a lovely piano at home and invited me back. I was pleased to discover that he not only had a lovely piano but a lovely daughter, too! This family was so hospitable over the festive season and I had a marvellous time with them. These little incidents of people's generosity were so important because they helped so much during the unhappy times of the war.

I dreaded the thought of going on an aircraft carrier to the fighting, which was still going on hundreds of miles away. But our unit never made it there, as a few months later to everyone's surprise *the Atomic Bomb was dropped on Hiroshima and Nagasaki,* which of course ended the war in the South Pacific.

When this happened, I was suddenly drafted to the South Coast where the main base of the Fleet Air Arm was to be demobilized. I remember changing trains in London from Scotland, where for a few minutes I managed to meet my fiancé, Pela. I had met Pela the previous year through my sister Judy, as they were very good friends. Once when I was on leave, we arranged to meet at Blackpool Amusement Park for the weekend. She was half-Russian as her father was a Cossack and we had some lovely times together. I suppose this was the first time I really felt I was in love and foolishly, we became engaged.

We couldn't get together very often as Pela was in the forces, so we wrote four- or five-page love letters to each other every day and I also wrote a piece for her called 'Temperamental Lady.' I think that probably says a lot about her! Sadly, I can't find this original manuscript and I would dearly love to find it because it would be interesting to know what my composing was like over 60 years ago. I feel certain it is buried somewhere amongst many other manuscripts in my studio or the loft and I am determined one day to find it!

I arrived at this main base and stayed in a Nissen hut with five other chaps for about a month. One by one, the others left, demobbed to different walks of life, complete with a new civvy suit and other domestic items. So there I was completely on my own in this Nissen hut. However, this proved to be an important period in my life as I had time to think and I began to map out my future.

When I was eventually demobbed, Judy came to meet me at the bus stop in Sutton and helped to carry my kit bag and luggage back to our little house in Clarence Road. How I counted my blessings for being in 'Civvy Street' again. It's a wonderful feeling to be home after being away for so long. It was heart-warming seeing my mum and dad again and shortly afterwards my mum suddenly said to me, "Oh I've forgotten something." She went upstairs and came back with an envelope that contained something rather special. When I opened it, to my surprise I found a lot of money inside. I was extremely puzzled and she said, "That's all the money you sent me over the years and I saved it for you." Feeling overwhelmed, I broke down, crying my eyes out while hugging her tightly. Laura was like that; she always thought of others first. Of course, I gently made her take it back and said it was especially for her. What a mother she was!

I hadn't been home long when my sister Maureen got married to a local chap called Tom at St. Nicholas Church in Sutton. It was a large family affair with Judy and Pela as bridesmaids and we had a lovely time and were as happy as sandboys! Maureen was such a bubbly girl who always smiled, and Tom was quite a character.

In the early days after the war, Tom and I became quite the comedy duo. I remember how we would have our friends and family crying with laughter with our antics. Both of us would ad lib and perform silly acts together that seem to come as naturally to me as my music. The humorous side of my personality certainly came to life! I think laughter is so vital to an enjoyable life. It is so important to have the ability to laugh and to see the funny side of situations. Later on, I was to compose many truly funny comedy situations for my publisher in Germany. Some of the comedy titles I composed are *Silly Season, Bassooner or Later, Flop and Go, Comedy Cartoon, Cartoon Brigade, Comic Chase,* and many short pieces called *Comic Cuts.*

Tom was a generous man and I liked him very much. Both of us were the life and soul of the many parties we used to have in those early years. He was also an excellent darts player and we would often have very good matches together. Our whole family loved playing darts and once a week we all went to 'The Mint,' a popular pub in Banstead about five miles from Sutton. Sometimes Tom and I would win every game of darts during the evening. Many times we got quite merry in that pub and couldn't walk a straight line home! This was because if you won, your opponents would pay for a round of drinks! That says it all, doesn't it?

6
Making Up for Lost Time!

While I had been sitting alone in that Nissen hut thinking about my future, I knew how lucky I was at twenty-two years old to be alive and engaged to a wonderful girl who loved me very much. But what concerned me most of all was, how could I possibly make up for the lost time spent in the forces? Even though I had been fortunate enough to play music throughout the war, I knew I needed to develop my technical knowledge of music. I would need to work hard and study twenty-five hours a day if I was to become the type of musician I felt and aspired to in my heart. I thought all these things out whilst sitting in this hut. How do I begin? I had heard wonderful music played by Robert Farnon, Sidney Torch, Glen Miller, Tommy Dorsey, Andre Kostelanetz, Leroy Anderson, and Stanley Black, along with many others, and knew I wanted to become as good as these talented musicians, or even better.

Could I make it if I studied hard? The Group Captain who had relieved me of my duties had spotted my talent and he certainly believed I really did have a gift. I had sat there day after day racking my brains. Where do I start? What can I do? After a while with all these thoughts going round in my head, it came to me there was only one thing I could possibly do and that was to just go for it. I would try, try and try again. How can I get to know important people in the music profession? The answer was to start from scratch and not to have any ties at all. Life would have to be all music. As the old song says, 'Life is Nothing Without Music,' which was composed by Fred Hartley a composer and orchestrator often heard on the BBC during the war.

One uncomfortable thought was troubling me. I had to talk to my fiancé, Pela, because I had made up my mind that not only did my music come first, but deep in my heart, I knew our relationship probably wasn't quite right. We had been engaged for six months and I knew it wasn't going to be easy telling her. I felt terrible but I had to do what I had to do. I met Pela at her home in Muswell Hill, London and took her to a quiet pub to gently break the news to her. We both cried, but it was probably more painful for Pela because it came as such a shock. For a long while afterwards, I missed her very much and was deeply saddened when I heard she had angrily burnt all my love letters in front of my sister Judy. I felt a little silly, too, because when we became engaged, I was given special leave to go home for a big engagement party.

We had about 120 guests and held the party at The Adult School hall in Sutton with lots of relations from both sides. In a way, I suppose I must have known that in my heart I wasn't really ready for a commitment, as Pela's two rather attractive younger sisters caught my eye that evening and I remember being quite enchanted by them! I did think at the time, "Is this the womanizing time in my life?" as I seemed to be easily bowled over by a pretty face, shapely legs and lovely eyes. Not long after we broke up, Pela married, probably on the rebound and had three children. We did remain friends in the end and we have kept in touch over the years. She still rings me up now and then to tell me she has heard my music on the radio on such and such a day or night.

Despite this major upset, it was good to get home again to begin my new life. So I immediately joined Sutton College of Music in Grove Road, Sutton to thoroughly learn theory of music. Over and over again, I would copy all the major and minor scales until I was blue in the face. It wasn't easy because it was so boring but I knew it was absolutely essential to have this grounding in music. The Associated Board exam tests each pupil on the theory of music and they have to pass this written test and oral exam before they can pass grade five on their chosen instrument. Most pupils hate this part of music in their lives, but without theory, there really is no music. Understanding this important subject is 100 percent necessary, particularly for a composer.

After being demobbed, I was often asked to play at the many American camps that were still about after the war. This work came about because of my ability to sight-read, as there weren't many musicians who had this skill. It meant that I could accompany cabarets and bands without rehearsals as I was able to sight-read the parts on the spot. Despite the fact this was a highly valued skill, I had to stand my ground very firmly with the organizers. In the beginning, they were only paying me for playing in the band and not for the extra work involved in sight-reading and playing for the cabaret. They soon took notice when one evening I refused to play until they put the matter right!

I also joined the Lenny Lewis Five for a short while as the pianist. Our group consisted of Lenny who was a brilliant clarinettist, Stewart Edwards on vibes, Ronnie Stone on double bass, me on piano and Tony Pike on drums. It was a wonderful group with excellent musicians and we played at the American camps, too. In the short time I played in the band, a commercial recording was issued called *Modern Party Sound* featuring four of my original compositions called 'Pick Up,' 'Jacqueline,' 'Bowler Hat,' and 'Sly Fox.'

I wrote down all Lenny's jazz choruses for clarinet, which sounded so much as if they were played ad lib but they weren't easy solos at all. I did enjoy making broadcasts with this unique group. In the end, I believe Lenny returned to his native land, Australia.

During this time, I still practised and practised and practised. I think I must have driven our neighbours mad in Clarence Road, but they were lovely and never once complained. In fact, I played all the great masters' wonderful music, including Bach, Mozart, Beethoven, Chopin and the French Impressionist School including Debussy and Ravel. I also played on gigs two or three times a week with various bands. For one particular gig at a very wealthy mansion, I got together an unusual group that consisted of me on piano, Alan Hartwell and Vic Reynolds on saxophones and an attractive young violinist called Rosemary Utting. Rosemary came from a very musical family and later on, I chose her to play the violin part of the piano and violin sonata I composed for my audition for a scholarship at the Royal College of Music.

Many years later, I used Rosemary's younger, attractive sister, Jill Utting, as one of the sopranos in my John Fox Singers. The strangest thing was for about six months, I had no idea she was Rosemary's sister. She came to me recommended by an associate of mine, John McCartney, who was involved in booking session singers and had always helped me with choosing my choir. It was a practice of mine to call my singers by their first names and I only knew this particular singer simply as Jill—it was only when I gave her a lift home one night that Jill chatted about her family and spoke about her older sister Rosemary who played the violin!

My singers were versatile and I broadcasted with them many times. They mostly vocalized as an added blend with my orchestra, or I would use them singing *a cappella* (meaning unaccompanied by any musical instruments) and for standard songs with an orchestral backing. It was very important that these singers could all sight-sing to save recording time in the studios.

I remember arranging 'Dreamsville,' a lovely song written by Henry Mancini, which is one of my personal favourites. Before the war, I would often play the piano in cinemas where singing competitions were held before the morning matinee. I would accompany singers who brought along the music for me to play to their song. It created a real buzz and atmosphere before the movie began and I really loved being involved in this part of cinema. Accompanying is very specialized and it has been a great part of my musical life. For many years, I have accompanied both men and women singers at social functions and theatres. I believe this was born out of all those wonderful family parties we used to have when everyone would be singing their hearts out in the front room, with me as a young lad enthusiastically playing the tunes on the piano.

7

Successful College Days

It was my sister Judy who first contacted The Royal College of Music (RCM) in Kensington, London and managed to get me an audition to study for my ARCM (Associate of Royal College of Music). What Judy did for me was more important and valuable than I can ever express in words. I didn't have any academic qualifications and I didn't have the confidence to promote myself, despite the fact I was working hard on my Associated Board piano grades. I was taking exams every three months and very proudly achieving distinction in most grades.

On the day of the audition, a professor asked me some questions about theory while also testing my knowledge of composers. He then asked me to sight-read a piece and play something of my choice on the piano and I chose to play Beethoven's *Moonlight Sonata*. When I finished, this professor was quiet for what seemed ages and the silence in the room seemed unbearable to me. Then he said quietly, "I'm going to take a chance on you, Mr. Fox, because your rendering of that Sonata moved me almost to tears. You'll start next term."

I was thrilled even though I knew this meant I would have to study very hard every day for the next year. At that time, I was teaching pupils at the Sutton College of Music in Grove Road, Sutton. I didn't enjoy teaching very much, mostly because many of my pupils lacked any real talent, with the parents very often wanting their children to play the piano more than the child! Only a chosen few would be dedicated enough to practise, with the remainder of my disinterested pupils rarely practising at all, leading me to become increasingly frustrated.

It is not easy to play any instrument well and even someone who is born with a gift has to work very hard at perfecting and improving on his or her talent. I felt extremely fortunate that I was lucky enough as an ex-serviceman to be accepted by a place such as the Royal College of Music, but if I hadn't practised and practised all those years I probably would not have made the grade.

Once I began my studies at the RCM, Judy, who was working as a shorthand typist, realized how tough it was for me financially and every week I would find a pound note on top of the piano at home. She had complete faith in me and never once doubted that I would make it in this wonderful profession. I have never ever forgotten her kindness and unfailing support during that vital stage of my life.

The Royal College gave me one year's study and after that, I won a three year composition scholarship. There were some good tutors and Dr. Edith Bathhurst and Percy Turnbull in particular taught me one of the most valuable lessons of all. They taught me what to leave out when composing. As mentioned briefly already, I composed a sonata for violin and piano for my audition with the RCM, for which I asked a very good student pianist, Fred Loftin, to play the piano and of course, Rosemary Utting, the violin part.

It was after I wrote this sonata that I knew my role in music was going to be composing, arranging and conducting. That sonata has always meant something rather special to me and I have an old recording, which I have recently copied to CD. Soon after that sonata, I wrote *Seven Easy Songs for Children* for soprano, sung beautifully by a student at the college with piano accompaniment. My first wife Jackie's eldest sister Eve, who was also a teacher, wrote the words of these songs. Although she wasn't a songwriter, she often wrote lovely poetry for children, which I would put to music. Thus began my love of children's songs and over the years, I have had the pleasure of composing in this genre many times.

Towards the end of my first year at college, Judy went to the expense of installing a telephone in Clarence Road because she thought it was necessary for the advancement of my career. She also spent many hours writing letter after letter to film producers on my account, until finally someone sat up and took notice. It was during this second year that I began composing music for quite a few 'B' films. This included one starring Richard Todd, another which was a murder mystery called *The Trunk* directed by Donovan Winter and *Death Drums Along the River,* which appears on Film4 quite frequently along with many of the other black-and-white movies. I still get a thrill hearing my music.

I would have to read the script of the film before driving to the film set at Elstree Studios to get the feel of the movie and meet the stars. This was the time to begin composing the music and when I had finished composing the score, a studio in London was booked where I would conduct a small orchestra set up with their backs to the screen. I would conduct them with one eye on the movie and on my score and one eye on my orchestra! It was quite a skilful job conducting a scene leading up to a certain climax and I had to ensure the right *rubato* (an Italian musical term meaning 'out of tempo') was reached at the right moment.

Unfortunately, the executive producer who commissioned me to write music for most of these films suddenly had a fatal heart attack. Sadly, these commissions very soon dried up and I didn't write film music again except for library music. Due to technology and the advancement of modern equipment, writing and recording film music is very different today, so I assume it is far easier now than in the days when I was writing it.

While studying hard at the RCM, I continued to write piano pieces by the dozen, including many compositions about the sea, which is, in my opinion, a wonderful subject for composers. One piece I wrote at the time was called 'Moon Over the Sea,' and much later in my career I arranged and conducted it for a large orchestra in Budapest, Hungary; it is included on a CD called *The Sea.*

Many well-known composers, who were also good pianists, often wrote piano pieces first and orchestrated them later. A good example of this is Ravel's *Pavane Pour Une Infante Défunte.* Stravinsky also relied a great deal on the piano for much of his symphonic orchestral music. To my mind, it doesn't really matter how the piece is written, providing the piece is not orchestrated in a 'pianistic' way, which put simply, means you need to have an orchestra in mind and not a keyboard when composing.

The piano is really just the instrument to help you keep in tune with what you are doing. For example, if you want a chord for the trombone section, the piano will help you to choose the right notes while experimenting on the composition. The piano is a means to an end with the end product being the real test of the piece's musical qualities for an orchestra.

8

Sally Barnes—Marriage to Jackie—Big Bands

In the early fifties, I got a phone call from Sally Barnes, the comedian charlady who entertained in the variety theatres, mostly in the Midlands. She was a very attractive blond who was extremely popular in her day and she probably heard about me through connections in the musical circles. I couldn't believe it when she asked me if I would take on the job of being her accompanist and arranger. I jumped at the chance! Sal (as we always called her) liked my piano playing immediately and must have recognized I had a comedian's streak as well as being a musician because she gave me the job on the spot! We rehearsed at her house in Surbiton with her husband Bobby Beaumont who was her manager. He was the younger brother of the wonderful musical comedy soprano Roma Beaumont. Talent obviously ran in the family!

Bobby was also a juggler and very good at playing darts in the restaurants and pubs. Whenever we had venues at various theatres, we would have a game of darts and he always beat me! And remember, I was quite a good player!

My act with Sally was very funny. Sally would go on to the stage and sing her signature song, 'The Best Things in Life are Free' dressed up as a charlady in rags with a bucket and mop. I would come on after her opening song, dressed as a workman in old overalls and a cloth cap patting her on the back saying things like, "Allo my old Sal, nice to see you 'ere tonight." The idea really was about a charlady and a cockney character who could play the 'joanna' then clean up after the 'stars' had gone home!

Sal would say, "Play on that old 'joanna' for me. Go on!" Part of my act was to play a little from the famous *Warsaw Concerto,* which always seem to go down well with audiences.

One particular night when it was my cue to join her on stage, I patted her on the back a little too hard, and she fell right into the orchestral pit! What a racket that made—the drums and the instruments making a real cacophony as they flew in different directions. The audience roared with laughter as they thought it was part of the act. Sal, being the pro she always was, got straight back on stage as bright and cheerful as ever. Fortunately, she was unharmed, only shaken up a little. Sal was a good sport and a wonderful comic.

There were also poignant moments in her act when she sang a song that brought tears to the eyes. Good comedians aren't funny all the time, as Charlie Chaplin proved. One of the venues was held at the Birmingham Hippodrome and a drummer friend, Tony Pike, drove my mum and dad, together with Judy Maureen, and her husband, Tom, to watch the show, which they really enjoyed as it gave them such a good laugh.

There was a time when Sal was upset because she wasn't advertised as top of the bill. She was performing with Alma Cogan who had been given the top billing. She was a singer of traditional pop music and was known as 'The Girl with a Giggle in her Voice' and was the highest paid female entertainer of her era. However, Sal quite rightly believed she was entitled to a joint billing at the very least. She complained bitterly to her manager and I do believe Sal and Alma had quite a row as apparently, they hated each other like poison! Anyway, Sal fought her corner well and they ended up sharing the top bill.

Shortly before my dad died of lung cancer, he saw Sal performing on *Sunday Night at the London Palladium,* on our small television set. He was so thrilled to see the show and hear the orchestra playing my arrangements conducted by Jack Parnell. Even though my dad was seriously ill, he made a big effort to let me know how happy and proud he was of me. It was some years later that I learned Sal had died in a nursing home for retired artists. What a professional she was and what a loss!

She had lived for some time on a houseboat on the River Thames and I don't know what happened to her husband and her two lovely daughters. When I found out later that she had died, I felt very sad indeed about it. No one can ever replace the talents of my old pal Sal and I have often thought about her over the years. She really was one in a million and we had such fun working together. I certainly could never forget her.

I didn't work with Sal for very long because many of the music halls began to close down. Times were changing and music halls were losing their popularity; consequently, Sally was getting less work. It was after my Sally Barnes period that bigger and better things began to come my way, especially when the well-known band leader, Jack Newman came into my life.

Like so many band leaders at the time, he played in the more exclusive areas of London including Mayfair and the West End. However, his real knowledge of music was limited and he wanted me to write some special arrangements for his band. I also became his pianist playing at places such as the popular dance hall, the Astoria in London. I remember arranging 'On the Sunny Side of the Street,' which was the band's signature tune with the boys in the band singing the chorus. It certainly was a jazzy period in my career and I even have a very scratchy '78' record of this band playing some of my arrangements including that very song!

'On the Sunny Side of the Street' reminds me of a place that had the nickname of 'The Musician's Street' in the West End of London. This was a valuable street for any musicians looking for work or 'gigs' as we call them. The real name of the street is Archer Street and here you would see clusters of musicians clutching their diaries to write down the available gigs. If there was some work coming your way, you would certainly be 'On the Sunny Side of the Street'!

Sometime after playing for Jack Newman, another band leader, Fred Hedley, came into the picture. In addition to arranging for him, I also played piano at Wimbledon Town Hall during the famous Wimbledon Tennis Tournament. It was a good band consisting of both professional and semi-professional musicians. We had a great summer season in Brighton with a packed ballroom every night including many of the afternoons. I enjoyed these sessions especially as one particular pub in Brighton kept open for our band when afternoon matinees were required at the ballroom! The opening hours in pubs were restricted then and we thought it was wonderful to be able have a drink or two in the afternoon.

During the time I was playing and arranging for Fred, the leader of the trombone section was a very young but superb musician called

Pete Smith. He also played the piano very well and often arranged for the small group within that band. Pete later became a professional arranger for the BBC Radio Big Band, the complete Radio Orchestra and later went on to record on well-known labels.

In addition to all this, he was a fabulous jazz trombonist and almost as good as the late trombonist Don Lusher, the great! Pete became a good friend of my first wife, Jackie, and me and even spent the first night of his honeymoon at our house in St. James's Road Sutton. His was rather a sad story because his father didn't want him to become a professional musician or get married and so they fell out in a big way.

Another important episode of my life happened about this time, too. I met my first wife. Judy introduced me to a friend of hers from the Rhonda Valley near Cardiff in Wales. Her name was Jacqueline but everyone called her Jackie and she was living next door to Judy in Wallington, Surrey, with her sister Eve. Jackie was a brilliant teacher who taught the reception class at a primary school in Wallington. A pretty brunette, she was a serene lady who had a degree in everything and seemed to have a special talent for teaching young children.

Before we were married, I once drove Jacqueline to work at the beginning of a new school year. In the playground, there was a hell of a racket with children crying and parents crying as they said their goodbyes. It was then I found out what magic Jackie had with children. Within ten minutes, she had her class of infants as quiet as mice and under control. Of course, I wasn't a good teacher and I felt in awe of her ability to command children's attention with such quiet authority.

Jackie liked cricket, which intrigued me as this was slightly unusual in a woman and also because cricket is the only sport that is of interest to me. Her lovely quiet lilting Welsh voice attracted me and it wasn't long before we were courting. Jackie understood what my music meant to me and even though I was still practising every moment I possibly could, we managed to spend quite a lot of time together. We fell in love and I knew instantly I wanted to marry her. We began married life at home with my parents, who gave up their bedroom for us. We stayed there for six months before we could afford to rent part of a detached house in St. James Road, Sutton. It was a pretty garden flat which we lived in for two years.

We didn't have much of a honeymoon because just a few days after we were married, Jackie's mother, who was in her mid-sixties, had a fatal heart attack. Jackie was very close to her mother so of course she went straight back to her hometown in the Rhonda Valley for the funeral and that was the end of our honeymoon. On her return, we settled down to our married life with Jackie accepting that music came first in my life, which meant I was out most evenings. We only had one evening to ourselves and that was Sunday. I was mildly amused and pleased to notice that under the influence of living with Jackie's lovely lilting accent, I gradually improved my own accent, which was rather more Cockney than Surrey in those days!

She loved Dylan Thomas the poet, especially his play for voices, *Under Milkwood,* which I also adored and even today I still have that book and read it sometimes. It is such an original play for voices, and Richard Burton, the great Welsh actor, read it so well, along with the other very good Welsh actors and actresses. I have the whole play on an old Argo LP which is a real treasure.

In 1958, we could at last afford to buy a small detached house of our own in Banstead, Surrey. This was largely due to the fact Jackie was on a regular teacher's salary, as just like any other musician, my earnings were often irregular.

When I was courting Jackie, I would sometimes visit the Rhonda Valley where she lived with her family and at this point I want to mention Jackie's younger brother Ray Isaac. He was a great athlete and after the war when he was still in the RAF, he was the person who ran round the ring at the Royal Albert Hall in 1948 with the Olympic torch to herald the beginning of the first games to be held since the war. He was a lovely man, married with two daughters, and he used to say in his wonderful Welsh accent, "Play some boogie woogie for me please, John." I would spend quite a long time just playing the piano for him and he never seemed to tire of hearing me play. Ray was an architect by profession and in the sixties designed and built a house with his own hands. It was a unique property in Carmarthen, South Wales, which was an architectural innovation at the time. We would often joke, "The house that Ray built!" Tragically, not long after the house was finished, Ray died of a massive heart attack at the tender age of 36 years.

Jackie almost fainted with shock when she heard the news because she was very close to Ray. We often thought afterwards that perhaps Ray's heart attack was brought on through working so hard building his lovely house, which he was never to enjoy.

On one particular visit to Wales, I decided to explore the lovely mountains and went for a walk in the Rhonda Valley in the early morning mists, very close to a coal mining area. After a while, I became aware an Alsatian dog was following me, which it continued to do for at least five miles. How I enjoyed that walk in the wonderful companionship of this unknown dog. From that day, I swore I would never in the future be without a dog and it wasn't long before we bought a Border collie puppy which we named Taly.

I learned before Jackie and I were married that unfortunately she would never be able to have children. This came as quite a shock to me and was a great disappointment at the time, but I was too much in love with Jackie for this to make any difference. Jackie didn't feel she missed out very much because, being a teacher, she was with plenty of five- to six-year-olds every day. Today, I feel an even greater sense of loss from not having children, particularly as the one time I could have had children with my second wife, Joy, we made a decision not to because of important musical commitments. There are very few of the Fox family left and I feel very sad about this, but I feel very lucky that I now have three stepchildren from my marriage to Joy.

Jackie loved my mum and especially my dad who at that time had lung cancer. A specialist had told him he had only three months to live and Judy suggested visiting a faith healer. I have to confess, I had no idea such a person existed and didn't think for a moment it would work. However, we were all desperate to help our dad and so as a last resort I agreed and we got in touch with a faith healer called Mrs. Shepherd.

I have to admit that I was surprised at the progress of my dad's health and the most wonderful thing of all was he lived for a further five years. Not many people believed what I told them until they saw with their own eyes his great improvement and then nobody thought it was nonsense. It somehow proves to me that there is something very special in faith healing.

We also took our mum who suffered horribly with arthritis and couldn't pick up the very large teapot she used for making tea for us all. One day after taking her to see Mrs. Shepherd for her arthritis, she put the kettle on and we were all talking away when we suddenly noticed what she was doing. "Mum," we yelled, "you're pouring out the tea!" We were all astounded.

Since then, I have visited the Harry Edwards Sanctuary for faith healers. This sanctuary impressed me very much as it is so spiritual and a wonderful place to visit as it is so tranquil. It is located in Burrows Lea, a beautiful part of Surrey near Shere, but more of this later.

Before we were married, Jackie was taken ill with T.B. Peritonitis, which was a serious disease and she had to go to Alton in Hampshire, very close to where Jane Austin the famous author lived, to convalesce for ten months. At the time, I drove an old Hillman and I would visit her every Sunday. Not long ago, I couldn't believe my eyes when I saw this very car in one of the period plays on television, the registration BKR 924 staring back at me from the screen. Even in my day it was quite old, but it was a glorious car with leather seats and without a boot, just a spare wheel at the back.

Every year, Jackie and I took my mum and dad to Cornwall or to mid-Wales for a holiday. We would tour the whole coast and countryside, staying in guest houses or bed and breakfast. My parents would be sitting in the back of the Hillman with their luggage on their laps! What fun we had with my dad insisting on stopping at every pub we passed, and me putting my foot down to speed past, while he grumbled away in the back, half hidden behind his luggage! My dad was an extremely generous man for someone who had very little money. On entering a pub, he was always the first person at the bar buying a round whether it was for one friend or ten. What a character he was and I had great affection and admiration for him.

My dad and I had bought that car together when I first came out of the RAF and I was a young impoverished composer! We were both so proud of our Hillman car and what a joyful moment it was seeing our early car looking as clean as a whistle on TV.

During my time playing in Brighton with Fred Hedley, even though I loved the Hillman, I had enough funds of my own to buy a new car. It was a white Ford Prefect and I was very proud of it, driving it backwards and forwards from my house in Sutton to Brighton every night. On these journeys, everyone was always happy to share the petrol costs. I have to confess that I did drive like a maniac in those days with at least three or four members of the band as passengers, including Fred himself.

But we were all young lads and it was all very exciting, as of course the roads were far less busy in those days and it was a dream driving on them. Back then, not many people had cars, unlike today, when many families may have three or four cars, whether they can afford it or not.

9

About Religion and Songwriting

Another interesting episode in the late fifties was my association with the Anglican Reverend Geoffrey Beaumont who preached at the huge church, St. George's in Camberwell, London. He was quite famous for his new style hymns known as Twentieth Century Folk Mass and even published a book called Eleven Hymn Tunes. He also went round playing singsongs in local pubs on piano and was very popular with everyone who lived in his diocese.

I wrote arrangements for him and conducted a band of professionals and semi-professional musicians including a small string section. The ten o'clock services on Sunday mornings consisted of me conducting this band on a balcony high above the aisle in this beautiful old church as I followed the church service with my baton!

Rev. Geoffrey Beaumont wrote lovely melodies to very popular hymns, and there was no organ, just this big band. The musicians were all volunteers (including myself) with no fees attached. We all gave our best, feeling good knowing we had given our spare time in the name of the Lord! Later, the Rev. Geoffrey had a half hour's programme on ITV television, called *About Religion*. I wrote and conducted all the arrangements for this programme, which also consisted of some of Rev. Geoff's original hymns. He would narrate, too, and even though it was live television, he didn't stick strictly to his script and the producer would have to crawl sometimes on his hands and knees to give me the okay to start on the next hymn!

I would be following the script so I knew when to begin playing but there was one occasion I shall never forget when Rev. Geoff was improvising. It was an awful moment because there was this complete silence as he had gone way off the script and I was still waiting for my cue. It was probably only for a few seconds, but it felt like a very long time. It was horrible! Later in his life, he became a monk and I was devastated to hear that one day he committed suicide. This has always been a mystery to me because in my opinion he was a one-off; he was such a lovely kind man, loved by everyone who met him.

While this was going on, I met an aristocratic gentleman called Derek Maxwell who wrote lyrics and we decided to write songs together. We traipsed round many publishers in Denmark Street, (known in those days as 'Tin Pan Alley' but which is now a rather trendy street) London searching for someone who would take us on. Eventually we struck gold with the British singer Ronnie Hilton who was very successful during the 1950s, owing his easy singing style to Perry Como and Bing Crosby. He enjoyed nine top twenty hits between 1954 and 1957 and continued to record until twenty-five years later when he became the voice of the BBC Radio 2's *Sounds of the Fifties*.

He recorded a song of ours called 'The Most Wonderful Thing in the World,' which was shown on ITV television one Saturday night. The stage had one big world all lit up and it was very colourful. It was a very exciting moment for both of us and we were very happy, especially later on when we received many royalties from that song. 'The Most Wonderful Thing in the World' really was "most wonderful" to Derek and me!

Later on we gave up writing songs together because The Beatles came on the scene and publishers became much less interested in the type of songs we were writing, and also because we just weren't able to make much money.

I continued to compose and arrange while Derek went into partnership with a friend making some real money from property speculation. He is still alive and the same age as me, but unfortunately he is seriously ill now and almost blind. Luckily, he can still hear and enjoy music. Some of the other songs, amongst many others we wrote together are 'Let's Dream Awhile,' 'You Send Me,' 'We Are Forever,' and 'This is The End.' They are all romantic songs and we were so proud of them in those early days.

10
Serious Composing and Arranging

All the years of hard work of practising and practicing, together with my studying at the Sutton School of Music and the Royal College of Music, were at last beginning to pay off. Music was pouring out of me and I was composing with so much excitement it seemed as if my very life depended on it. Ideas for composition kept coming and I would write theses ideas down immediately. I decided it was time to do something serious about my music.

One morning, I picked up several pieces of my most recent solo piano pieces and set off to Denmark Street where Derek Maxwell and I had found publishers for our songs. I had been told about Anglo-Continental Music so decided to try them first. I stood, hesitating on the threshold, before boldly knocking on the door.

A Polish man called Richard Frank who was the main publisher agreed to see me saying, "What have you got?" I showed him some of my manuscripts, which he asked me to play. He sat at his desk smoking calmly as he listened intently. When I finished he said, "I like your music very much; it is most original."

My first compositions were published and he sent me off to write about half a dozen ordinary, novelty piano pieces. One day he casually asked me to write a composition for a symphony orchestra. I couldn't believe it because I had never composed anything like that before. To be suddenly asked to write for a mighty orchestra was a very big step for me and I was in total awe, almost speechless. He must have noticed the look on my face.

"Go on," he said, "you can do it, you have the talent. Just do it. Choose any subject."

I rushed home bursting with excitement and telling myself, "I have to do what I have to do. What can I write? What can I write?"

It felt so urgent, this desire to write the piece immediately. I think it was probably because I was so afraid that if I stopped to think too much, I wouldn't have the confidence to do what Richard had asked of me. I wrote the first thing that came in to my mind, scribbling furiously as the ideas came flooding out of me. What helped me most of all was my extensive knowledge of orchestration, which I had studied very seriously during my college days.

As a lover of the English countryside, I chose to write a composition called 'A Pastoral Impression.' I took it to Richard who checked through the score suggesting just a few changes here and there. He was impressed and very pleased with it. Imagine my joy!

At that time, the BBC was looking for new composers and used the BBC Concert Orchestra to play through four or five works from young composers every month. Each composer's work was auditioned and if liked, it would be passed for broadcasting. Richard submitted my piece and it passed the BBC audition. I nearly jumped over the moon. My first serious piece for a full-sized concert orchestra and here it was being played over the radio! Not only that, my piece was playing amongst the music of the great masters such as Sir Edward Elgar, the popular English composer.

Richard was a marvellous mentor. He was a very good composer himself and he had the ability to spot what was right or wrong with a piece. He would spend hours with me always with a cigarette in his hand, going over my pieces, even taking the telephone off the hook so he wouldn't be disturbed. He was so interested in talent and would make time to see any musician who showed promise. At the time, Richard had another protégé, a young composer who visited him at his office now and then. His name was Howard Blake. Blake is famous for his very popular piece from *The Snowman* called 'Walking in the Air,' and amongst many concert works, he wrote a piano concerto for Princess Diana. We met quite a few times in Richard's office but our paths went in different directions and although I am still loosely in contact with Howard, since those early days we have only met again on a few occasions.

That composition of mine, 'Pastoral Impression,' was recorded on CD with works from other well-known composers by the White Line label in 2003 entitled *British Light Music Discoveries 5* played by The City of Prague Philharmonic Orchestra conducted by Gavin Sutherland. My piece was retitled 'A Pastoral Reflection.' Over the years, many orchestras have played this composition and I have also conducted some of them, too, but this particular recording really is magnificent. Since that composition I have written many other successful light classical pieces for orchestra including 'Portrait of Eve,' 'Characters from the Fairy Tales' and 'Strings in Three Four,' to name a few which have been recorded on commercial CD.

In 1963, I worked as a pianist six nights a week at the Piccadilly Hotel, which had a lovely grand piano. I played with the Harold Turner Quartet of which Harold was the leader, drummer and vocalist. I have always loved the exciting atmosphere of the West End shows and concert halls and it was a real pleasure working in such a classy hotel with many celebrities dancing to our quartet. However, we found it irksome when one night the manager insisted we had to enter the hotel through the tradesman entrance! Imagine how amused we were the next night when for security reasons the same manager said we had to enter through the main grand entrance in Piccadilly!

After that, the Harold Turner Quartet played for some time at a well-known night club, the Jacaranda Club in Chelsea. It was a select place where quite a few named people went to dine, including film stars and radio celebrities. It was here that I met the famous bandleader Jack Payne who was the first British bandleader to perform for troops in France during the war. He was married to the equally famous pianist Peggy Cochrane.

Jack would visit the Jacaranda Club quite often and enjoyed listening to my solo piano playing during the interval. He was so impressed he said he would help me and later on he actually became my agent. He wrote a letter to Norman Mead, the BBC Orchestration's Manager, who interviewed me a few weeks later at Broadcasting House. He gave me a popular song referred to as a 'popular evergreen' called 'You are my Lucky Star' to arrange for the BBC orchestras. I was definitely 'under a lucky star' because after that I wrote hundreds of arrangements, which helped make my name as both an arranger and composer. This is a most unusual combination because generally anyone with musical ability would be either one or the other, but rarely both.

After the Jacaranda Club, our quartet played in a hotel at Tags Island close to Richmond with the popular woman trumpet player Gracie Cole. Gracie was the lead trumpet in the Ivy Benson Girls Band from 1945 to 1950, before leaving to form her own 'all girl' band, which made music press headlines with a performance at London's Jazz Jamboree. In 1951, she married Bill Geldard, a first-class trombonist and a fine musical arranger who played with saxophonist George Evans.

During this time, I was arranging quite a lot for the BBC orchestras, and Gracie always showed great interest in my scores. One day, astounded by the harmonies I wrote, she told me she believed I had discovered what sounded good and what didn't in my arrangements.

I was so sorry to hear of Gracie's death at age 82 in December 2006 after a long illness. However, true to her love of music, she was still playing the piano in nursing homes two weeks before she died. She was a tremendous trumpet player and certainly one of the 'boys'! She had a real ear for music and could busk anything!

Another place I had some interesting times in was the Empress Club in London where I took a tinkling piano job in the evenings. This was a place for rich and aristocratic clientele including many film stars. Many of these celebrities knew me by my first name and would call out, "Good evening, John." and "Goodnight, John."

After a while, I got to know their favourite songs and sitting by the window of this popular club playing the grand piano, I could see these celebrities coming and going. When I spotted a familiar famous face, I would make sure I was playing their favourite song as they walked through the door. This obviously pleased them very much and on the way out, they would often leave a large tip on top of the piano. Sometimes it was a pound note, sometimes a fiver or even a tenner and on some occasions, it might even be a twenty-pound note. It didn't take me long to remember who liked which song!

My lovely mother, Laura, in her teenage years.

My dear dad in 1914–1918 war.

The family in Brighton with baby John on Mother's lap.

The Fox family at home, with John as a small boy.

The Robin Hood Hotel, which was the local pub where my parents used to go for a drink.

Me (with hat on), recently, on the corner seat where my parents used to sit for a drink.

Young John in the garden at home in Sutton.

Today's frontal view of 62 Clarence Rd. in Sutton Surrey, where I was born.

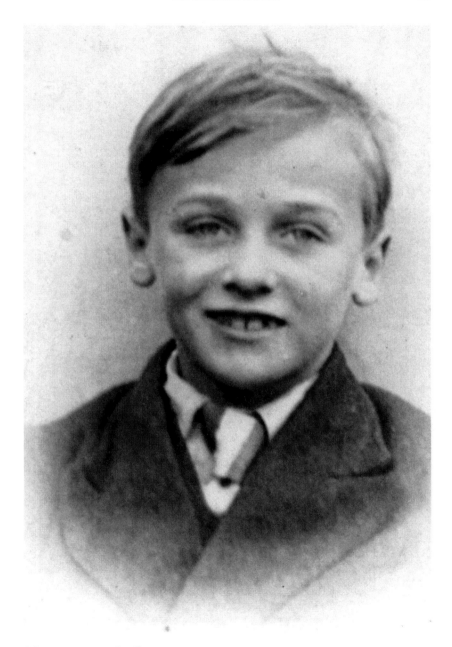

John, as a young schoolboy.

John with his wonderful parents.

John as a teenager with first love (Hilda).

Hilda—John's first love.

Young John in the RAF (Royal Air Force).

John with RAF colleagues.

John's RAF Band.

My Mum and Dad in Brighton on holiday.

John with his three sisters Maureen, Judy, and Lee.

His Mum and Dad relaxing in front of John's old Ford Prefect.

Many of the Fox clan with Uncle Harry when he came over from Canada to visit.

Dad, Mum, Jacqueline, and me in front of my old Hillman Minx car.

11

Teaching and My Trip to Krakow

It wasn't long before I gave up evening work because of the late hours it involved. It was a change not to have to dress in an evening suit followed by the long boring journeys driving to London and back. Another reason for giving up evening work was because a different opportunity came my way. The head of the very large secondary Wandsworth Comprehensive School phoned and asked me if I would like to be a temporary music teacher for a term until the permanent teacher was able to take up the post.

The money was good but unlike Jackie, I really had no experience teaching classes in school. But as it was only for a short while, I thought the challenge would be interesting. I had to play the piano for the hymn in the main assembly hall that involved sight-reading first thing in the morning. I tried to teach eight- to fifteen-year-old boys something about the theory of music. It is true that one has to love teaching to make a proper go at it. Thank God for good teachers because unfortunately I wasn't one. However, this temporary post did remind me of the school featured in the magazine Magnet called Greyfriars, which took me back to when I would read these stories with my sister Judy, many, many years before.

The headmaster of a comprehensive school still wore a cap and gown in the fifties and I can still fully visualize an incident when I witnessed the headmaster in his full attire flogging a boy. This boy had stolen money from another boy's locker and he was hauled up in front of the whole school in assembly and given '12 of the best' with a long cane. I remember the young boy didn't make a sound.

Another incident involved one of the boys in my class playing a prank on me. Just as I was about to sit at the piano, I heard a few giggles and instantly spotted four or five drawing pins on my piano stool. I pretended I hadn't seen them and made as if I was about to sit down then said, "*Who* did this?" There was complete silence. No doubt others in the class were in on the 'joke' but I knew the main culprit and I asked him to stand on his chair and sing all the music notes in their various pitches, which I pointed out on the blackboard. There were no more practical jokes that term!

You have to love your work, just as I love music, to be good at it. If you are a good teacher, you are simply worth your weight in gold. Jackie was certainly in that class—excuse the pun! She was a magnificent schoolteacher because she had a certain way with young children and seemed to have that natural ability to hold their attention effortlessly.

While teaching, I was still writing quite a number of serious pieces for my Polish music publisher Richard Frank of Anglo-Continental Music. Richard didn't drive and one day he asked me if I would take him to Krakow in Poland in my car because he had organized the Krakow Symphony Orchestra to record about eight of my compositions. We set off with the car piled high and almost weighed down to the ground with all the presents Richard was taking home for family and friends.

It felt very exciting, leaving very early in the morning and after crossing the channel, I drove for many, many hours. We crossed the border at the spot where the Germans first entered Poland to invade the country and it was a fascinating sight because the great big ditch the Germans had built was still there. The bridge between the two countries is very long and high. Looking down, there were many rocks and I remember feeling there was 'danger in the air.' Another colourful spectacle on our journey was the jostling and constant stream of many peasants going to market with their fruit and vegetables in wooden carts with enormous, almost vertical shafts attached to the horses.

We stopped in Warsaw, where we paid a visit to Richard's brother who was a professional teacher and while we were there a rather amusing incident occurred. One night, Richard asked me if I would like to attend a sex education class! We didn't go, of course, but I learned these classes were an integral part of Polish life and I was quite astounded at the time.

These were magical days for me with the musicians playing my compositions beautifully, the recordings taking place in a magnificent old church with superb acoustics. There is a great cathedral in this lovely city and the dome is made of pure gold! Although it was a communist country, I liked Poland very much and to me it seemed to be full of gentlefolk. In fact, one of the compositions I wrote for the Krakow Symphony Orchestra was called 'Gentle Folk,' which is still played in many countries today.

I found it to be a wonderful country and it was difficult to comprehend that not so many years ago, during the Second World War, thousands and thousands of Polish Jews were exterminated in concentration camps by the Nazis. Strangely enough, the Nazis liked music, especially Wagner, and if a Jew could play an instrument well, he or she was more likely to escape the gas chambers.

12
BBC Orchestras and Solo Piano

During the early sixties, while I was composing and arranging prolifically for the BBC, my music career took off in another direction because Chris Morgan, one of the senior producers of Radio 2, was a great advocate of my music. He liked my style of composing and arranging, which was very popular with the station's audiences, and he asked me to audition for one of Radio 2's half-hourly programmes. This involved conducting the BBC Variety and Revue Orchestras as well as my own orchestra, accompanied by well-known singers such as Rosemary Squires, Cleo Lane, Nick Curtis and Lindsay Benson.

I am very thankful that conducting other people's music as well as my own is among my specialties because I passed the audition effortlessly. It was a very proud moment for me. These programmes were a combination of all kinds of different music, which included the conductor following singers in 'rubato' and conducting well-known pieces of light music by composers such as Eric Coates. He wrote the music for *The Dambusters* and the famous signature tune for the Radio 4 programme *Desert Island Discs,* which is still going today.

Another music writer who also had his own programme at the BBC was Canadian Robert Farnon, known to all of us as Bob. During the war, he conducted the Canadian Band of the Allied Expeditionary Forces and was seen as one of the greatest composers of light music in the latter half of the last century.

Following this success, I was given many conducting programmes, which involved me working very closely with different producers. Most of the time, the producers let me choose and conduct the music selections, which would very often include some of my own arrangements and compositions. Not only was I recording music for my own half-hour programmes but also for the many programmes played throughout the week on BBC Radio 2.

It was wonderful to have this freedom to help choose the music and devise compilations that worked very well and were so popular with both the BBC and the audiences. However, there were occasions when perhaps a young producer wanted to make his mark and he would insist I include something I felt wouldn't go so well. There wasn't much I could do on these occasions but go along with the changes, but luckily this didn't happen very often.

One particular junior producer sticks in my mind because he behaved towards some of us in the BBC in a very arrogant and dismissive manner. He obviously felt he belonged to the elitist class of those days and didn't fraternize with those he thought more menial than he! One day, I needed to speak to him and knocked at his door. He answered rather gruffly, "I haven't got time for you today."

Some while later, when my name was famous within the halls of the BBC and its listeners, I came across this same producer on the stairs and he was very friendly. "Well hello, John, and how are you?" In no uncertain terms, I quickly replied, "You didn't say that to me a couple of years ago when you turned me out of your office." Embarrassed, he bumbled some kind of "haw-haw" reply, and I was glad to have had the opportunity to give him a little of his own medicine!

During my time at the BBC, I became good friends with George Smith from Chappell's Music Publishing, founded in 1811, which is the best and most famous music library in the world. George knew all the people at the top in the BBC and he was an avid fan of my music. He was always happy for me to arrange any piece from Chappell's massive music library for strings, harp and rhythm. In fact, he would often say to me, "John, don't forget to always use something from Chappell's to be played on your radio programmes."

Ernie Ponticelli, a fantastic pianist from Campbell Connelly, told me the same thing. This music publishing company was co-founded by singer-songwriter Jimmy Campbell and his friend Reg Connelly, who wrote the song 'Show Me the Way to Go Home,' which sold two million copies in one year.

This helped me a lot because whenever I had any spare time, I was able to earn money picking and choosing my favourite evergreens to arrange from these two famous publishers. I have written some of my best arrangements under these conditions and loved every second of it because I was able to arrange my favourite songs 'my way'!

One particular broadcast was called *The BBC Radio Orchestra Show* and I was asked to be the guest arranger and composer for part of the show entitled *A Man and His Music*. This show was broadcast every Saturday at lunchtime and the compere who interviewed me was Michael Aspel, well-known for hosting the long-running children's television series *Crackerjack* in the sixties and *Aspel And Company*. He was a regular host for *Miss World* and latterly hosted the *Antiques Road Show* for several years. After Michael finished interviewing me, he went on to play six pieces of my music including 'Pastoral Impressions' and 'Tonight' from *West Side Story*.

Not long afterwards, I became one of the musical arrangers for the BBC, writing for the BBC Variety Orchestra conducted by Paul Fenoulet and later Malcolm Lockyer, and the BBC Revue Orchestra conducted by Harry Rabinowitz. Malcolm was an excellent all-round musician, being a fine pianist, composer, arranger and conductor. He would often ask me to compose music for him. He lived in Sutton, close by to me, but sadly, he died quite young of throat cancer.

I also wrote quite a lot of incidental music for the English composer and arranger Arthur Wilkinson, who began his musical career in the RAF during the Second World War and went on to write music for films and West End shows. He was a much-loved arranger who lived in Banstead and we became very good friends. He would begin his work at four in the morning until ten o'clock when he would stop and spend the rest of the day in his local pub, The Queen Victoria. He also wrote the highly successful *Beatle Nutcracker Suite,* which was a parody of The Beatles in Tchaikovsky style and I wrote many arrangements and some compositions for him including some incidental music for the Ice Skating Shows that took place in London. He died of a massive heart attack in his fifties while conducting one of his ice shows.

Both the BBC Variety Orchestra and Revue Orchestra accompanied all the variety radio programmes and they both had exactly the same combinations with the same sound and the same number of musicians. It was the BBC producer Lawrie Monk who came up with the marvellous idea these two orchestras could be split up and made into one whole unit that could be divided into quite a number of combinations.

They became the BBC Radio Strings, BBC Radio Orchestra and the BBC Radio Big Band. Lawrie was a fabulous musician and he played for me at the Grand Hotel in Eastbourne for a while on bass guitar. Lawrie began his career playing the trombone in the famous Johnny Dankworth Seven Band and when he left, he became a producer for BBC Radio 2. Johnny Dankworth, an English jazz composer, saxophonist and clarinettist, is married to Cleo Lane and is linked with all the great names synonymous with jazz, including Louis Armstrong, Ella Fitzgerald, Duke Ellington and Nat King Cole. Johnny, who is now in his eighties, was made a Knight Bachelor in the New Year's Honours List in 2006 and is the first British Jazz musician to receive such an honour.

Lawrie's idea was to use the whole orchestra once or twice a week with the addition of bassoons, French horns and tubas while also including my John Fox Singers. The Head of Radio 2, Edward Nash, asked me to write some stringy type arrangements as the string section of this newly arranged orchestra had twice the strength of an ordinary orchestra. Instead of having ten violins, three violas and three cellos, I had the great luxury of having twenty violins, six violas and six cellos!

I also had the pleasure of arranging and conducting many times for the full Radio Orchestra, which included the Radio Big Band with players on four trumpets and four trombones in addition to five saxophonists who were also happy to double on other instruments if required by the composer or arranger.

At this time, many other notable musicians also had programmes of their own including pianist Alberto Semprini with the BBC airing his light music programme, *Semprini Serenade,* from 1957 for twenty-five years. Neil Richardson, an English composer, was best known for his library music and in particular his 'Approaching Menace,' which became the famous theme tune for the BBC series 'Mastermind.' Others included Angela Morley who wrote many television and film scores, John Gregory who was also a guest conductor for the BBC Radio Orchestra with his cascading strings style and Frank Chacksfield, one of Britain's most famous orchestra leaders.

Lawrie Monk did an exceptional job of changing the music combinations through the orchestras in addition to helping both male and female vocalists, including my second wife, Joy Devon, who was also a vocalist and who the Radio Orchestra adored. Lawrie died suddenly a few years later. What a loss of a brilliant musician and producer!

By now, Jackie and I were living in a large house in St. James Road, Sutton, renting the ground floor and she must have gone through many lonely times during the evenings as I was driving to London six nights a week to work. This was in addition to teaching private pupils and at the Sutton College of Music during the day while still finding time to compose and write arrangements. It was a tough work schedule and a big strain on me, both mentally and physically.

Another wonderful well-known pianist at the BBC was Alan Clare who would sometimes deputise for me at the Jacaranda Club if he was free. I often did the same for him and we became great friends. Alan was the 'piano player' on the renowned BBC Radio and Television *Goon Show* starring Spike Milligan, Sir Harry Secombe and Peter Sellers. Alan was also quite a comedian in his own right, which was a great asset when working with the Goons! How great the Goons were! They made me cry with laughter whenever I listened to their radio shows or watched them on television. Sir Harry Secombe lived in Sutton and I knew him well. He was also a very good tenor, although he sang 'sharp' at times.

The BBC frequently played my pieces, which provided very good royalties for me. It never ceased to be a very proud moment for me whenever one of my compositions was announced. In those far-off days, each piece was announced individually such as, "That was 'Chanson de Matin' by Edward Elgar. The next piece called 'Safe Grazing' was written by the young English composer John Fox or "That was an English pastoral composition by John Fox." How thrilling those few words can be when you know there could be thousands of people out there listening to your music!

13

Grand Hotel Eastbourne and Dangerous Journeys

Now come some very interesting phases in my musical life, beginning at the Grand Hotel in Eastbourne, one of the most splendid Victorian hotels in the United Kingdom, which stands out magnificently against the coastline with its completely white façade. Linked to many great and prodigious politicians, film stars, world-class tennis players and musicians, including Winston Churchill, Charlie Chaplin and Elgar, it sits on the seafront with views out to Beachey Head.

Debussy, one of the most important of all French composers was also a visitor and during one of his visits actually wrote the wonderful *La Mer* meaning 'The Sea,' which is generally regarded as one of the greatest orchestral works of the twentieth century. I can understand why he was able to write such a marvellous piece with such beautiful views of the sea from the hotel.

The BBC would broadcast salon music from there each Sunday afternoon featuring violinist Albert Sandler. Albert was a household name during the thirties conducting the Palm Court Orchestra. Reginald Leopold, who was known to millions through his broadcasts for the BBC, later took over the Palm Court Orchestra. They broadcast from the foyer in the hotel amongst the potted palms with an invited studio audience and the instrumentalists were required to wear full evening dress. It was an immensely popular programme, which ran for eighteen years.

I heard through the grapevine of available evening work six nights a week at the Grand Hotel and I asked Harold Turner, who was a good vocalist and drummer, if he and his quartet would like to audition with me. Who do you think was there taking the auditions? None other than the British band leader Geraldo whose autograph I had waited for by the stage door on my eighth birthday with my broken arm! More surprisingly, when I walked in, he recognised me straight away, saying, "Aren't you the little boy with the broken arm who came to see me many years ago?" He had heard of 'John Fox' on the radio but had no idea that all along he 'knew' me! Life is full of amazing serendipities.

Geraldo's two grandsons were with him and he asked me to play a solo waltz with just bass and drums. When I had finished, Geraldo said to the two boys, "See, that's the way I want you to play when you grow up." How proud I felt and of course he gave us the job. Although we were billed as the 'Harold Turner Quartet,' I shared the leadership with Harold as it was through my original connection we were given this work.

It was a 116 mile round trip to Eastbourne and the members of our group would take it in turns to drive. Harold who lived in Kensington, London, drove to Purley for the meeting place. From there, we took it in turns to drive to the hotel and back each night, six nights a week in all types of weather. At times during the winter, the driving conditions were very dangerous with ice and snow on the road.

Other than the occasional dreadful car journey, I must admit we felt very lucky because most of the time, we only had to play for two and a half hours each night. Sometimes the manager would ask us to play for longer and eventually we had an arrangement whereby I kept a little book to keep an informal record of our hours. When the hotel was not very busy and we weren't required, I would record this in my little book. Somehow the hours balanced out nicely and we would have 'nights off.'

The third member of our 'quartet' was Alan Hartwell who lives in Ashstead, Surrey. He was the saxophonist who doubled on clarinet; then during the interval he would also double on piano. We had a bass player who lived in Purley, the late Brian Smith, who became a great friend of mine and we used to walk our dogs together in glorious Banstead Wood.

It was during my time playing at the Grand Hotel that a number of events occurred ranging from comedy to tragedy that are forever imprinted on my mind. Late one afternoon, I was relaxing in the bath getting ready for the long evening ahead when I heard the shrill bell of the telephone. I didn't think anything of it, but a short while later I could see smoke coming through the bathroom door.

I leapt out of the bath opened the door and saw smoke all over the house. Forgetting I was completely nude, I rushed down the stairs and found the kitchen on fire. What a terrible sight that was, seeing our lovely kitchen completely ablaze. The back door suddenly opened and our neighbour Mr. Maskery came rushing in with a bowl full of water and aimed the contents at the gas stove where the fire had started. Jackie had been frying some chips when she answered the telephone and it was her sister Eve. Completely forgetting the pan of fat was still on the stove, she had chatted happily away.

It was complete chaos as you can imagine, with me running about all over the place without a stitch on! The fire brigade arrived very quickly to put the fire out, but not before our kitchen had been completely destroyed. Burnt to a cinder, the whole ceiling, the rafters and loft were hacked to pieces, leaving the kitchen looking like a smoking dungeon.

I certainly didn't feel like travelling down to Eastbourne but when I rang Harold to tell him of our disaster, he begged me still to go to work because the Grand Hotel had a special function on that night. Although shaken up, Jackie was fine and our dog Taly was safe so I reluctantly relented. On my return, what a sight greeted me with the kitchen looking like a burnt-out shell. Of course, we eventually had a new kitchen and Mr. Maskery never forgot the time he walked in to our kitchen to help put the fire out and found me running about in utter panic completely naked! He had a great sense of humour and we had many funny moments recalling that scene!

Most evenings, I wouldn't be home until 1:30 a.m., sometimes even later, but I would always take Taly out for a short walk. It was good to get some fresh night air and although I was very tired, it helped me to relax before I went to bed. No matter what time I went to bed, I would rise in the morning to drive Jackie to school in Wallington about four miles away and picked her up again in the afternoons. Later on, Jackie learned to drive and I bought her a lovely white mini so she could drive herself to work.

Sometimes during the summer months, we would go to Eastbourne for the weekend taking Taly to stay over in a small hotel. During the day, I would sometimes swim with my Taly from one pier to the other pier and he would not allow me to go out very far, only about twenty feet. Taly always swam on the outside and one sunny day, the whole of the sea front was full of people admiring and applauding us. Taly certainly was a marvellous Border collie to us.

During those long, long car journeys to Eastbourne, we all learned 'punning.'

One of our favourites was, "I'm getting my royal teas (royalties) tomorrow." In the end, we could hardly stop talking in a 'punny' language!

One evening, it was my turn to drive and on the way, at a place called Forest Row in Sussex, which is very much deer country, a huge deer was crossing the road. There wasn't very much traffic about and it stopped suddenly in the middle of the road. I could see the whites of his big eyes and in a flash I steered the car to the left missing him by an inch and avoiding what might have been a very nasty accident. A few seconds afterwards, the double-bass player sitting in the back of my car said softly, "Oh! Dear!" His comment was completely serious but as we were all "punsters" we made an incident of that for many years with exclamations of, "Oh deer!"

Not far from where that incident took place, there is a dangerous bend in the road. One time, returning from the Grand Hotel in the early hours of the morning, about a mile before that bend, two cars passed us at high speed obviously racing each other. One of the cars tried to pass the other car and careered straight on just before that bend and hit a huge oak tree.

To our horror, when we arrived on the scene several seconds later, we found all the young occupants killed outright. The second car returned to this terrible scene with the young occupants crying out "No, no, please, it can't be!" It was some time before an ambulance came and it was just awful waiting there as we all stood about in total shock. The occupants had all been drinking heavily and the car in the accident was impossible to recognize. None of us spoke a word in the car when we continued our journey. There was no punning that night, only silence. It was an awful tragedy and the event made headlines in the papers the next day.

On another occasion on a cold winter's night, Alan Hartwell, the clarinet player, was driving and the road was like an ice rink. Suddenly our car, a Ford Corsair, went into a spin going round and round at least three or four times before shuddering to a halt. Fortunately, there weren't many motorists on the road that night and Alan, being a very good driver, managed to keep the car from running off the road. Remembering that dreadful night when those youngsters were killed, we felt so relieved to be unhurt.

Sadly, there was worse to come. In the late sixties, I bought a new Vauxhall Victor in a smart two-toned red and grey colour. It was Harold Turner's turn to drive on this particular Thursday night and I asked him whether we could swap because I wanted to show off a bit and use my brand new car for the journey.

Harold, as always, was exceptionally nice and was very happy to swap. The following night, Harold drove as agreed in his two-door Hillman Imp, which had the boot in the front and the engine in the back. On the journey home, very late at night, I remember falling asleep at the shortcut we used to take, which involved driving up a steep hill and then going down the other side to the main road.

I knew nothing until Roy Carter, the current saxophonist, shook me, screaming, "John, John, we have to get out quickly; we've had an accident." I somehow managed to scramble out and all I could hear was this terrible noise of the wheels going round and the car revving with sparks flying everywhere. I thought the car was going to blow up any second. Brian, our bass player, was still in the back, unconscious, but it was the sight of poor Harold Turner that turned me cold. He was lying slumped over the wheel. The impact had broken his neck, killing him instantly.

Most of my ribs were damaged and some broken; my nose was broken, too, and streaming with blood. The ambulance eventually arrived from Redhill Hospital in Surrey and I heard the ambulance driver saying, "Don't worry about the driver in the front, he's gone; we must cut the chap out from the back."

It was chaos on that dreadful night. Harold's brother and son together with my wife, Jackie, and my sister Judy came to visit us in the casualty ward. I was still stunned and in awful shock. The next day, they took me home in an ambulance and the shuddering on that journey was very painful. Roy was in hospital with a broken leg for some time, while Brian remained unconscious for ten days, suffering from a fractured skull. He wore a thick wig on his head to cover up his baldness and that is what saved his life.

We had collided head on with a Velox, which is an extremely strong car. The driver said he came over the brow of the hill and saw our car on the wrong side of the road and we believed Harold must have fallen asleep at the wheel. This had happened before on a number of occasions but only for a couple of seconds, as one of us normally remained awake to keep an eye on him. But, alas, it seems on this particular night, we were all fast asleep.

I felt terrible because I had asked Harold to switch his evening to drive and of course thought, 'But for the Grace of God go I.' How can we ever know that by changing one small arrangement, our lives might be altered in some tragic way? I am a great believer these events happen for a reason and although Harold's time was cut short on this earth, I like to think he's in a far happier place.

14

BBC Radio Orchestra and Female Vocalist, Joy Devon

It was very difficult coming to terms with Harold's death and I was also in a lot of pain from my injuries. However, the following Tuesday after the accident, I was due to conduct a broadcast session with the BBC Radio Orchestra at the Aeolian Hall in New Bond Street. This is where the BBC recorded most of their orchestral sessions and despite my broken and sore ribs, I was determined I was going to attend as this was one of my favourite orchestras and I didn't want to let them down.

Of course everyone said I was mad to go, but I wouldn't give in and as Jackie didn't drive, my next-door neighbour said he would take me to the recording studio and wait until I was ready to go home. Because of my injuries, I was unable to walk and my neighbour had to help lift me up the steps to the studio.

Most of the members of the orchestra knew about the serious accident and when I got to the studio, they all applauded me for the heroic effort I had to make to attend the session. The producer made up a couch for me because I was unable to stand and had to lie almost flat on my back. I was nearly out of sight of the orchestra and all they could see was my baton cutting through the air. Despite this, they followed the music perfectly. It seemed the orchestra never played as well as they did on that day with a horizontal conductor! What a picture it would have made.

At the end of the session, the members of the orchestra came up to me to shake my hand and to express their heartfelt respect and affection. It was a very emotional evening. A month passed before I was able to return to the Grand Hotel and by then I had formed a new group to take Harold's place. Johnny Frenchie was a wonderful session player and he joined the band playing clarinet, bass clarinet, all saxophones and even a mandolin. Lawrie Monk, the BBC producer whom I have already mentioned, played on bass guitar as Brian was still very ill after the accident. In fact, Brian didn't ever return; even when he had recovered physically, he couldn't bring himself to face that car journey with its memories of our awful tragedy. Finally, I took on a local drummer and singer called Geoff Swift and little did I know he would also bring into my life the woman who would become my first *real* love and my second wife.

Apart from the dreadful car accident, my music career was going very well. My name was becoming well-known through my broadcasts with the BBC and I was arranging and conducting many wonderful sessions including my own compositions both home and abroad. But life was not good at home. I was away so much and Jackie was becoming increasingly lonely even though she lived for teaching and also enjoyed cooking, gardening and reading. In our happier days, we would often recite poetry together on a Sunday but now we hardly saw one another as I was very often working that day, too.

I don't remember exactly when I began to notice Jackie smelled of alcohol but it became more apparent on some nights when I returned home late from Eastbourne. At first I didn't think too much of it as I was so busy with my music and just thought Jackie had had a couple of drinks to keep herself amused during the long, lonely evenings without me. She played a lot of Frank Sinatra's hits from the *Only the Lonely* LP and I knew it was almost worn out from being played over and over again. Gordon Jenkins, an American arranger famous for his lush string orchestrations, composed this song for Sinatra. A few years later while working at the BBC, I enjoyed recording it for the BBC Radio orchestra with the John Fox Singers singing the words.

We were still renting the garden flat in St. James's Road at the time and had become very friendly with the couple, Derek and Pat, who lived in the flat upstairs. They were very sociable and had a cocktail cabinet filled with about twenty bottles of spirits.

One day, when Jackie was teaching at school and I was home, Derek came to see me and was behaving in a very uncomfortable manner. He had something awful to tell me and didn't know how to say it because he liked Jackie very much. Everyone did. She was a wonderful teacher, together with being a highly intelligent, warm and attractive person.

Apparently, Jackie had been going upstairs to their flat while they were out and helping herself to their alcohol. They had suspected for some time and had begun to mark the bottles. Of course, I was mortified and said I just couldn't believe it, but nevertheless promised Derek I would tackle Jackie.

Jackie was terribly embarrassed when I broached the subject with her and promised it wouldn't happen again. I was so wrapped up in my work, I don't think I was accepting the enormity of Jackie's problem. When I am conducting, composing or arranging I can think of nothing else. My whole being was consumed by music and I selfishly blocked out anything that might interfere with my work. This of course included the fact Jackie was struggling with alcoholism.

Our relationship with Derek and Pat was never quite the same again and went rather sour, which was a great pity. Very soon after this incident, we moved to Winkworth Road in Banstead as we were able to afford our own small detached house. The strangest thing of all was we bought this house from an Irish couple who were alcoholics themselves. I felt slightly uncomfortable about it at the time, but dismissed any hesitations because the house seemed ideal for us. Perhaps it might have been better to have listened to this initial misgiving as I was never really happy in that house, but nevertheless I did write quite a lot of good music while living there.

Not long after we moved in, I began to find whisky, gin and wine bottles hidden in the house. I found them in cupboards, behind clothes and even lodged in the chimney. I now knew something was drastically wrong, but Jackie wouldn't stop drinking. Some demon was driving her and while I am certain that my preoccupation with my music was partially responsible, there were also other factors to consider.

Jackie's father worked in the mines and would drink most of his wages away in the pub on a Friday night, forcing Jackie's caring and loving mother to knit clothing to sell so she could feed her family. When she died prematurely, Jackie's father couldn't forgive himself for the way he had behaved over the years and would spend every spare moment at her grave seeking some form of forgiveness.

Jackie lost her mother, and two of her brothers died young in close succession and I believe these losses affected her deeply. These events, together with her lonely marriage tipped her over the edge. Also, it seemed alcoholism ran in the family as her father drank immensely and one of her brothers, John, had died through alcoholism. It now seemed to have a very firm grip on Jackie.

Usually we didn't argue and Jackie was always soft-spoken but as soon as she drank she would become very angry, shouting and yelling at me. Sometimes after the long drive back from Eastbourne, I would find myself locked out and I would have to break the lock to get in. I knew these were the nights when Jackie had been drinking heavily and her drinking brought with it a terrible anger towards me. Greeted by this dreadful sickly smell of alcohol and a tirade of verbal abuse, I was dismayed at having to break into my own home. For someone who was normally so beautifully spoken, to hear Jackie slurring her words was very distressing. Although one thing always struck me: no matter how drunken Jackie was, I never once heard her swear.

On one occasion, I found six bottles of whisky, gin and vodka in our shed. I immediately took them to the kitchen and poured the whole lot down the sink. When Jackie discovered what I had done, she went mad pushing our small wardrobe from our bedroom along the landing before throwing it down the stairs. It amazed me alcohol could create such rage that Jackie, who was so very slight, could summon the strength to do such a thing.

For a long time, I ignored the signs because the whole situation was too painful to me. By the time I accepted Jackie was an alcoholic, my work was completely preoccupying me. I was composing and arranging all day and driving down to the Grand Hotel at nights, as well as often travelling abroad to Europe. Alan Clare, a self taught pianist who had a long association with Stephane Grapelli and who teamed up with Peter Sellers at one point, played in the West End clubs of London during the fifties and sixties and he would very often stand in for me at the Grand Hotel when I was working abroad.

Then life took a different turn. In the early seventies, Geraldo phoned to tell me the Grand Hotel wanted a female vocalist to accompany our band. Geoff Swift, the drummer in our group, recommended a Scottish singer called Joy Devon who was born in Edinburgh. Although at this time she wasn't a professional singer, Geoff told me she was a fine female vocalist and very attractive. He even confessed he had tried to date her without success and told me directly she was not taken in by any male charm!

In fact, I did know a little about Joy because through Geoff, she contacted me by telephone, often on a Saturday, to ask my advice about which songs I could recommend to her. She sang at gigs and private functions along the south coast and told me she had heard my music on the radio and liked it very much. I remember thinking at the time she had a lovely, soft speaking voice.

A while later, I agreed to audition Joy at the Grand Hotel. Geoff knocked on the door and told me Joy was in the foyer waiting. I said, "Tell her I'll be with her in a minute." I had just arrived from Banstead and was sorting out the music for the evening, but to be truthful I wasn't very keen on introducing a singer to the group. I was happy the way things were and it felt slightly irksome to think we would need to work differently, so I wasn't that enthusiastic to see her.

I don't remember how long I kept Joy waiting but eventually I asked Geoff to bring her in. Her entrance knocked me out. My mind racing, I thought, "I have never seen anyone so beautiful in my life and if she can sing as good as she looks, wouldn't that just be great!" It wasn't just her looks; she had great charm and presence and that evening, I felt this immediately.

As we shook hands, Joy went down on her knees, and smiling said, "Haven't you got a strong handshake?" What an introduction! She got the job of course and from that moment, I knew I wanted her more than anything in the world. So despite all my misgivings, Joy joining our band was a very successful venture and the audiences loved her. One famous visitor to the Grand Hotel, amongst many, was the bandleader Eric Robinson, who was also once the co-owner of the famous IBC music studios in Portland Place, London, which recorded some of the best-known groups in the world including The Beatles and The Rolling Stones.

He often stayed at the Grand and we would have conversations about music during the interval. He was taken with my music and played some of my compositions including 'Strings in 3/4' and 'Portrait of Eve' with his orchestra on BBC Radio 2. His brother was Stanford Robinson the famous English conductor.

In particular, there was one very prominent guest at the Grand, who enjoyed Joy's singing. He was Jack Cohen, the British businessman who founded Tesco. Born in the East End of London, Jack established himself as a market stallholder in Hackney and in 1924, the same year as I was born, created the brand name Tesco from the initials of a tea supplier, T.E. Stockwell and the first two letters of his own surname. As it is often said, the rest is history!

Jack spoke in a cockney accent and was a regular visitor to the Grand with his wife, visiting at Christmas, the New Year, Easter and the summer holidays. He often stopped to say hello to me, have a brief chat and compliment Joy on her singing. A huge crowd always accompanied him and whenever he walked out of the ballroom at least a hundred guests would follow! It was quite usual for individuals in the audience to buy the musicians a drink, especially if they were really enjoying the music and it always amused me that despite his great wealth, Jack didn't once think to treat any of the band members to a tipple!

One evening, a middle-aged gent who was staying at the hotel came up on stage and standing behind me, watched me closely as I played the piano. When I finished the piece I was playing, he spoke to me and I have never forgotten his words: "I am a very rich man but if I could play the piano like you, I would give you my whole fortune in return." Of course, I was very flattered and laughing his words off replied, "I don't think you would!" But apparently the piano was a great passion of his and he was quite addicted to the old ivories! I certainly did meet some characters during my time at the Grand.

15
Arranging

As well as composing my own music, I was also arranging other composers' music. Many producers and publishers seemed to like my arrangements and I believe this was because when arranging popular songs for the orchestra, I took particular notice of the lyrics, enabling me to make full use of many lovely words in the orchestration.

For instance, 'All the Things You Are,' the lovely standard by Jerome Kern with wonderful lyrics by Oscar Hammerstein II that includes the lines, 'You are the promised kiss of springtime that makes a lonely winter seem long,' with the middle words saying, 'you are the angel glow that lights a star, and all the things I know are what you are.' Then the ending, 'when all the things you are—are mine.' It's a magical song with the words 'you are' as the main theme and a gorgeous melody.

When I wrote this arrangement using only strings and harp, I concentrated hard on the meaning of the words and many producers have often told me it's my best arrangement. I believe this is because the words meant so much to me and I felt it was my role to bring these words to life. At this moment, I feel it's important to mention it was actually Jackie with her great knowledge and love of poetry who first helped me to fully appreciate the mighty influence of words.

I look at the lyrics very carefully and arrange my music around each word. What does the word sound like? If it is heavy or slow, I might use the trombone to convey its meaning. Or perhaps the word is light and frivolous, so I might choose the flute. I may use the brass to announce a bold bright word and with words of love, I might use the influence of strings in different octaves to express romance and heartbreak. Working with music and words in this way brings with it an immense pleasure and since many arrangers either don't have the inclination or the talent to approach their arranging in this manner, I became famous for my 'John Fox' sound.

In 'Love is a many Splendored Thing,' for instance, the words in one phase read, "And the world stood still." I slowed the melody down in this part of the song to portray a musical image of the world standing still. Cole Porter and Irving Berlin both wrote their own words and music with great success, and for me being able to both compose and arrange was also a great asset. How beautiful the lyrics were in those days. Sadly, today's lyricists do not seem to have the same ability to produce such charming words to songs.

More and more people use such unattractive language including the incessant use of the words 'you know' at the end of every sentence! It's little wonder that good lyrics are almost a thing of the past! In the days when I was writing songs with Derek Maxwell, he would send me his lyrics before I wrote the whole melody so I could judge where an important note was to go, and equally where the less important notes went, too.

16

BBC Recording of "George Gershwin"

In early 1972, many executive and junior producers of the BBC held an important meeting. There was excitement in the air because it was about making a commercial record with the music of George Gershwin. This great American composer wrote songs for the classical concert hall and Broadway. He also wrote many classics with his elder brother Ira, who wrote among other things, the wonderful lyrics for the highly acclaimed opera *Porgy and Bess.*

George was 39 years of age when he died of a brain hemorrhage in 1937, but the wonderful songs he wrote will never be forgotten and over the years, his music has been used extensively in films and television. Many of the arrangers within the BBC speculated on who might be the lucky one to receive this prestigious commission. To my great delight and honour, the BBC chose me! They told me I was to write the arrangements and conduct the BBC Radio Orchestra with my John Fox Singers.

I suspected Chris Morgan, the senior producer at the BBC, had played a part in my selection. This is because, knowing I loved Gershwin, he felt I had something rather special and original to offer. Chris Morgan was the producer of this record, which was simply called *George Gershwin.* We both spent quite some time selecting which songs of his to use because there were so many good ones. This BBC

Gershwin album is played still, especially in the United States, to this day. The sleeve for the original LP was rather special, too, because when it was fully opened, it featured a complete picture of Manhattan and the Brooklyn Bridge, all in shades of blue after the title of Gershwin's *Rhapsody in Blue*.

Some of the titles on this album, which was recorded in 1972, include, 'Fascinating Rhythm/Rhapsody in Blue,' 'Summertime,' 'Oh! Lady be Good,' 'S'Wonderful' and 'I Got Rhythm.' All magnificent hits and with my interpretation coupled with original scoring, I freshened the notes to develop modern harmonies that sound, I am often told, as good today as they did then. One of the last songs Gershwin wrote before he died is 'Love Walked In,' which Joy also recorded later on a CD called *The Magic of Joy Devon*. She sang beautifully, with my strings accompanying her in the background.

My *George Gershwin* album proved to be a very popular recording, which the BBC played extensively on its radio stations when it came on the market in 1973. For over a year, stations all over the world including the United States played this album. During that time, the renowned publisher and musician, Gerhard Narholz, was in London from Munich, Germany and happened to hear it. Gerhard knew Chris Morgan and contacted him asking him about this 'noteworthy arranger.'

Gerhard's *nom-de-plume* was Norman Candler under which name he arranged, composed and conducted his large string orchestra 'The Magic Strings,' recording over twenty albums. In 1971, the BBC awarded him the '3 Star Award' for the 'Best Album of the Year.' Gerhard was also a songwriter and among the artists he wrote for were Petula Clark and Bill Ramsey. As soon as Chris gave him my address, he contacted me asking me if I would be interested in writing library music for his company Sonoton Music Publishing.

He even wanted me to compose lots of music and travel to Munich to conduct it with the Munich Symphony Orchestra. That was in 1973 and since then I haven't yet stopped writing for this great man. I have composed music for him on every conceivable subject including emotions, sad occasions, pastoral pieces, openers, closures, slapsticks, comedy situations, westerns, children's fairy tales and animals to name just a few. As the years have gone by, more and more subjects have been added to my *oeuvre* including *Earth and Space*, which was recorded in Leipzig East Germany and I feel this is the best music I have ever composed, partly because conducting the splendid 130 piece orchestra through that music was perhaps my 'finest hour.'

In 1973, at about the time I recorded my BBC Gershwin album, Norrie Paramor, the arranger and popular recording producer, took a job at the BBC to conduct a new orchestra, the BBC Midland Radio Orchestra in Birmingham. Originally, it was the BBC Midland Light Orchestra and had been latterly conducted by Gilbert Vinter and Jack Coles. One day the telephone rang, and it was Norrie asking me to visit him in London.

He was also the Recording Director for EMI Columbia Records and produced hit singles for Cliff Richard, The Shadows, the hits 'Don't Cry for Me Argentina' and the theme from 'The Deer Hunter' (Cavatina). Norrie asked me to arrange fifty songs for this new orchestra at the BBC and what an honour for me, being asked to work for such an impressive musician. After I had arranged these 50 titles, Norrie gave me many more commissions to arrange and I would often go to the BBC Pebble Mill Studios in Birmingham where these arrangements were recorded. He was a very quiet and likeable man but smoked heavily and sadly, he died of lung cancer in 1989.

Norrie's nephew is Nick Ingman, who has come a long way arranging and composing. He is a music professor at the Royal Academy of Music in Kensington, teaching composition and arranging, so I believe music runs very strongly in this family.

17

Jackie and Joy

My situation at home was becoming increasingly unbearable. Jackie was still drinking, but more heavily now because she was no longer working. Her doctor had signed her off because of her drinking problems, but she was still on a full salary and spending most of her money on alcohol. It seemed she was never sober and we were rowing constantly. If Jackie was really drunk, she would start throwing anything she could lay her hands on at me. This was a truly awful predicament for me to be in as I was very busy with so much composing and arranging. I felt under constant pressure.

To create great work, any artist needs peace and harmony and here I was totally distraught and shattered from the disruptive atmosphere of my marriage. How terribly unhappy we both were! Jackie wasn't behaving rationally and at one time constantly rang the BBC studio in Maida Vale when I was recording the Gershwin album insisting she had to speak to me. In the end, Chris Morgan refused to take her calls and I knew nothing of this until some while later because Chris had kept it from me, fearing it would upset me during the recording.

Even my mother and sisters would no longer visit our house as it was too awkward with Jackie's unpredictable behaviour. This was very sad for everyone concerned, particularly as my family was extremely fond of Jackie.

By this time, I was working with Joy every weekend and it was very obvious that we were both strongly attracted to one another. Perhaps if I had been happily married I might have just flirted with Joy without taking it any further, but with the situation at home where my marriage was no longer a marriage, even in the bedroom, I found myself increasingly tempted to take my relationship with Joy further.

My opportunity came when I received the Gershwin contract. I was so elated and called Joy to ask her if she would come out to lunch with me to celebrate this wonderful occasion. I took her to a restaurant between Tunbridge Wells, where she lived, and Banstead. I felt on top of the world and I couldn't remember the last time I had felt so happy. We had a wonderful bubbly lunch with champagne before going for a car ride. And what a car ride it was! Before the afternoon was out, we did what all young lovers do with nowhere to go and resorted to the back seat of the car. So began what was to be a lifelong love affair.

When Joy was singing at the Grand, the management gave her a lovely room so she could change before singing and then change again at the end of the evening. Of course, this was a great opportunity for us to be alone together and on some pretence or other I would often go to her room after we finished playing. I don't think we were fooling anyone, as most of the chaps in the band knew what was going on.

I even began to drive to the Grand Hotel alone in my own car so I could stay behind at the end of the evening. Unfortunately, I think the matron also got wind of it and some while later told Joy a room was no longer available to her. How wretched we felt, because that small incident made our love feel cheap, which it wasn't, but of course we understood the matron's decision.

All the while I was feeling terribly guilty about Jackie, but I could no more stop my relationship with Joy than stop composing music. Then I had to go abroad for a week to record in Munich and I asked Joy to come with me, expecting her to say no. But she said yes and I was so happy and contented to be with her. We both had such a wonderful time and when we returned, I knew it was time to leave Jackie.

Joy was concerned because she knew Jackie was unstable and was worried she might do something mad such as come after me with a gun and shoot me! We wanted to be together and Joy suggested I live with her in Tunbridge Wells, as she also knew my music was suffering because I was unable to concentrate at home. The day I left Jackie was very calm. When the van drew up to collect my piano and personal belongings, although Jackie had obviously been drinking, she was gardening in the front of the house and she didn't say a word.

Silently, she just let me go even though I also took our dog, Taly, who she really adored. It had to be that way because I knew she wasn't capable of looking after him properly.

Joy was divorced with three young children, Andrew, Marion and Richard, and lived in a townhouse in the centre of Tunbridge Wells. Of course Jackie became suspicious because she found out the telephone number and would ring me often wanting to know where I was. I didn't tell her so she sent a private detective after me. One night when I was leaving a gig at the Bridge House in Reigate, this private detective followed me, although I had no idea at the time. A couple of days later, there was a knock on Joy's front door and it was this private detective telling me Jackie had sent him to find out where I was living and that I would be hearing from a solicitor.

Despite everything Jackie was doing and had done, I didn't hate her. I just felt so terribly sorry and yes, at times, desperately guilty about the whole business.

But Joy and I were very much in love and at last I was in a place where I could work and concentrate on my precious music. However, it was very unfortunate that close to Joy's town house was a bus station, which woke me up at four in the morning with the early buses revving up and coming and going. There was also a milk depot where the clinking of bottles and the milkman preparing for their rounds would often wake me, too.

There was one occasion when I needed to return to Banstead to visit my bank. I parked my car in a side street with the back window open, as Taly was with me. On my return from the bank, I saw Jackie leaning through the window stroking and talking to Taly. She was crying. I stood there unable to move. I felt too ashamed to go up and speak to her knowing I had hurt her so badly. After a couple of minutes, she turned and walked away. It was such a painful touching scene and I felt the tears well up in my eyes, too.

My mother came to visit us and although she was very fond of Jackie, she was very glad I had found some peace and was away from all the troubles at home. Of course, she immediately took to Joy. My sisters visited as well with their husbands and they, too, immediately liked Joy and were so glad I was happy. Even Gerhard, my German publisher, and his lovely wife, Heidi, came for dinner when they were visiting London, and Joy, I might tell you, was a fine cook! Sometimes in the evenings I would relax for a couple of hours and play table tennis with Andrew, Joy's youngest boy, and in the end he was beating me at the game!

Then Jackie stopped drinking. When I left, I guess this gave her a huge jolt and she probably realized our marriage was over because of her drinking. Before long, she began to attend an Alcoholics Anonymous club in Epsom.

I had been living with Joy for ten months when I decided to return home to Jackie, who by this time was completely dry. Joy and I had long, long conversations about the pros and cons of our relationship, including the fact she didn't think I was really in a position to take on her three young children. To be truthful, I felt very mixed up about the whole situation and had been worrying about it for some while. Jackie had rung me and pleaded with me to go back. It wasn't that I no longer loved Joy; this was far, far from the truth. But I felt I owed it to Jackie to give our marriage another try, particularly as she was now sober, and I couldn't forget how much she had helped me in my early years.

Also my music had begun to suffer because I was finding it increasingly difficult to work in Joy's house with the outside disturbances coupled with the noise of young children. I was really struggling because once more it felt as if my music was being taken away from me and this was making me very unhappy.

It was a real wrench leaving Joy and returning home to Jackie but I wanted to be in my own home again and also wanted to see what Jackie was like sober after all those years of being an alcoholic. I obviously took Taly back home with me and it was heartbreaking when I left Joy's house as we hugged each other tightly and cried.

When I arrived home in Banstead, Jackie was waiting and had bought a couple of pieces of antique furniture for me. One was an elegant coffee table, the other, an attractive wonderful telephone table and seat combined, which I still have in my studio to this very day. Jackie, now sober, was the kind, warm, generous person with extraordinary talent and personality that everyone loved. She was more like the person I had fallen in love with all those years ago.

Shortly after returning home to Winkworth Road, we organized a big surprise party, a stone's throw away from where I was born, at the Robin Hood Hotel in an upstairs room for my mother's eightieth birthday. Jackie looked especially lovely that evening in a long, green evening dress I had bought her for the occasion. Once again our marriage was good and she never once asked me about my relationship with Joy. Sometimes the phone rang late at night and it would be Joy, who was missing me desperately and wanted to speak to me, but again Jackie didn't mention it or even ask me who was on the phone.

Of course I didn't show it to Jackie, but my heart still ached for Joy. I missed her so much and couldn't get her off my mind and she couldn't get me off hers either. Often after speaking to her on the phone, I was left wondering whether I had done the right thing returning to my marriage.

With all this upheaval in my private life, I had gotten behind with my music. I had many commissions to catch up on from my publishers, who had been very patient with me during my troubles, telling me they would wait until I was ready. I happily settled back to my music on a large scale and when I was composing, my personal troubles faded into the background. I did have one sticky incident that, perhaps, is quite amusing looking back on it now, but it certainly wasn't at the time! I was conducting at one of my sessions held at the Aeolian Hall for the BBC and Jackie said on this occasion she would like to come with me and listen, which was something she rarely did. Jackie settled in the studio watching, when the door opened and Joy came in with her daughter, Marion.

The Radio Orchestra knew about my affair with Joy, and quite distinctly the lead trumpet player looked at me and said, "What are you going to do now, John?" I probably looked a little flustered and I think many in the orchestra were enjoying the little show. I was very worried the two of them might end up sitting close to one another, so I went over to Joy to guide her to the other side of the studio. Jackie had never met Joy so didn't know what she looked like, but I often wondered afterwards if in her heart she knew it was Joy.

The chaps and women in the orchestra were all watching me closely with slightly sardonic grins on their faces. But in fact, if I am honest, once I regained my composure and began conducting, I probably showed off a little that day as I performed to the two women in my life!

To launch my Gershwin album, the BBC held a big event opposite Broadcasting House in Portland Place, London. Along with the press, many publishers and producers were invited and it was a great occasion with a wonderful buffet.

Jackie and my mum attended and I made a speech thanking every one concerned. I was also very glad I gave special thanks to my mum and said many lovely things about her for all her love and support she gave me over the years, because not long after this period my mum began to suffer from tic douloureux. This is a rare disease caused by worry, which affects the cheek, lips and gums on one side of the face. But despite this disease, she lived to the ripe old age of eighty-eight.

I was full of excitement after that wonderful event but something was missing. I just had to see Joy to share this great episode of my life with her. I told Jackie and my mum I had to go to Eastbourne to play, but I paid a deputy pianist to do the job. Without a moment's hesitation, I went with excitement to Tunbridge Wells to see Joy and tell her all about my special day. At that moment, I knew how terribly important she was in my life and how I needed so desperately to be with her always.

Once again, I was in torment, but even though I was going through difficult times, my music didn't suffer. It's as if all the heartache I was going through and causing helped me to write and arrange music with more passion and feeling. If a musician doesn't understand or feel such emotions, it is much more difficult to write music that will arouse and engage audiences.

About a year after the George Gershwin launch, Jackie began drinking again. I don't know exactly when this started because she never drank in front of me. But I first noticed it again in her eyes and smelled it on her breath. I don't know what might have triggered this, but I suspect she knew I was seeing Joy again.

18

A Dangerous Mission!

Around this time I was writing music for Apollo Sound Records based in Germany. My publisher, Richard Frank, had a contract with Apollo Sound through his Anglo-Continental Music business in Denmark Street and on one occasion, he asked me to travel out to Stuttgart to record a large selection of my latest compositions. I was to meet him in a small village some distance from Baden-Baden. I travelled by air and leaving the airport I hailed a taxi to take me to my destination, which was quite a distance away.

Unfortunately, it was quite a remote village and the taxi driver didn't seem to know where he was going. He kept driving round and round until he eventually stopped to ask someone the way. *The omens are not good,* I thought to myself as mile after mile of the bleak countryside enveloped by cold grey weather sped by my window. Eventually we drove up to a rather grand 200-year-old mansion where Richard was staying with a Polish friend and his German wife.

We stayed at this place for a couple of days and there was a beautiful grand Bechstein in the drawing room. I seem to remember I spent most of my time playing on that lovely piano. There were a few other guests staying and our Polish and German hosts were very hospitable, plying everyone with large quantities of vodka. During those two days, there was a terrific snowstorm. It surrounded the house in a real blizzard and it was the worst I've ever experienced in my life. On the day we were leaving, we had to get up at 4:00 a.m. because the narrow roads were full of ice and snow and we would only be able to drive very slowly.

Our descent down the drive to the car was precarious because it was so icy. My two bags full of music for the two sessions in Stuttgart were very heavy and I spent most of the walk on my bottom! Richard was very worried about the weather and said, "We can't possibly go in this, I'll phone the studio and cancel the session." But I insisted we should still go and finally persuaded Richard to make the journey. The snow was about four feet deep and so thick on this enormous black limousine we could hardly see it. We collected shovels and began digging out the car, which seemed an almost impossible task.

Our Polish host had also promised his neighbours a lift to the railway station at Baden-Baden about forty miles away, so finally seven of us piled into the eight-seater limo. There was our Polish host who was driving and his charming German wife, a very big, strong woman from Berlin and a young boy of about ten years of age and his mother.

The roads were very slippery and it was still very dark, as it was so early in the morning. Everywhere I looked was white with snow. We were driving along quite a narrow road through the mountains where on the right we could see a very steep drop. Suddenly the car skidded and went into a spin and we found ourselves completely out of control on a bend. The next minute, the car had left the road and the long bonnet was facing down the mountainside, the front wheels hanging over this steep drop.

There was stunned silence as everyone realized the enormity of our situation. My heart was in my mouth and the only thought I had was to get out quickly with all my music. I was sitting in the second passenger row and had to climb over the back seat to the third row to get out. Our Polish host and his wife had to scramble over two rows of seats and all the while the car was slowly slipping further over the edge as it made this dreadful revving sound. The tough strapping German woman saw a sign post about four yards away and without a moment's hesitation, she manually hauled it out of the ground. Our Polish host quickly found some rope in the boot and between us we managed to put it round the bumper and pull the car back a little from the edge and slide this large sign underneath the front wheels.

In the middle of this high drama, a milk van came along from the opposite direction and the driver, catching sight of this odd group of people struggling to prevent their car from falling off the edge caused him to skid himself and go off the road into a ditch! He left his milk van and came running over to help heave this big car back on the road. Our Polish host scrambled back into the driver's seat and managed to reverse the car.

It amazed me that he seem to have no sense of fear and just did what he thought had to be done. Once our car was back on the road, we helped the driver of the milk van haul his own vehicle out of the ditch. What a morning! Soaked to the skin, we continued our journey, thankful for our very narrow escape.

As we arrived at Baden-Baden railway station, we saw the steam train was ready to leave for Stuttgart. Clutching my music for dear life, Richard and I sprinted to the ticket office and just managed to board the train as it was moving off the platform. Finding a carriage, we needed to do something about our wet clothing. Much to the astonishment of our fellow passengers, most of whom were on their way to work, we took off our shirts and trousers and put them on this long radiator at the back of the carriage. By the time we got to Stuttgart our clothes were comparatively dry.

Despite our adventurous morning, we were only twenty minutes late for the sessions and I managed to conduct all day with the orchestra playing magnificently. However, there was an uncanny end to the day. I had written quite a difficult piano piece, which I had to play with orchestral accompaniment. It was a complete coincidence, but I had called this piece 'Keep it Cool' and as I played it, the dramatic events of the day unfolded in my mind. It was recorded for an album on that same day using a big orchestra consisting of saxophones, woodwind, a wonderful brass section including French horns, strings, harp and a rhythm section. The album was called *Instrumental Pops No. 6* and I still have it in my studio reminding me of a 'never to be forgotten day.'

How lucky I felt to be alive and I knew none of us would ever forget our eventful journey. It was definitely a case of coming out unscathed because everyone 'kept it cool'!

19

The Loss of Jackie and Taly

Once more, the situation with Jackie was becoming difficult. I had been home about a year and during that time, she had only remained sober for a relatively short while. I had so much work and I was once more in a situation where I was unable to concentrate on my music. At my wit's end, I called Judy and she told me I could move into her house.

A few days later, I moved out. Jackie was under the influence of alcohol and said only, "Off you go then." For the second time in our marriage, the removal van came for my upright piano. Judy lived in quite a large house in Fir Tree Road not very far from Winkworth Road with her husband, Roy, my sister Maureen and her husband, Tom, my mother, and at times my eldest sister Lee. Then there was Taly, my dog, and Judy's cat, Cindy. With such a full house, the only place for me to sleep was at the top of the stairs on a bunk bed. This wasn't ideal, but at least I had a place where I could write my music in peace.

My mother was not so well at this time, but she made me cups of tea and coffee in a very shaky way. It was upsetting to see her not well as I loved her dearly and I had been greatly influenced by her wonderful disposition, coupled with her loving and practical way of dealing with life. She was so proud of what I had achieved in my music profession and to the end of her days, she would not let me forget how special I was to her and how gifted she thought I was to be so blessed with such musical talent.

I had been living at my sister's house for some while when one day, Taly refused to eat. It was more than the fact he wasn't eating his food; he just wasn't himself at all so I took him to the vet. There is no easy way to tell someone their dog is very seriously ill and I could hardly believe it when the vet told me Taly had a tumour and the kindest thing to do would be to put him to sleep. He was over fourteen years old, but he had always been a very active and lively dog and had been my constant companion over those years. I was bereft. After a few days, I asked the vet if I could spend one more day with Taly and he agreed. At this point I rang Jackie, praying that she was having a good day and not on the drink. I knew if she hadn't been drinking, I could communicate with her. Jackie adored Taly and the news hit her hard, too.

I felt so sad to think I had taken him away from her on two occasions. She wanted the three of us to spend the evening together at our house before the vet came to put him to sleep the next day. It was a poignant evening. Jackie did have a few drinks but she didn't get drunk and spent the whole night stroking Taly and saying loving words to him. Even when I was so tired that I had to go to bed, about three in the morning, Jackie stayed up with Taly until the next morning when the vet came with a girl assistant and gently put our lovely Taly to sleep. What an awful day that was and I have no way of describing in words the sense of loss and depth of pain one feels when losing a treasured pet.

Taly was a wonderful friend and over the years I had written so many pieces of music about him. In my early days of recording at the Aeolian Hall for the BBC, I would often take him to my sessions. We would travel by the Underground to central London and he would trot by my side. I never had to put him on a lead and everyone loved him, from the passengers on the train to the members of the orchestra and staff at the BBC.

One Saturday afternoon, a short while after Taly had been put to sleep, I began thinking it was about time I had some fresh air and decided to walk to Banstead Downs where Taly and I had enjoyed so many lovely mornings and afternoons together. I walked along, imagining Taly was still by my side and without even fully realizing what I was doing, I found myself walking from my sister's house to my own house, which is about two and half miles away.

It was as if something very spiritual was compelling me to go to my own home. I walked past the house thinking it seemed very quiet, with no sign of our cats that were often about. For a while I walked on, but for some inexplicit reason I turned on my heel and went back.

Everywhere seemed to be locked, so climbing over the tall fence next to the garage, I looked in through the kitchen window. A horrible sight greeted me. Our two cats, Tigger and Thomas, were hovering about looking frightened and distressed. There seemed to be cat's mess all over the kitchen surfaces and there was newspaper scattered about the floor all scrabbled up and torn. I knew instantly something was desperately wrong.

I looked to see if there was any way I could get in. Luckily, I saw the small top window open to my studio and I managed to squeeze my arm through to open the larger window beneath it and somehow pushed myself through the small opening. As I jumped into the room, a terrible smell hit me and I called out to Jackie, "Where are you? Where are you?" Forgetting about the cats, I ran round the house calling Jackie repeatedly. I even ran down to the shed thinking she might be hiding there. Nothing. Nothing but silence, the pitiful meowing of our cats, and this awful, awful smell.

For the third time, I ran upstairs and back into our bedroom. Then I saw Jackie. She was lying on the floor close to the bed and I couldn't understand how I hadn't seen her before. But in that split second I knew she was dead. I fell to my knees saying over and over again, "Forgive me, forgive me, forgive me." I picked her up and couldn't believe how light she was. I gently hugged her and laid her on the bed. Later I found out she had been dead for three days. I had never smelled death before, but now I knew why the house was filled with this awful stench.

As I stood there for a few moments, which seemed like hours, I felt deeply responsible and guilty. It was the darkest moment of my life and I was inconsolable as I sobbed my heart out. Jackie had committed suicide drinking several bottles of alcohol but had left no note. It was utterly devastating. I found many empty bottles of whisky, gin, vodka and wine of all types hidden in cupboards about the house. I called the ambulance, my doctor, Dr. Latham, and my sister Judy who was equally distraught as she was very fond of Jackie. The ambulance came and took Jackie's body away and my doctor said, "I have seen many suicides, but I've never seen such a clean house." Jackie had obviously cleaned the house painstakingly before she took her own life. She was only fifty-three years old.

The last time I saw Jackie alive was just the week before. This was strange, too, because since living at Judy's, I had very little contact with her. But Jackie had called me saying she would love to see me and as she didn't appear to be intoxicated, I agreed to spend an evening with her.

Well, she wasn't completely sober, but she wasn't at that awful drunk stage either. We had quite a good evening, which ended in us going to bed and I stayed until the following morning when I kissed her goodbye as any husband might kiss his wife before leaving for work. It was what we both wanted, starved as we were at the time of any physical love and I was glad to have that positive last memory of Jackie. I often wondered over the years whether she actually knew then what she was going to do and had wanted this last night with me.

My mother was still very unwell, and I had to break the terrible news of Jackie's untimely death to her. Jackie's sisters and relatives travelled from Wales to attend the funeral and we laid her to rest at Randall's Park, Leatherhead. It was 1977. Over the years, I have often agonized as to why Jackie didn't leave a note, but I shall never know what she was thinking that day. This period of my life took a dreadful toll on me, however it is often said, born composers who have truly suffered are able to express intense and deep feelings through their music.

20
The Loss of Mum and a Vision

It was fortunate I was so busy with commissions for conducting, composing and arranging, because I hardly had time to dwell on the recent distressing events in my personal life. I threw myself even further into my music and at this time Chris Morgan, executive producer of BBC Radio 2, gave me a couple of weekly radio broadcasts. One was the *The John Fox Hour* presented by Jean Challis, and broadcast every Friday night before the programme *Friday Night is Music Night,* which is still going today.

This programme is well known as 'FNIMN' and together with an audience, it was broadcast live from the Golder's Green Hippodrome. There were many occasions when the producers would use my John Fox Singers entirely as a choir event with me conducting. The producer was Robert Beaumont and he not only used my arrangements and compositions for this broadcast, but for other programmes as well.

The John Fox Hour featured mostly my arrangements conducting the BBC Radio Orchestra and my John Fox Singers. I would include one or two of my own compositions and throughout the hour, the acoustic classical guitar duo Stella and Bambos would sing three or four of their folk songs. The other programme featuring my arrangements was *String Sound,* broadcast for half an hour on a Sunday afternoon and repeated mid-week at two in the morning. I also wrote the signature tune for this broadcast called 'String Magic' and while the programme contained mostly my arrangements, a few other conductors and composers also took part in this string based broadcast.

I conducted and arranged the BBC Midland Radio Orchestra and The Northern Ireland Orchestra for a number of other programmes and during these times there were not many days that went by without my music being featured on the radio.

I was also writing library music extensively for my German publisher, Gerhard Narholz of Sonoton Music Publishing. Library music is used throughout the world by producers for advertising, feature films, television, radio, background music and for public places. Each time a piece of library music is played, the composer will receive a royalty; if the music is played on a live show, the royalties are greater than if it is a repeat, and this continues until seventy years after a composer's death.

Many of the library pieces I wrote over fifty years ago are still being played today in the United States, including on the Oprah Winfrey Show. The producers of this show tended to pick more of my romantic pieces and in particular a piece called 'Kiss Away Each Tear.'

When I was first composing and arranging many years ago, I had no idea that in latter life I would benefit from these royalties. I wrote the music because music was in my blood and while I was very happy earning a living, I gave no further thought to any monetary gains beyond what I was currently working on.

Not long after Jackie's death, my mum took a turn for the worse. It was now 1977 and she was eighty-eight years old. Despite being very lucid mentally, physically she was having a dreadful time, even though she was living with my sister Lee, who looked after her. My mum had cancer of the left eye, which is a very rare cancer and her eye would often weep blood, which was very gruesome for both my mother and Lee. The doctors would come but couldn't do anything about her condition as there was no cure.

A few times, she went in to the cottage hospital in Epsom to give Lee a break from looking after her day and night. It wasn't a very nice place for my mum to go because many of the patients were mentally ill. My mum was the loveliest and sweetest person you could ever wish to meet and it was terribly upsetting to see her so physically uncomfortable, particularly as I felt I had caused her so much worry over the years. One day, a short while towards the end, I collected up lots of old photographs and went over to Lee's place to visit her. She was sitting up in bed and looking at me. Very haltingly, because she could hardly speak by this time, she said, "I'm finished."

Of course I replied, "No, you're not—wait until I show you the photographs I have with me." I sat there holding her hand and telling her our news. Then I went through the old times with her, showing her photographs of our family times together, especially one lovely photograph of her when she was sweet sixteen. I noticed how she nodded and smiled as we relived funny and sad times.

It was very emotional, but I was so glad to see her looking happy. At this time, I was arranging a piece of music called 'Happy Talk' from the show *South Pacific,* and whenever I hear this particular arrangement of mine, it takes me back to those precious last days of my mother's life. Again it was an uncanny moment in my life as this piece of music was so appropriate to the 'happy talk' of that visit when we went through the photographs together.

My three sisters and I were with my mother when she slipped away quietly and peacefully at about four o'clock in the morning. Despite the fact that we were all expecting her death, this made little difference to our immense grief. In turn, we gave Mum our final hugs, then clung to each other and cried.

After a while, I wanted to be alone. I went into another room and sat down in a chair, my mind was full of sad thoughts. A small lamp lit the room, which was quite dark, when all of a sudden out of my mind came this wonderful vision of colour. It filled the whole room with a thousand and one rainbows and out of nowhere came my mother looking radiant and beautiful. At first I thought she was running towards me, and then I realized she was looking to her left and she was holding out her hands as if she was greeting old friends. It was an unknown landscape, completely new to anything I have ever seen and all the time my mother was running through this colourful mist.

It was all over in seconds and I sat there in total awe. It was a unique spiritual experience and it was as if God had come into the room. From then on, I knew my mother was in a safe place and since that day I have been a firm believer in spiritualism. I am slightly ambivalent about the 'God' that we have learnt about as children and much of the dogma that surrounds the teachings of 'God,' but nevertheless *I know* there is something that is bigger than just our physical presence on this earth.

Once or twice over the years when I have mentioned my vision, people have said, "Oh yes, I've had a vision too," in a casual way as if the experience was commonplace. I know by the slight flippancy of their remark, it probably isn't the same kind of experience I had. My experience was so deeply moving and powerful, it is very, very difficult to adequately express its meaning.

When I recovered, I ran back to where my mother was lying to tell my sisters. "I've just seen a vision." They looked at me and I knew in that second they believed me. The vision had completely drained me, but I also felt lightness as if everything was all right.

After losing Jackie and my mother in such a short time, I spent many lonely days and nights at Winkworth Road, but several months after the loss of Jackie and my mum, my three sisters thought it was time to cheer me up a little. I had moved back home very soon after Jackie's death, but hadn't done much to the place as I found it difficult living there and often felt very lonely. My sisters came round and they gave the place a good spring cleaning and swept away all the cobwebs.

They also suggested I invite some friends and colleagues over for a party. I set to work inviting fellow musicians, friends and publishers including Richard Frank, Chris Morgan and many more executives from the BBC. My sisters did most of the work, preparing a wonderful buffet and organizing the drinks. They looked after everyone admirably and I felt very proud of them on that evening. George French, a great friend of mine and a good composer who was the leader in my John Fox Orchestra, became quite merry and actually said to me, "I love you, John." How I teased him once he had sobered up! We had everything in common as far as our music was concerned and he is a very talented violinist.

I didn't have background music or anyone playing the piano that evening and somehow this seemed right. We were all very happy talking about music and meeting old friends again. Some people had travelled a long distance to be there and I was very glad to see everyone. When it was over, the place somehow seemed renewed and I felt this party had cleared the air of the terribly sad events that had happened in the house.

John playing in his band with Rosemary Utting (violin), after the war.

At Laughing Waters near Dorking where I played with Vic Reynolds. Me, Jacqueline, Vic's daughter.

John at the piano (on extreme left) with the Jack Newman Band.

Me with the Harold Turner Group at The Grand Hotel Eastbourne.

The Mint pub in Banstead where we had many games of darts.

Our local church over 800 years old —All Saints Church in Banstead Surrey.

John with Tigger and Taly—what an animal lover!

John and Tigger, our lovely tabby cat at 30 years old!

John with John Sbarra, the American composer, who sadly passed away recently.

John with Neil Richardson (left)—a very good arranger.

John conducting a recording session with the BBC Radio Orchestra.

John conducting a large orchestra for an important recording in Budapest Hungary.

Mixing the recording of the Gershwin album in the control room with Chris Morgan, the BBC ex.

Celebrating the launching of the Gershwin album with Chris and the production team.

John with his dad in the shadows, shortly before he died.

Marriage to Joy Devon at their wedding inside All Saints Church Banstead Surrey.

John and Joy with family on their wedding day.

Family and friends after the wedding to Joy.

John conducting one of the many orchestral sessions.

Conducting in Leipzig East Germany.

John composing at the piano with persian cat Thomas looking on.

Andrew in his cap and gown after graduation.

John with Graham Belchere in the control room during a BBC Radio Orchestra session.

Recording in Leipzig with the producers and Joy.

The tall Philip Lane with John and Joy at a Robert Farnon society meeting.

John composing in his studio.

Andrew and Jill after their wedding in Sutton.

In Budapest Hungary with Gregor Narholz, the producer (an interpreter looks on).

John with Steve Race before a Musical World of John Fox concert.

With Joy, Alicia, and MarlinTaylor (my publisher) in New Jersey in the USA(on a visit to England.

21

Marriage to Joy and a Wonderful U.S. Contract

In 1973, Jim Schulke and Phil Stout of Schulke Radio Productions (SRP), based in the United States, approached the BBC, as they were interested in using some of the easy listening music the BBC played behind their Test Cards on the television.

SRP suggested the BBC might like to generate extra income from these tracks by selling them on to SRP to play in the United States. The BBC loved the idea and formed a partnership between the BBC Transcription Service and SRP. This partnership lasted until the early 1980s when the BBC began to disband its orchestras.

At the BBC, it was a monumental event for the executive producers, including Neville Rayner and the selected conductors, arrangers and musicians, when the deal went through. Knowing our music would soon be heard around the world, everyone was very excited about the contract and the day the contract was signed, we went out to celebrate with the whole lot of us becoming completely plastered!

I was involved in writing many of the arrangements for the BBC Transcription Service and Bonneville Radio Station in the United States, the top easy listening radio programme, would frequently play my arrangements. In the very late seventies, Marlin Taylor, the boss of Bonneville, heard my Gershwin album on Schulke Radio Productions. Contacting the BBC, he asked, "Who's this John Fox? We do like his music. We want this man!" Many other producers at Bonneville who also heard my music playing on the SRP network were very enthusiastic, too.

Marlin sent a top producer to the United Kingdom to see me. He brought with him a contract asking for exclusive rights to any arrangements they commissioned me to write. Although this contract was something entirely independent of my work with the BBC, I wasn't happy when I read the exclusion clause and rang Marlin Taylor saying I wanted to be able to use these arrangements for my BBC broadcasts. In the end, they relented because they were so keen to play my music in the States and they amended the clause in the contract.

The contract consisted of me being in charge of the sessions, which covered booking orchestras, the recording studio, arranging the titles and copying. I used the best session musicians in a recording studio called CTS, which had the most up-to-date facilities and techniques. Located in Wembley, London, CTS was originally known as Cine-Tele Sound Studios and at the time, considered the top recording studio in the world. The mixer of these sessions, a top balancing engineer, was a very good-looking young man called Dick Lewsey and today he is described as having an 'enviable reputation in the music recording industry,' especially music for films.

He has recorded film scores and albums for many famous artists including Maurice Jarre, Julie Andrews and Henry Mancini. With Dick's expertise and my innate sense of what my arrangements required to produce the right sound, we both knew the finished results would be very well received. In fact, they were so well received, my contract with Bonneville involved arranging and recording every three months and lasted for many years giving me a very good income.

Bonneville would choose a selection and send me the sheet music of the titles to be recorded and I have to say, some of the American songs were completely new to me.

This didn't seem to make any difference to my arranging, as Bonneville were always pleased with the pieces I wrote. Dick and I were great friends and made a very good team together. Some of the song titles we worked on included 'Love is a Many Splendored Thing,' 'Manhattan,' 'Lucy in the Sky with Diamonds,' which is not a favourite song of mine, and 'I've Grown Accustomed to Her Face.' We had a little joke with this title and would often jest, "Let's play 'I've thrown some custard in her face'"! I also arranged many Bert

Bacharach songs, which were very enjoyable to work on, not only because of his wonderful melodies, but also because of the lovely lyrics written by Hal David.

It was difficult living at Winkworth Road on my own, but luckily I was very busy and my personal life was once more beginning to look promising. I was back in constant contact with Joy and very happy. The time I went back home to Jackie, I did miss Joy terribly and although I confess we met on a couple of occasions, for nearly two years, we hardly saw one another. We had spoken regularly on the telephone and I know my mum was very cross about this when she found out, but the days I didn't speak to Joy were very hard.

During the time I was living at Judy's house, Joy and I would often talk on the phone late at night about wanting to be together. At one point, I even thought about getting a divorce and we began to talk about looking for a home together in Kent or Surrey and viewed quite a few properties. However, I also still felt a very strong bond to Jackie and in many ways, I was racked with guilt. She had helped me so much in my early years and I couldn't forget this fact.

Equally, it was torment not being able to see Joy. How terribly mixed-up and deeply troubled I felt. Then of course, the harrowing blow of Jackie's death was very difficult for me. After this tragic event, Joy and I continued to keep in contact by telephone, but I needed time to come to terms with this shocking tragedy, and it was several months before we agreed to meet again. During this time, I threw myself into my work but would take off Friday nights so I could listen to my show *The John Fox Hour* on the radio. I never ceased to marvel that it was my music coming over the airwaves and never ceased to feel immensely proud of my achievements.

I had always known since the day I first laid eyes on Joy, I wanted to be with her. After all that had gone before, it was bliss to be able to begin a proper courtship with Joy, who, I began to realize, was the first *real* love of my life. We continued to live in our separate houses, but soon we were often working together, so managed to spend quite a lot of time in each other's company.

Life at last was on an even keel and late in 1979, we went for a walk in our favourite place called Oaks Park, a beautiful spot near Banstead. I didn't get down on my knees, but I chose a pretty spot then asked Joy to marry me. How thrilled I was when she said yes! We both felt over the moon about it. It was now time I thought about selling my house in Winkworth Road, which didn't hold many happy memories for me and I certainly wasn't sorry about getting rid of it.

Some weeks later, I saw for sale in the local paper a detached house called "Coniston," built in 1938. There was something about the house that attracted me and I called the estate agents immediately to arrange a viewing. Even though it had only just come on the market, there were already three people interested in it. The wife showed me around this fair-sized lovely gabled house and I couldn't believe it when she showed me into a music room! The son was playing the cello at the time and his father was playing the piano. I felt this was a wonderful sign and I knew this 'musical' home had to be mine.

Walking through the long garden, which was beautifully kept, I saw a gate in the fence at the bottom. I went through it and, lo and behold, I saw a wonderful field. It was the private Priory School's ground for junior boys and a perfect place for dog walks. By this time I had another dog called Taly Two and felt this was another sign the house was ideal for me. I told the owners there and then I loved it. By Jove I wanted that house!

I rang Joy in Tunbridge Wells to tell her the news and she immediately dashed over there as fast as she could. She was always a fast driver and it seemed she arrived in Banstead in a flash! She loved the house as much as I did so I contacted the owners to say I would buy it. Unfortunately, because there were these three other people after the house, they told me we would have to join a queue.

However, I was determined to have this house. I decided there had to be a way. Finally, I telephoned my bank manager to ask for a rather large bridging loan. This was the time when your bank manager knew his customers personally, and after a short stunned silence he replied, "Of course you can, John!" I immediately told the owners not only was I in a position to buy the house instantly, I would also pay them an extra couple of hundred pounds in cash. They jumped at my offer and how excited I was to know the house was finally mine.

The difficulty was Winkworth Road had been up for sale for some time with no sign of any interested buyers. I became increasingly worried about this massive loan I had taken out and wondered if it had been wise to be so hasty in buying Coniston. Just as I was starting to regret the situation, a young man appeared out of the blue and bought the house on the spot!

In April 1980, Joy and I had a rather grand wedding, holding our marriage ceremony in the registry office followed by a lovely service in All Saints Church, Banstead. My very good friend the Rev. Peter Naylor gave a very touching service and we had our wedding breakfast at the White Hart Hotel in Epsom. George French was my best man and Joy's father and his wife came over from Australia.

We left for a honeymoon in the United States where I was well-known because the radio was constantly playing my arrangements, especially the string-based arrangements. We arrived in New York and there was a grand limousine waiting for us at the airport, which took us directly to Bonneville radio station and to our astonishment, there were balloons flying and neon lights flashing: "Welcome Mr. and Mrs. John Fox."

We stayed in a hotel opposite Central Park with such a large bed that at one point in the middle of the night, I thought I had lost Joy because I couldn't find her! I had made many American friends in the profession and we had such a marvellous time with them. One morning, I even appeared on live television in New Jersey and the announcer interviewing me asked me interesting questions, which luckily I found very easy to answer. Some of my compositions were played and they particularly enjoyed my *Earth and Space* suite.

Joy and I had a car to use in the United States and it gave me a real thrill when I heard my music playing so often on the radio. I found the Americans very kind and pleasant people. Walking down Park Avenue on a Friday evening with people walking slowly and the traffic also moving slowly was really something to remember. A perhaps more unsettling experience was the sight of the police with guns and when we first heard real gunshots we thought, "This can't be right; this sort of thing only happens in movies!"

While we were in New York, we made new friends and met the well-known John Sbarra who composes light music and he wanted me to arrange some of his melodies for an orchestra consisting mainly of strings. Later, we recorded two sessions in London, where at that time the best recordings in the world were being made in the recently discovered 'stereo' sound. We also met Marlin Taylor, the boss of an easy listening music station in New Jersey, and his wife, Alicia, who was a well-known professional soprano.

Since that time in 1980, we have become good friends. Once when we stayed at their house for a couple of nights, they were away one morning and I wrote two compositions in their names, which thrilled them both. Marlin now runs the XM Easy Listening programme radio station, which plays my music frequently from Washington, D.C.

Our honeymoon turned out to be a marvellous occasion, with Joy bowling everyone over with her charm and presence. I felt very proud to have her as my lovely wife. While we were away, our new home was being decorated, which included tiling the kitchen, cloakroom and bathroom. Judy at the time was working for a local tile company that gave us tiles for these three rooms as a wedding present. How lovely our new home looked on our return to the United Kingdom.

22

The French Grand Piano and Something Rather Fishy!

Just before Joy and I were married in 1980, I met John Bradbury, a piano tuner and repairer of pianos. At that time, he had for sale a fantastic French Gaveau grand piano, attractively inlaid in mahogany wood. Gaveau was established in 1847 in Paris and is famous for its beautifully crafted pianos. I found out it was made in 1924, the same year I was born, and knew it was meant for me!

On the left of my studio this magnificent grand piano sits, which I use when I play for pleasure, and on the right is my working upright Bechstein piano. My music desk and cupboards are full of music scores, with shelves where hundreds of my CDs, LPs, 78s, 33s, reel-to-reel tapes of my broadcasts and sessions abroad are stored. Overall, my study contains the evidence of thousands and thousands of music pieces composed or arranged over the years.

Sometimes when I am in the middle of composing, I might swear and curse when the piece is going badly, or jump for joy if I felt I had written something very special. I become cross very easily and quick tempered if everything is going wrong. I might spend a whole morning working and working on a composition or arrangement, only to decide in a split second it isn't good enough, tear it into little pieces and throw it on the floor in a complete rage. I would be as mad as a March hare!

The only thing I can do at these times is to stop and take my dogs for a walk to *compose* myself. What an appropriate pun! I always take a pen and manuscript paper to scribble or write down any ideas that come to me. Often, this means later in the day I am searching for several pieces of paper I have written scores on, as they could be all over the place! Sometimes I will think of a line, hum the tune and dash to my piano to write down the notes before I forget a wonderful piece of music that had just come into my head.

Or at times, when I am in the middle of a commission and the piece just isn't coming together, I will get up in the middle of the night to work. This scenario often happens when I have a commission to arrange or compose a piece I am not particularly keen on, which means I have to work hard to make the piece sound good. Funnily enough, producers often comment, "That's one of your best pieces," when a commission has gone that way.

From my studio, there are French doors leading out to our garden and at certain times of the year, it is very beautiful. All sorts of birds come to feed here: blue tits, blackbirds, thrushes, doves, robins and a lot of goldfinches, which are my favourites as they are so colourful. Watching the birdlife helps calm me down during my more frustrating musical moments.

It certainly isn't easy living with someone who is a musician but my artistic temperament generally never fazed Joy, who most of the time would remain very calm and serene, with the utmost confidence I would get where I wanted to with any piece I was writing. At times, I had so much writing to do, I felt swamped but found it difficult to refuse commissions, often finding myself writing through the night in order to finish my work. I would often say I needed twenty-five hours to my day! Joy sometimes wouldn't like the piece I was writing and would tell me so! I took a lot of notice of what she said because often she was right, as she had a wonderful ear for music.

There was one strange period, though, when we had been married for many years, when I was probably working just a little too hard and once more was hardly home. Looking back, this was obviously getting to Joy, although she didn't say anything to me. One evening when I came home, she wasn't there. I didn't worry too much at first, thinking she had gone out and would soon be back. The hours passed; then I noticed she had taken some of her clothes, but there was no note and nothing to give me any indication as to where she might be. We hadn't had a row; she had just disappeared. I immediately rang my sisters and our close friends frantically trying to find her. Nobody knew where she was. The next couple of days were awful and I even contacted our hotel in Puerto Pollensa, thinking that perhaps she had gone there.

I agonized over whether she had got to a point where she not only felt unwanted, she couldn't handle being the wife of a composer who spent most of the time working in his studio or conducting sessions. Recently, I had taken on a lot of work and during those first agonizing hours, I had to admit to myself that I had been neglecting my marriage.

What an awful time I had until about a week later when the phone rang early in the evening and I heard Joy's voice saying quietly, "Hello love, do you want me home?" I was astonished and said "Of course I want you home." I told her how much I had missed her and how worried I had been. "Please come back," I said (later I was to write a piece called exactly that!). "Can you come home straight away?"

She told me she was calling from a telephone box just three minutes from the house. How relieved I felt! It took me some while to get over that little episode. We never really spoke about it, only that Joy did tell me she had been to visit her aunts in Scotland because she had felt a little fed up with life at home, with me working all the time. I don't think I ever took Joy for granted again.

Going back to my infant days, we had an old piano that was not overstrung, terminology used to describe pianos of lesser quality. When I came out of the RAF, I bought an upright overstrung piano from Norman Baldrey, who had a second-hand shop selling pianos in North Cheam. I kept this magnificent instrument right up to until 2002 when I gave it to Parkside Nursing Home in Banstead, where my sister Judy was staying and replaced it with a fine upright Bechstein that belonged to the son of my artist friend Peter Atkins.

My old piano sat in the main lounge at the nursing home and I would sometimes go and play on someone's birthday or for a special occasion. Or on a visit to see Judy with the two dogs, I might stop and play her favourite song, 'Somewhere Over the Rainbow.' It was great to once again sit at that piano, which had given me such fabulous service for so many years.

Not long after Joy and I settled in Coniston, we met a S.A.S Army Scotsman called Angus who taught students at Epsom College. We became quite good friends and he would often drop in for supper, amusing Joy and me with his stories, as he had a great sense of humour. He also enjoyed my music, which seemed rather at odds with this very tough strapping Scotsman. On one of his visits, he suddenly said, "Don't you think it's about time you had a goldfish pond?" We had not thought about it and agreed our garden certainly had the space. Gradually the idea began to appeal to us.

Angus said he would build the pond and just a few days later, we had a fish pond without any goldfish! Angus said he had far too many fish himself and would donate a few to us. The next day, he arrived with about eighty fish in a large container and threw them into our new pond. His generosity touched us both and we were very excited about our new fish.

A couple of days later, we began to notice the fish were dying. Joy and I went round the garden digging little graves in which to bury these poor goldfish. Unbeknown to us, the builders who were working on an extension for our next-door neighbours were watching our strange ritual. Peter Price, the boss, was also watching us as we went through the same routine throughout the afternoon, as each dead fish rose to the surface of the pond. I think he must have felt very sorry for us because finally he came over to see what the problem was and said he would bring us a tank for our remaining live goldfish. Then he told us a fishpond built with cement needs a lining and this might be the reason the fish were dying.

Peter kindly helped us transfer our fish from this poisoned pond to the tank, and then offered to rebuild the pond using the correct materials. We have been firm friends ever since while he also became our friendly builder, building our porch, the conservatory and an extension to our house, amongst other things.

When we saw Angus again, we told him the story, which seemed to surprise him. Then he confessed on his way over to us with the fish, the tank fell off the trailer and all the fish were squiggling and wriggling in the road. With some help from passers-by, he managed to save most of them, but of course the fish would have had an awful shock and this probably contributed to their deaths. We also learned later that he wasn't being as generous as we were first led to believe, as he had wanted to get rid of his fish for some while. A fishy tale (tail?) indeed!

23

The Royal Bath "Classy Gig" and a Comedy Situation!

In the early '80s, a short while before Christmas, I received an unexpected telephone call. It was from David, a thick-set, likable, good-looking young man who had been the under manager of the Grand Hotel Eastbourne during the time I played there and was now the hotel manager at the Royal Bath Hotel in Bournemouth.

David asked me whether I'd like to get together a trio and vocalist to play over Christmas right up to New Year's Eve. He said we could take Joy's three children, Andrew, Marion and Richard, with us, together with our dog Taly II. Apart from the Grand, the Royal Bath is probably the most luxurious first-class hotel along the south coast and we were all thrilled to have such an invitation. I selected a bass player called Bill Brown, who played in the BBC Radio Orchestra, and the drummer, Rex Bennett, who played for me in the John Fox Orchestra. We came with our families and the hotel management invited us to use the facilities of the hotel and eat in the main restaurant just like any other guest.

My trio for this 'gig' was purely a piano, bass, and drums combination, with Joy singing the vocals. I took with me my 'Dulcitone keyboard' an instrument similar to the Celeste that sounds high and tinkly. We would be playing in the evenings for about three-and-a-half hours and after Boxing Day night, we were to stay on until New Year's Eve to play our last evening.

Joy and I had a special room on the ground floor for dog owners. It was large with French doors and we were able to let Taly II in and out of a little garden. What a treat! However, disaster struck on the very first night. Andrew caught his finger in the door of his room nearly breaking it. We panicked a little, as it was almost time to begin playing. Joy rushed Andrew by car to a nearby clinic, which of course made her late for our show.

Being our first night, it was a little nerve-racking and we had to begin the show without her. Luckily, it was only about half-an-hour and we played many jolly arrangements to keep the guests entertained. Andrew's finger bled a lot and we were all scared it might be something serious, but we managed to get through that evening very well under the circumstances.

We were at the Royal Bath for about ten days and we thoroughly enjoyed it. With the hotel fully booked, the ballroom was packed and every night the guests danced their way through the evenings to our music. During the day when we were not working, we would take the children and Taly II over Bournemouth to see the sights and walk Taly II on the beach. The atmosphere of the festive season helped everyone to be very happy and many evenings when the dancing was over, Joy and I would sit with David and his friends around a large round table passing the port! On Christmas night, we were all particularly merry and had one too many. Poor Joy felt terribly unwell that night.

On the last evening, David gave us a special farewell supper with his friends. We sat up drinking, smoking and singing our hearts out all through the night; then David insisted we all had an early breakfast! Finally, the party broke up just as the dawn was breaking. Somehow, I then had to give Taly II his 'midnight' walk! The weather was very stormy and it was dark, teaming with rain driven by a very strong wind. I put on my raincoat and managed to battle against the driving rain and walk over the cliffs. It was completely deserted. Then, out of the darkness, this tall figure loomed in sight with a collie dog just like Taly II, off the lead. This person walked past me, saying quietly, "Goodnight, John!" I simply replied, "Goodnight, David," as if it was the most natural thing in the world that we were both walking our collies in a raging storm at the crack of a winter's dawn! That was the end of a perfect evening.

About eighteen months before this episode, I had taken Joy, the children and Taly II, on the spur of the moment to Bournemouth for a holiday. When we arrived, we began our search for a suitable hotel. We drove round and round for hours. Everywhere was either full or they didn't take dogs and children. As a last resort, I thought we could try the best hotel in the area, the Royal Bath. Walking through the foyer, I heard this voice saying, "John! What on earth are you doing here?" I spun round and there was David. He had recently moved from the Grand Hotel in Eastbourne to become manager at the Royal Bath.

He immediately gave us the lovely ground-floor room with the French doors leading out to the small garden. We stayed for a week and can you believe David didn't charge us a penny? What a fine and generous friend!

The Easter following that wonderful Christmas, Joy and I were in Munich as I was conducting and composing some important sessions for my publisher, Gerhard of Sonoton Music. I was recording in the famous Trixie Studios with the help of a very talented balancing engineer called Willy Schmidt. Working very hard, I recorded many different types of my music, at times with large orchestras, some chamber ensembles, string quartets and also big bands.

When I had finished, I was very happy with the results and very tired. I had a meeting with Gerhard to clear up some outstanding business matters and he was so thrilled with my work, he gave me another commission on the spot. Germans lavishly celebrate Easter and Gerhard had organized a big party at his office. At one point, he stopped the party with an announcement, "Would everyone please speak English? John Fox and his wife are here and they don't speak German." Everyone tried to speak to us in English, even if it was just broken English. I was so happy that evening after all my hard work and with my new commission, I kept drinking glass after glass of champagne.

I don't often become 'Brahms and Liszt' but that night after drinking copious champagne, I was well gone. When Joy and I left, we had to walk about 100 yards to our hotel and on the way, I jumped over bollards singing my heart out. Probably remembering Christmas night when she became ill on port, Joy was sober as a judge and when we reached our room, she couldn't believe her eyes as I struggled into the bathroom and filling the bath tub, proceeded to climb in fully clothed complete with bow tie! Joy laughed herself to tears and so did I afterwards!

24

Memories of Tigger and Benjie

When Joy and I married, we had Taly II, four cats and a budgie between us. Being animal lovers, we were very happy with our menagerie. Two of the cats were mine from Winkworth Road; one called Tigger was a tabby and Thomas, a lovely ginger and white Persian. Joy's cats were Bubby, who was also a male, together with a female called Tara.

Somehow, Joy had a talent for teaching budgies how to talk, and her budgie, Benji, talked nearly all the time. I often found this slightly off-putting when trying to compose music! One evening when we were entertaining our friends, the artist Peter Atkins with his wife Pam, we were in the middle of a conversation when suddenly from the cage Benjie began talking. He kept saying things like, "Benjie, Benjie, stop talking, stop talking—lovely, lovely Benjie—shut up, shut up."

It was hilarious, with Peter and Pam completely astonished at this little creature speaking out words so clearly. We kept rather quiet following that little episode, with each of us wondering if Benji had picked up any of our conversations during the evening ready to repeat them at another time! Thomas and Bubby were great friends and would often cuddle together on top of my working armchair while I was composing. They never disturbed me, as if they knew exactly what I was doing.

I wrote a composition called *Memories of Tigger*, which proved very popular and has been played many times all over the world. Tigger was a real character, living until he was almost 30 years of age and all the while being the boss of all our cats! As a kitten he arrived one day out of nowhere at Winkworth Road and we of course decided to keep him.

When he was about twenty-nine years old, I contacted our local newspaper as I thought they might think this very old cat would make a good story. *The Banstead Herald* came to see me with a photographer and within a couple of days, there was a photograph in the local paper of Tigger sitting on my piano. *The Daily Express* splashed it over the front page with the headlines, 'Is this the oldest cat in Britain?' It was a great moment and many of the other national dailies, also ran the story. We actually found out later that Tigger wasn't the oldest cat, as apparently there was a cat living in the Ladies Toilets at Victoria Station in London that was thirty-six years old! Still we were very glad Tigger had his moment of glory and of course we did too!

While I was still living at Winkworth Road, Tigger went missing. For days, we looked for him, searching the garden and nearby front gardens. After ten days, we had given up all hope of ever seeing him again. One night after returning home from Eastbourne, I decided to walk down to the bottom of our long garden and look for him one more time. I was calling "Tigger, Tigger," and just as I was about to go back in the house I heard a very faint "meow." It seemed to be coming from the shed of the house at the end of my garden. I leapt into my car and drove round to the house in the next road where I thought I had heard the faint meowing.

By this time it was one o'clock in the morning, but I still knocked on the door. It was some time before a man answered the door sleepily and apologizing for my intrusion at that early hour, I explained about hearing this pathetic meowing coming from his shed. The man fetched a torch and we walked down to the bottom of his long garden. He unlocked the door, and there was Tigger! How relieved I felt, and as you can imagine I was elated. This neighbour had been away and we could only assume Tigger had slipped into the shed and fallen asleep.

I picked him up and hugged him very tightly before rushing back home with the good news. Despite his ordeal, he seemed to be in perfect health, although he did eat a large meal very quickly. This happened about halfway through his life when he was fifteen years old and it certainly didn't seem to have done him any harm. What a tough cookie!

Taly II wasn't quite so lucky. When he was about seven or eight years old, I took him for a short walk as I did every evening before going to bed. As usual, he wasn't on a lead because I could always trust him not to go very far. This particular evening, he did disappear for a few minutes but it didn't concern me. By the time we were back home, Taly II was being violently sick. After a while, I went to bed thinking he had obviously picked something up on our walk.

The next morning, poor Taly II could hardly move and he had been sick all night. Joy and I bundled him into the car and sped off to the vet. We couldn't believe our ears when the vet explained Taly II had been poisoned and there was nothing he could do for him. He would have to put him to sleep. Yet before he could do this, Taly II died just a couple of seconds later while he was still on the table. Joy and I were both there and afterwards we scattered his ashes in many of the places where he loved to walk and play. He was a lovely dog and we loved him very much. We were broken hearted.

I can only think when he disappeared the previous night, he had eaten some rat poison. It was difficult to comprehend as it all happened so quickly and the image of Joy and I leaving the surgery with just Taly II's collar is a lasting sad memory for me. We have a lovely array of photographs of our cats and Taly II at the top of our stairs in Coniston to remind us of our lost pets.

Taly II's death devastated me but I couldn't be without a dog. A few days later, Joy left for Tunbridge Wells to visit her daughter Marion, who was expecting her first baby, James. I decided there and then, I would find a puppy and surprise Joy on her return home. The first place I visited was a pet shop in Epsom. Sadly, they didn't have any Border collie puppies. However, they told me of another place nearby in Stoneleigh that might be able to help.

How happy I was to discover they had just one Welsh Border collie puppy that was black, white, and brown, and I drove home with this tiny pup, only six weeks old, in an old blanket on the front seat of my car. When Joy came home, she opened the kitchen door to see newspaper all over the floor and this tiny black and white puppy. Thrilled with her surprise, she immediately picked him up and we spent the evening choosing a name. We called him Robbie and in a short while, he proved to be one of the finest and the most intelligent dogs we had ever owned. We loved him so much that when he passed away, we bought an album for the photographs we had of him from when he was a puppy up to the age of almost fifteen! We also have a monument in our garden, in memory of our lovely Border collie, Robbie.

Later, Peter Atkins painted a large picture of Robbie standing very proudly in Banstead Wood near to the pond surrounded by autumn trees. We have this lovely painting hanging over the fireplace in our sitting room, which often attracts compliments from the many visitors to our home. In fact, I have a few of Peter's paintings in my studio and I often stop and look up from my work to admire these lovely works of art. My publisher, Gerhard Narholz, knew how much I loved animals and commissioned me to write and compose 'animal' pieces, which became a Sonoton CD released in 1998 called *Animal Lovers*. The titles include 'With Tender Love,' 'A Man and His Dog' and 'Nobody Wants Me.' The cover is a close-up photograph of me and Robbie. I continue to receive many royalties from across the world for the playing of this CD, proof enough for me that it is still very popular.

As a composer, I'm very fond of the English countryside. Living so near to such picturesque places as Banstead Wood, Ruffetts Wood, Walton on the Hill, Shere, and Oaks Park where Joy and I walked our dogs, helped me to become passionate in composing many pastoral pieces. These pastoral and panorama compositions have always been a very important part of my writing.

To portray this type of music, composers have to be able to orchestrate well, especially when handling the large orchestras required to paint a portrait in music of breathtaking scenery. When I am out in the countryside, I take in all the sights and sounds from water mills to tiny babbling brooks, from gabled cottages to the rolling fields of Surrey. Tiny animals of the wood might tiptoe across my mind together with ponies of the forest or a deer like Bambi!

When I am composing, I pluck them out of my mind and these images help me pick the right notes and instruments for my piece. I am certain this is a gift from God, for which I'm truly thankful. Of course, in my early days it was practise, practise, practise and only later, when I knew music notes through and through, did this ability to apply my imagination effortlessly seem to materialize in an almost unconscious way. I have to say at this point, *"If music be the food of love, play on!—John!*

25

Rain Fantasia—Selections and Television

At times, the executive and junior producers from BBC Radio Two would organize a brainstorming session with arrangers for new musical ideas. On one particular occasion, they were looking for a musical piece that sounded original, about fifteen minutes long. It was decided to hold this meeting at lunchtime in the local pub a short distance from Broadcasting House.

Among us there was the brilliant arranger Neil Richardson who wrote the theme tune for the television series 'Mastermind' and Johnny Gregory who was a guest conductor of the Radio Orchestra. Johnny's career included accompanying many famous vocalists such as Matt Munro and Nana Mouskouri.

He maintained the time he spent with the BBC was the best period of his career.

Before I continue with this particular episode, there was a little incident in the early eighties with Johnny Gregory that tested our friendship. I was conducting and arranging a series of six concerts called *Memories of Mantovani,* and the agent who commissioned me called my orchestra, 'John Fox and the Cascading Strings.' When my agent released the publicity for these concerts, the very next day we received a threatening letter from Johnny Gregory saying I would be sued for using the name of his orchestra, 'The Cascading Strings.' It came as a complete shock and I was beside myself with worry, particularly as Johnny and I were quite good friends. It was a complete coincidence my agent had decided to call the concert the same name as Johnny's orchestra.

We were in a bit of a fix because we had printed the leaflets, the tickets, and the billboards together with placing a large article in the local press. I also felt very cross at the time to receive such a letter from a friend. I was beginning to wonder what to do when the telephone rang and it was Johnny. He was very sorry about the whole incident, confessing he along with an associate had made a big mistake as he had not actually registered the name of his orchestra and therefore my agent could legitimately call my concerts what he wanted.

We called a truce. The concerts went ahead as planned throughout the south of England, including the famous Fairfield Halls in Croydon and the Congress Theatre in Eastbourne. Most people from this era will remember Mantovani's signature tune, 'Charmaine,' which I arranged in a very 'stringy' way as my introduction to the concerts. The leader in the orchestra for these concerts was George French, and I also arranged a special solo item for him, which he played beautifully.

Desmond Carrington, the well-known actor in the long-running television drama *Emergency Ward 10* and broadcaster for twenty-three years from 1981 to 2004 for the BBC Radio 2 programme *All Time Greats,* on a Sunday afternoon, compered my first concert at the Fairfield Hall. It completely sold out. Desmond often chose my music to play on his Sunday programme and also presented one of my BBC *The Magic of John Fox* concerts with my own orchestra and singers broadcast from the Golders Green Hippodrome.

The Congress Theatre in Eastbourne was the last of the six concerts and completely packed to capacity. What a night! Most of the staff from the Grand Hotel who were off duty and who I knew so well from my years of playing there were sitting together on the right-hand side of the hall. From the managerial staff to butlers, to chefs, to waiters and waitresses, to chamber maids and cleaners, they were clapping, shouting and cheering me on with sheer delight. What a thrill that gave me and how touched I felt by their enthusiasm.

When the concert ended, I made a speech, talking about my bygone days at the Grand working six nights a week and how I knew the staff by their first names. It was a poignant moment with the whole event bringing tears to my eyes as I thanked everyone for their unfailing support. The audience demanded two encores and I obliged, playing firstly, 'When I Fall in Love' and secondly, most appropriately, 'I'll be Seeing You.' What a marvellous evening and one I shall never forget.

Returning to our BBC brainstorming session in the pub, we sat there racking our brains, trying to come up with some new ideas for special arrangements that were original. Jim Dudderidge and Norman Mead, who were in charge of commissioning, the late Graham Belchere, who was the producer of the Radio Orchestra Show, and I were sitting at the bar suggesting different themes, when Jim suddenly came up with the great idea for 'rain tunes.'

He said to me, "You could do this, John; we need a large orchestra and your John Fox Singers for the choir to vocalize as well as sing words."

Both Norman and Jim liked and knew my work very well and felt they could trust me to come up with what was required without too much direction, which suited their busy schedule. It took some time to prepare for this huge commission, but having thought up titles connected with rain, showers, thunderstorms and rainbows, I finally produced a large score, which in some parts had two melodies playing at the same time. I called it *Rain Fantasia*. The piece lasts about 20 minutes with well over twenty titles including 'Stormy Weather,' 'April Showers,' 'Singing in the Rain' and 'September in the Rain.'

This huge work required skilful conducting, with the famous Bob Monkhouse interviewing me on BBC Radio 2 before the opening broadcasting saying, "We are very much looking forward to hearing the first performance of John Fox's *Rain Fantasia* with the BBC Radio Orchestra." I had never before been interviewed by someone who was so enthusiastic, asking me question after question about how I came to arrange it in such an intriguing and compelling fashion.

I talked about using solo woodwind instruments above soft strings, such as the piccolo in the arrangement using little snippets of 'drip, drip, drop, little April showers' to mimic rain, gradually leading to a climax using the whole orchestra with the string section playing three octaves apart and exploding into the piece, 'Somewhere over the Rainbow.' Later, he told me that initial performance completely bowled him over.

At the time, I recorded the piece on cassette and often over the years when I have listened to it, the thought has struck me, "How did I do that? Where did that come from?" It's as if it was 'another you' who wrote the work, because at times the piece sounds so sublime I just won't believe my ears I was ever that good! How fragile an artist's ego is with our minds constantly filled with doubts and no matter how well received or how well a piece of music goes, we still continue to disbelieve our own talent.

Other selections that I have arranged and require immense work together with skilful conducting include, *Memories of Robert Stolz,* the last Viennese composer to write in the style of Johann Strauss. It is generally accepted there are very few conductors outside of Austria and Germany who can successfully conduct Austrian music. This is because much of their music is based around the waltz, such as the 'The Blue Danube,' which requires conducting in *rubato* and this is a very, very special talent.

Interpreting Austrian music needs more than conducting just in 'dead time'; it requires an innate emotional understanding, something that comes straight from the heart. In my experience, many conductors don't get this, not just because they don't get the message, but because they perhaps haven't taken the time to get to know this stunning country with its scenic beauty, or feel the atmosphere of the great musical city Vienna.

The soloists, who took part in my work of *Robert Stolz,* included the internationally renowned brother and sister duo Marietta and Vernon Midgley, who also sang many times on the radio programme *Friday Night Is Music Night.* Marietta lives very close to Banstead, but sadly our paths haven't crossed since.

One of my personal favourites that was very popular with radio audiences is my arrangement selection from the musical show *Guys and Dolls,* first produced on Broadway in 1950, which between the years 1951 and 1992 won a total of fifteen Tony Awards! Another favourite arrangement of mine is *Tribute to Irving Berlin* in celebration of Irving Berlin's one-hundredth birthday. For this broadcast, I conducted the full BBC Radio Orchestra, with the John Fox Singers. They performed so well. Who can go wrong with Irving Berlin?

Introduced by the very popular composer and radio and television presenter Steve Race (famous for his Bird's Eye frozen peas jingle), this tribute was broadcast from Golders Green Hippodrome. His exact words were, "Good evening and welcome to Golders Green Hippodrome. Different though we all are, we have one thing in common and that's an affection for melody. How fortunate then we are to have the BBC Radio Orchestra with Leader Michael Tomalin and their conductor this evening is one of Britain's leading composers and arrangers, John Fox, with his selection of melodies by the great Irving Berlin. We welcome you to the Musical World of John Fox."

When the concert was over, Steve simply said, "Thank you, John, for that most ingenious and brand new tribute to Irving Berlin." In fact, he complimented me greatly when the commission first came in, as he said he felt I was the only person who could do it. Steve must have liked my music very much because he was very keen on selecting it for his radio orchestra show and would often comment, "That's another lovely arrangement by John Fox." At this point, I do hope you don't think I am shooting a line!

Before that era at the BBC, probably one of the most talented arrangers and composers was Angela Morley. Angela was born Wally Stott and had a sex change operation in the seventies. As you can imagine, this was virtually unheard of in those far-off days but it certainly didn't detract from her musical talents and she went from strength to strength with her composing. Angela wrote many television and film theme tunes including *The Goon Show, Hancock's Half Hour,* and *Watership Down,* which I love. She also worked with the famous Geraldo Band towards the end of World War II as Wally Stott. We knew each other well and of course, we had a common connection with Geraldo, as he was also my agent during the late fifties and early sixties. She is my age and now lives in the United States.

In 1990, Brian Smith, the bass player in my band at the Grand Hotel in Eastbourne, recommended me to a young producer who was looking for a well-known composer and arranger to take part in a film for Channel Four Television. This young attractive female producer came knocking at my door to ask me if I was interested. It was a documentary film about Muzak and they wanted me to arrange a heavy metal song. Muzak is a form of music where instrumental arrangements have been made of pop songs and is generally known as elevator or lift music, since it is played in public places such as shopping malls, department stores, cruise ships and airports.

My arrangement was to be of a song written and performed by the famous Ted Nugent, an American hard rock guitarist who was a major rock performer of the '70s. Nugent was renowned for his bizarre costumes on stage, including wearing a long furry tail like a squirrel's tail when performing.

He had recently formed a new group called Damn Yankees, which went on to sell five million albums. The song in question was 'Cat Scratch Fever,' and my role was to arrange this song in a more easygoing harmonic melody for solo piano in an hour long film called *Muzak and Beautiful Music.* When this young producer played the song for me, I couldn't believe my ears. What a dreadful noise, I thought! Then again, I have always enjoyed a challenge and immediately said, yes, I would do it. I have to admit it turned out to be a great pleasure arranging this piece and it was quite a novelty for me to be on television.

A couple of days later, the camera crew, including the executive producer, arrived at the house and decided they would begin the film in the field at the back of our garden where the schoolboys in their whites were playing cricket. It was a typical rural English scene. The award-winning broadcaster John Walters, perhaps best known as the producer for John Peel's music show, interviewed me. He was also a frequent contributor to music and arts, television and radio shows, but sadly, he died suddenly at the young age of sixty-three in 2001.

He was very nice, so easy-going and amiable, asking me many questions on the differences between pop and easy-listening music. Also, we talked about what I thought of Ted Nugent's shocking heavy metal act on a video from New York, where he was wearing his big bushy tail like a lion. I admitted I wasn't taken with this type of music with loud bangs and aggressive style, saying for me it was a little like describing the difference between heaven and hell! They televised me as I got up from my piano and with my hands flying everywhere, making loud banging noises as I had done so easily as a young child, demonstrating through sight and sound the ugliness of this heavy metal sound. It certainly amused the television crew greatly and they thought the general public would love it, too.

This part of the film opened in one camera shot with the camera panning for about one hundred yards or so past the cricketers, through our gate along our garden to my studio where the French doors were wide open, right up to me playing the chosen piece, 'Cat Scratch Fever,' on piano. Later, John Walters went to the United States and interviewed Ted Nugent for the film, who admitted my arrangement was very well played. He even said, "I must admit this guy knows what he is doing even though I don't like keyboards." This somewhat surprised but really pleased me, as we were so completely opposite in our approaches to music. Mind you, I nearly descended into a raving parody of his music when he referred on television to my beautiful French Gaveau piano as a 'keyboard'!

In the film, Ted Nugent's act suddenly ends with a clash of loud noise and the scene changes immediately to the peace of the English countryside with the young schoolboys in white playing cricket and my arrangement playing softly in the distance. As I said earlier, an ascent from hell to heaven!

26

My Special Joy, Music in East Germany and Richard's Baton Case

Joy and I had settled happily into married life and I was very keen to help Joy make the transition from being a semi-professional to a professional singer. Joy loved singing, but she had been a full-time secretary and bookkeeper in Tunbridge Wells, as she had needed to support herself and her children after becoming divorced.

I had accompanied singers all my life and it was something I enjoyed immensely, so I would often accompany Joy on the piano when she sang at local gigs. I now wanted to get her out of the habit of being a semi-pro and concentrate on her singing career seriously. I worked hard on her voice, encouraging her to sing right way down to bottom E-flat below middle C, which is a lovely register and quite a sexy pitch, up to top C, two octaves above middle C, which is quite a difficult note to reach.

Apart from the big stars such as Ella Fitzgerald or Barbara Streisand and with the exception of opera singers, there are not many sopranos who can reach these notes easily. I recognized straight away Joy had a natural talent. I weaned her away from singing tempo songs and trained her to sing in *rubato*. It wasn't always easy and I would insist Joy went over and over a note until she got it right. She would say, "I can't do it, I can't do it. Let's have a cup of tea." However, I would persist and we often had many disagreements over the whole process. In the end, Joy recognized I was helping her to reach her full potential.

For a while, Joy also went to a professional for coaching and then it wasn't long before she was working with me when I required a solo singer for my vocal music. She was not one of my John Fox Singers because her sight-singing wasn't one of her strong points. Sight-singers have the ability to read the music in front of them and perform it from sight, which is a very important skill especially when recording and broadcasting. Singers such as these are generally called session singers and often sing in choirs. Joy was a versatile all rounder with a terrific vocal range with the ability to sing *arias* as well. Essentially, she was a soloist and had to learn the song by heart before performing or going live. The big difference between sight-singers and soloists is the fact soloists can interpret the song in their own special way, whereas sight-singers work directly from the sheet music where no deviation is expected.

They must of course be able to sing in tune, which many session singers can easily do. Amateur choirs generally take their vocal parts home and practice with lots of rehearsals before performing their show pieces. The Leith Hill Festival in Surrey is a good example of this type of singing. Joy would generally come with me on my sessions and of course later we worked together in concerts abroad, in Birmingham Golders Green and broadcasts when I conducted the BBC Radio Orchestra. Joy also supported me in my administration duties, especially when I took on session musicians to form my own orchestra and she would have their cheques ready at the end of each broadcast or concert.

It was important to me that the musicians were paid promptly and in our profession this wasn't always the case. I valued the musicians who contributed to my success and felt strongly it was important to treat them well and I certainly didn't ever have any problems getting a full orchestra together. I had what is called a 'fixer': someone who engages all the best musicians who are available on the required date or dates. My 'fixer' was my leader, George French.

It is of the utmost importance to have the ability to recognize and select excellent musicians; otherwise, it is not possible to have a good orchestra. Everybody got on so well with Joy, too, and when she was included in my orchestra, and also the BBC Radio Orchestra, as a solo singer it seemed as if they made a special effort and played their hearts out!

Joy had a very positive influence on everyone around her and whenever she walked into a room, there was something about her that made you completely aware of her presence. She was soft-spoken, very graceful, and she laughed and smiled easily, which increased the loveliness of her already very attractive features.

When we had large parties at Coniston for birthdays, Christmas and New Year's Eve, I would generally employ a piano player to play background music throughout the evening; then Joy and I would always perform a duo at some stage.

Many times, she would bring tears to the eyes of our friends and neighbours with her rendering of songs such as 'Send in the Clowns.' Equally, she could make people laugh, singing comedy songs and especially, 'Typically English,' when she would vary her accent on the lyrics from a Glaswegian to a hoity-toity English toff!

Her rendering of Andrew Lloyd Webber's 'All I Ask of You' from *Phantom of the Opera* with the popular baritone Lindsay Benson is really quite something. When Joy received commissions of her own, I would accompany her on the piano and we would often travel to London together to play a duo act.

One very good episode in our great partnership was after completing some sessions in Munich, my publisher, Gerhard, asked me to call in to see one of the Cologne Radio senior producers, Dr. Bungart, before we returned to the United Kingdom. Dr. Bungart was very nice—a short, typical-looking North German with a lovely black beard—and he wanted to know if I was interested in building a music programme for five concerts to be broadcast live from a large concert hall in the centre of Cologne.

He took time off and came over from Cologne to our home for a fortnight so we could discuss and go over my arrangements and compositions for this proposed broadcast. It felt wonderful to be compiling a programme two hours in length knowing it was for the German public. Dr. Bungart knew the exact type of my material he wanted to use for this important occasion and I found the whole experience very interesting.

Arriving in Cologne, Joy and I were given this spacious and very comfortable apartment. Equipped with mirrors everywhere, it was furnished for artists of all kinds. Mirrors are very useful to conductors and singers, as it is customary to practise in front of mirrors to help not only perfect movement and style but also to help alleviate feelings of nervousness before a performance.

We had a whole week to rehearse with The Köln Concert Orchestra and we both enjoyed every second of it. The idea of the concert was to perform my music in lots of different styles including jazz, classical and arrangements of Tchaikovsky's *Romeo & Juliet* and of Elgar's *Chanson de Matin*. It was a very exciting time.

For five nights, we played in different venues throughout Cologne before the big night at Cologne's Opera House built in 1957. On the last day of rehearsal at the Cologne Radio Station, I accompanied Joy at the piano and we experienced one of our finest moments ever performed together. Nobody seemed at all interested in what we were doing, with the producers and mixers busy with their heads down in the control box upstairs. Suddenly there was a flurry of activity and Dr. Bungart and a few other radio engineers rushed down the twenty or so steps to where Joy and I were performing our duet, 'Send in the Clowns.'

They were utterly amazed at Joy's rendering of that song with just piano accompaniment and as we ended the piece, there were at least three or four seconds complete silence. They said her voice had come from heaven! Dr. Bungart immediately said to his engineers, "We must record this now!" He sent everyone rushing about the station to put in place the equipment for the recording.

The night of the last concert had a full house and the audience was terrific. It was quite obvious they loved every moment. When I put down my baton and walked up the four steps to where the grand piano was situated and Joy began her rendition of 'Send in the Clowns,' this interval completely surprised the audience. The combination seemed to be just right with the whole orchestra remaining completely silent for a couple of minutes while I played and Joy sang.

I had bought Joy a couple of sparkly evening dresses to wear, one blue and one pink. When she walked on that stage in the long blue dress, complete with silver high heel shoes, she looked fantastic, and every eye was on her.

When we had finished, I lost count of the times we walked on and off that stage for an encore. The audience clapped and clapped. We took many, many bows because the applause went on for so long! We both felt like a million dollars and I have to say The Köln Concert Orchestra was equally fantastic. The way they played with such professionalism and enthusiasm, it was a real pleasure working with them.

I could only make my speech in English but the audience didn't appear to mind and somehow seemed to understand what I was saying. It certainly was a night to remember. Some time later, Dr. Bungart engaged Joy and me for another concert in Cologne with the same orchestra and which was just as successful.

Not long before Joy and I went to perform in Cologne, her son Richard did something that was very special. He presented me with a conductor's case in mahogany with my name written on the top in brass letters. It holds many different batons and they are 'cushioned' in so they don't get broken, as batons are very fragile. It was indeed a lovely surprise, especially when Richard told me he had made the case himself. He and his wife, Tracy, drove all the way to Cologne for this very special concert, which they enjoyed enormously.

Over the years, I have taken this marvellous-looking case with me to concerts and broadcasts everywhere. It holds many precious memories and I still have it propped up in my studio today. How talented and thoughtful of Richard to make such a wonderfully useful gift.

Of course, with Gerhard as my publisher, I spent quite a lot of time in West Germany arranging, composing and conducting. One day, my first opportunity came to go to East Germany. Gerhard had secured a commission for me to record a CD of my music in Leipzig, the home of Johann Sebastian Bach! He was too busy to go and after giving me all the details, left me to find my way over the Berlin Wall. I found a publisher called Dennis Berry, who was also a composer and arranger. He founded his own record label called Conroy Music, sometimes known as Berry/Conway. Berry also arranged for Ted Heath and at times worked alongside Johnny Dankworth with many of his compositions played on the BBC test cards. As well as being my producer, Dennis was also my driver and interpreter, as he was fluent in the German language.

Joy and I flew into Berlin and arranged to meet Dennis at Berlin railway station. I had never met him before but recognized him straight away with his big mop of white hair. He drove us the whole way to Leipzig without stopping, apart from refuelling, and the journey was six or seven hours long. It was an interesting journey through East Germany's countryside, which seemed to have very few towns. Unfortunately, Dennis insisted on playing Frank Sinatra the whole way and while I like Sinatra, I have to say by the end of that journey, I had had quite enough of him!

When we arrived in Leipzig, I had to stop at a place similar to our post offices and produce some papers. The man behind the counter gave me back my papers and a large package containing 30,000 East German marks. I was totally amazed, but apparently it was customary to give any celebrity entering the country a gift of some kind as a gesture they were pleased to have such people visit them. There was even a write-up in the daily national paper announcing my stay in Leipzig.

I don't think I have ever met such nice friendly people as the East Germans. They were still under Communist rule and most seemed to be very poor. Many times, we saw queues of people waiting to buy bread. It certainly was the case that unless you had money, life was very tough. Another thing I noticed was the way East Germans spoke. They had a real dialect and their language sounded so very different from the West Germans.

We were staying at an inn that was very comfortable and quite luxurious in comparison to how the rest of the population in East Germany lived.

The music I had composed for this recording was my suite, *Earth and Space*. This suite came about because Gerhard wanted something along the lines of *The Planets* by Holst. As *The Planets* was still in copyright at the time, it wasn't any good writing an arrangement as I would not have received any royalties from my work and neither would have Sonotone. We were discussing our next move when suddenly I suggested a suite called *Earth and Space*. Gerhard immediately said, "That's a wonderful title!" I set about writing this suite, which could also be used for library music. As I wrote the music, I imagined lifting off from earth into space and thought about the moon, Mars and the stars.

I really enjoyed writing this massive piece, which was to be recorded by a 130-piece orchestra and I had to use the largest score paper I could find because I had so many strings to write for. I had to divide the parts so I could develop a much more modern harmonic sound. As far as I am concerned, the more strings the better! I used double staves for the first violins, second violins, violas, cellos and double basses! What a sound!

I would like to explain a little about 'The John Fox harmonies' or 'sound' as it was sometimes called. I have often been asked, "How did you get that sound?" It is very difficult to explain, but I believe I was born with an inherent understanding of how to produce music both melodically and harmoniously. I have a 'musical' mind, so I know almost instinctively what every instrument sounds like and how each instrument produces different sounds.

For instance, when I was growing up listening to songs, I wouldn't like certain old-fashioned harmonies that had changed very little since the thirties or forties. There was little reason to this, only that to my musical ear, it didn't sound good. My idea was to improve the harmonies by adding more notes to the chords to produce a fuller sound while still keeping to the same melody.

It was my own interpretation of the notes for each instrument that helped to create the 'John Fox' sound. However, to explain how to write melodies or harmonies to the lay person is almost impossible, as the basic rules for the structure of music and composition principles are too complex to explain here. The only way I am able to describe this 'sound' (which I must stress was only one of the many styles of the thousands of compositions and arrangements I wrote) is to say there is a strong influence in the use of strings, which I would use to blend in softly with four other instruments.

In my music, I created a 'special blend' using four unusual instruments: a muted flugelhorn, alto flute, alto saxophone and a cor anglais (which is larger than an oboe and creates a much lower sound). This 'blend' would play in unison and create this almost 'secret' sound, which many listeners and producers loved but couldn't really explain why! The range was also limited from B-flat below middle C up to D, which is a tenth above.

This 'blend' of four instruments, which is set apart from the remaining instruments in the orchestra, must not last too long, otherwise boredom might creep in. I would use this 'blend' much more in my arrangements than in my compositions because there were far more of my arrangements of popular songs that were commercially recorded than my own compositions.

It is a strange thing, because my compositions do not relate in anyway to my arranging and they are completely different, in my opinion. I think if one heard one of my serious classical compositions and it was followed by an arrangement of mine, you would think it was written by two different people. Over the years, I had a tendency to put my compositions and arrangements in two categories, thinking of my compositions as J.F. wearing a top hat and my arrangements as J.F. wearing a cloth cap!

This recording of *Earth and Space* in Germany was truly a great period in my life as I was given free rein to really do what I liked. Gerhard trusted my ability to orchestrate a large orchestra and I was able to conduct my own music as I wanted it. The orchestra also worked so hard on my behalf to get everything right, including working alongside Joy who was vocalizing some of the wordless voice parts.

The recording was actually taking place some way from Leipzig and it took two big coaches to get the whole orchestra to this enormous mall, which was built for Stalin. In the centre of this mall, which was closed to the public while we were recording, there was a large stage as long as my own garden in England!

While we were there, we stayed in this little inn where the food was good despite the fact the place was quite primitive and was very much like a place you might have found in England one hundred years earlier. We had a small room and I had to sort out the music for this 130-piece orchestra. There were pieces of music all over the place and I was up with Joy until three o'clock in the morning trying to sort it out!

Another strong memory of that place was this constant smell of gunpowder. Apparently, we were close to a factory where ammunition was made and this sulphurous odour was constantly in the air. After we finished recording *Earth and Space,* I asked everyone who was involved in this large production to have a drink on me for all their great efforts. There were 130 musicians, plus six librarians, three men in the control mixing box and three producers. Everyone had a drink, with the cost, to my utter amazement, only amounting to ten pounds!

When the orchestra stopped for lunch in a large canteen, it would irritate me the whole 130-piece orchestra was served first and the rest of us would be waiting until nearly the end of the break before we were given our lunch. This was because it was still under Russian Communist rule at the time and it was the custom to serve the 'ordinary' people first.

My *Earth and Space* music has been very popular over the years and I have received many royalties from many countries throughout the world. It really was the first of its kind and some of the ideas I conjured up at the time even surprised me because they sounded so original. I believe this took place before the composers of the music for *E.T., Close Encounters of the Third Kind, Space Odyssey,* and *Alien* came on the scene and while it has never been acknowledged, I believe many of the current day composers have been influenced by my *Earth and Space* music.

We visited Leipzig three times, and on the second occasion, we stayed in a large luxurious Japanese hotel, and the last time we recorded there, it was just three weeks before the Berlin Wall came down. We still had quite a few East German marks, which were worth very little because they were about to become invalid tender. Joy and Dennis decided they would try to get rid of them in exchange for deutsche marks at Leipzig railway station, which is one of the biggest stations in the world. I stayed in the car while they did this and looking back, I realize it was probably quite a scary thing to do as it was late at night.

Everything turned out fine, including sending the tapes to Sonoton in West Germany. During the whole trip, Dennis helped us immensely and as I have said before, my *Earth and Space* is amongst the best recordings and compositions I have ever been involved in. Later, I also made a six-movement suite of my *Earth and Space,* which you can hear on my commercial CD, *Voyage of a Lifetime.* This 'voyage' contains many of my compositions, arrangements, folk songs, with pieces featuring The John Fox Singers in a cappella style and my suite, *The Love of Joy.* I believe this CD certainly represents the versatility of both my composing and arranging styles of my musical career spanning over sixty years.

27

Prostate Problem and Loss of Pets

In my early sixties, I suffered from a slight health setback. It wasn't too serious, but I had to be admitted to hospital for surgery. I had been experiencing problems with my waterworks and for a while dismissed it, as I wasn't experiencing any pain. I decided to do something about it when it became obvious my urine flow was not normal.

My doctor gave me an internal examination through my 'tail end,' which wasn't very pleasant at all! He then referred me to a prostate specialist, Mr. Boyd, who practiced at St. Anthony's in North Cheam. He told me I had Benign Prostatic Hyperplasia and I would have to have an operation. Thankfully, he assured me it would not affect my love life.

A short while later, I went to St. Helier's Hospital in Carshalton to have my prostate removed. As I was coming round from the anaesthetic, I could see this pair of vivid blue eyes looking at me. What a wonderful sense of relief when I saw my lovely Joy by my bed and how comforted I felt at that first moment of awareness. Like most people when going under general anaesthetic, I did worry about the fact there was, of course, the risk I might not regain consciousness.

I had a private room with many friends and colleagues visiting me. It made me feel very special having so many visitors who gave me so much attention and I certainly realised what good friends I had. When

I was allowed home, I still had to wear a catheter for a short while and felt very tender and tired. However, a few days later on my first Saturday morning home, the Channel 4 video film about Beautiful Music and Muzak arrived through the post.

How timely this was, as watching the film certainly helped to cheer me up and I felt quite overwhelmed. It was indeed very good therapy for me and very shortly afterwards, it was shown on television, which I found just as thrilling. After I left hospital, I wrote a romantic piano piece for Joy called 'Your Smiling Eyes,' in memory of that lovely vision when I was coming round from my operation. This was recorded on an album called *Heartstrings* and is the last track on the CD.

I had to take it easy for a while to enable me to fully recover from my operation and I was so glad to have our lovely pets about me. It wasn't long before we realized Thomas, our gorgeous ginger and white Persian wasn't well either. We were told he had a tumour and we had to have him put to sleep. He was eighteen years old, and yes, he had had a good life, but it was hard losing him.

Tigger was over thirty years of age when he died and Bubby was run over when he was about twelve. They had lived happily side by side, with Tigger as the boss! We had our budgie, Benjie, who as you know was an absolutely brilliant talker! I wrote a composition called 'Our Benjie' for him that was played by a woodwind quartet, with flute, oboe, clarinet and bassoon. When Benji died, I composed another short piece called 'Lament to a Loved One.' Over the years, I have written numerous pieces of music for our companionable and loving pets, which have been published on different CDs.

I must tell you about Benji's death, which was rather unusual. Joy and I think Robbie our collie frightened Benji one day. He may even have caught him in his mouth. Benji would always have his hour or two of freedom in the mornings when we let him out of his cage to fly around the kitchen. This particular day, we saw him collapsed on the kitchen table. We put him back in his cage and he quickly seemed to recover. A couple of weeks later, he had developed a tumour and we took him to see the vet. Benji suddenly sprung to life and flew around the room a couple of times, then flew into Joy's hand and died!

At one time, we bought a kitten from our local vet and named him Ginger. He was such a character and a pure delight to have around. This little cat would disappear on many occasions into the large field at the back of our house and we had no idea where he was. This worried me quite a bit, especially as he didn't come when I called him. One day, I walked round the field banging a saucepan lid against the saucepan, calling him. As if by magic, he appeared out of nowhere! From then on, when I wanted him to come home, off I would go, saucepan and lid in hand and he would appear sometimes from a long way away. He would jump up and over our tall back gate and stand there expectedly as if wanting a reward for returning home!

My next-door neighbours, Molly and Bob, called this act of mine *The Saucepan Symphony,* and many a time we laughed about our lovely little Ginger and that symphony! Unfortunately, when he was only ten months old, Ginger's bouncy character got him into real trouble when a dustcart ran him over. We did miss his exuberant character. Our last cat was a lovely black moggy called Tara, which Joy rescued from her workplace when the office was closing down.

When Tara was fully grown, she developed this habit of walking round the field with our dogs and at night if she was out, I would know it was her because of her very bright yellow eyes, which shone out like car headlights. Sadly, she was another one of our pets who died from leukaemia at thirteen years old. I have never forgotten the pleasure my cats have brought me over the years. Although we didn't get another cat after Tara, I often think of my cats that have gone and recall our happy, funny times together. I am glad to say all our cats were friendly lap cats and we laid them to rest at the bottom of our garden at Coniston in remembrance. We also looked after a lovely bitch called Lady, a beautiful collie type of dog, for a couple of friends who were moving to Ireland to build a house. One evening, about two years later, they turned up unexpectedly to take her back. This was very sad for me because it was so sudden and I had so enjoyed looking after her. She always slept in our room and if I ever got up in the night, she would be watching me! She always seemed to sleep where she could keep an eye on me. Unfortunately, we heard that Lady was kicked by a horse in Southern Ireland and it killed her outright. We loved her very much and miss her dreadfully.

28

The Loss of Lee

One evening not long after my prostate problem, the telephone rang. It was my sister Judy panicking about our elder sister. "Come quickly, something has happened to Lee," she shouted down the phone. Lee had gone through some troubled times with her marriage and was now living on her own in a flat in North Cheam. Often she would stay at Judy's house for two or three weeks at a time, as she was very lonely. Twenty years earlier, Lee and her husband, Harry, had immigrated to Johannesburg, South Africa with a couple of friends. Harry had his own sheet metal business—the very one I worked in when I was just a lad, tearing my hands to pieces!

I took the four of them to Southampton to catch the boat and that was the last I saw of Lee for nearly three years. Then one day, she turned up in the United Kingdom on holiday and stayed for about a month before returning to South Africa. Three months later, Lee returned for good without Harry. Eventually she found a job at a printer's that had a flat over the shop where she could live.

She spent her time knitting Harry jumpers and socks and we couldn't understand it. We kept asking her, "Why are you knitting for Harry?" and Lee would answer, "Oh, he's coming back—he's coming back. I know he's coming back."

Harry never did come back. Apparently, he had met another woman; so after nearly twenty-five years of marriage, it was over for Lee. I knew Harry had always desperately wanted children and Lee didn't, which was a great pity. I have often thought it might have played a part in the final demise of their marriage. She didn't say very much about her time in South Africa and I always had the feeling she had never been happy there.

Life would have been very restrictive there for Lee because she wouldn't have been able to go out, especially in the evenings because it was too dangerous. She only spoke on occasions about the young domestic girls who worked for her in the house. They were young girls who did all the cooking, cleaning, washing, and ironing and I think she formed quite a friendship with them. I had always been on good terms with Lee and felt we got along very well. She was a very kind, warm person with a great sense of humour and a good sport.

Also, despite the fact she had very little money throughout her life, she was like my dad and always very generous when she bought presents. In her late teens, Lee loved going to dances at the Locarno Dance Hall in Streatham, which was opened by the band leader Billy Cotton in 1929 and was very popular during the war years. It was a high profile place that had regular appearances of musical stars such as Duke Ellington, Matt Monro and Chuck Berry. It also became the venue for the famous Miss World heats during the 1950s and was well-known as a social location where people met their future husbands and wives.

She would spend hours dressing up, then order a taxi to take her to Sutton train station. Lee just loved dancing and she really was an excellent dancer! She invariably caught the last train home at midnight, then totter back home in her very high heels. One time, unfortunately, our little dog Bonzo, who was still only a small puppy, raced after Lee as she was getting into the taxi and somehow she managed to step on him with her very high heels and break one of his legs. There was lots of yelping and shouting. Poor Bonzo!

If our dad had known about Lee staying out so late, he would have been angry, but he was always fast asleep and I don't think he ever knew about this episode in Lee's life. However, because he locked the doors at night believing we were all upstairs in bed, Lee would have to throw stones at Judy and Maureen's bedroom window so they could let her in. She would clamber over the coal bunker and use a ladder to reach the window so Maureen could pull her in! Mum must have known about these antics and she never once said a word. This happened at least twice a week on a regular basis and to this day I am amazed at how she got away with not waking our dad up!

Although I wasn't as close to her as I was to Judy, she would always listen to the programmes on BBC Radio 2 when my orchestra was playing and when she died, we found over fifty cassettes in her home, which were recordings of my broadcasts.

There were times when Lee and I didn't see eye to eye and this normally occurred when she put on 'airs and graces.' This would happen when she came to my sessions and met some of the executives from the BBC. She would adopt this rather la-di-da accent, which wasn't her at all, and none of the family could understand why she did it.

She was probably a bit of a show-off and she had become what is termed a snob, throwing a line to everyone about her life in South Africa and behaving as if she knew a lot about music, which of course she didn't, which would really rile me. When she was home, she would behave in her normal way, dropping the pretence and once more becoming the Lee we all knew and loved, but it was often quite difficult to handle this behaviour of hers.

After receiving the telephone call, Joy and I rushed over to Judy's house in Fir Tree Road. When we arrived, Judy was visibly distraught and told us Lee had just that moment died. Apparently, she had been in her room doing the crossword and smoking. Lee hadn't been feeling very well that day and had even called out the doctor who told her there was nothing wrong. Because she was such a heavy smoker, Lee always had this dreadful cough and had a tendency to talk about her health quite frequently. I was quite incensed the doctor had dismissed her illness and afterwards I went to see him to tell him what I thought of him. He was of course very embarrassed.

The news came as a double blow to me. Firstly, losing Lee and secondly, because just the weekend before, Lee and I had an awful quarrel. We had not spoken again. I sat in Judy's sitting room with my head in my hands, wishing I could turn back the clock, not wanting to believe this dreadful loss had occurred. It is a terrible thing when you lose a member of your family, but I can't even begin to tell you how painful it is to lose someone under these circumstances.

It was a Sunday afternoon and the row was so silly, too. I can't even remember how it began, although it did have something to do with an incident that happened years ago with Lee's tendency to show off. She was talking about her life in general but knowing she was exaggerating, I became angry with her, telling her I knew she wasn't speaking the truth and how I disliked her trying to be someone she wasn't, which resulted in us shouting at each other. Exasperated, I told Joy we were going and I angrily left the house. That was the last time I saw or spoke to Lee.

She died of a sudden heart attack as the aorta, the main artery to the heart, failed, probably due to her excessive smoking. She was seventy-five years old. For the next four or five days, I visited Lee in the funeral parlour at Trueloves in Sutton until the day of her funeral, talking and pleading with her to forgive me. My tears flowed and flowed in that funeral parlour and even today, I have not been able to reconcile or forgive myself for the last day Lee and I spent together.

Smoking is a real killer; we know that now. When I was in my teens, I did smoke and I would play piano with a cigarette dangling from my mouth, with the ash going all over the place. Then one day, the headlines on the front page of every newspaper read, *"Smoking Causes Death!"* This really hit home and I have never picked up a cigarette since! Lee, just like Jackie, felt very lonely and I think she smoked as a form of comfort. Most of the human race is addicted to something as it seems to be in our genes. The big ones and the most well-known, of course, are smoking, drinking, drugs, womanising, eating, gambling, or overworking. Personally, I probably come under the last category of overworking. I feel being addicted to music can't be that bad, especially as I am in my eighties and still very fit, both mentally and physically.

29
Puerto Pollensa and "Sad Occasions"

Luckily for me, I was always busy composing, writing arrangements, and conducting here and there. At least twice a year, normally in the spring and autumn, Joy would book a holiday. We had our favourite holiday resort, which was Puerto Pollensa in Mallorca. We would stay at the same place in a luxury four-star seaside hotel called the Illa d'Or.

It was located right on the beach, surrounded by palm trees with the mountains behind, and we would book the same room with a balcony and sea view. To us, it really was the most beautiful place on earth. Spanning more than two decades, we went back there over twenty-two times.

Because I was so busy, Joy would make the travelling arrangements and handle the packing. We had such wonderful times at Puerto Pollensa and we both loved this place so much, I was inspired to write a composition called 'Siesta in Puerto Pollensa.' There was a grand piano in the restaurant and just for the fun of it, I would often sit at that piano playing whilst Joy sang. The manager was a short Spanish chap who made a big fuss of us, particularly as my playing would bring all the clientele in to listen.

Everyone thought we were the resident musicians and were paid for our services. Once we even had a little incident when the owner from a nearby music and dance bar came in angrily and told me I was taking all his customers away!

Joy and I had a very romantic encounter on one of these holidays, one we shall never forgot. One lovely, sunny, hot morning after breakfast, we drove off round the island to find a quiet cove or beach to sunbathe. The hotel did have its own beach, but there were times when we just liked being on our own. In fact, this one morning we hadn't gone very far, only about five or six miles down the road, when we spotted a very quiet place. We were lying in the sun on a smooth ledge above a cove listening to the seagulls and the waves with nothing on our minds. It was completely deserted, then looking out to sea we saw this couple, a middle-aged man and an extremely attractive, sexy, young girl in a small boat.

They were both in their bathing costumes and sometime later, they dived into the water. Before the blink of an eyelid, they swam the short distance to the rocky shore *and made love!* They were only about ten yards from us and they had no idea we were there, just above their heads looking down on them. The sight of these two lovers without a care in the world was really quite something. Without saying a word, Joy and I glanced at each other then packed up quietly and hurried to our parked car about one hundred yards away.

I drove back to the hotel like a madman and we both rushed to our room and with our pulses racing fell passionately into each other's arms. What a *siesta* that was! What an experience! What pleasure! Wanting is such a great feeling. Oh, to be young again!

Ah, sex! That wonderful, vital force of life, which of course brings to us other considerations in our daily existence that are sometimes not quite so happy. Just before Joy and I were married, Joy discovered she was pregnant. It was a total surprise to us and we were both taken aback. Joy was in her late thirties and already had three children from her first marriage and I was in my mid-fifties. We were both very busy with successful careers and having a baby was far from our thoughts. For a couple of weeks, we agonized over the situation.

Our relatives were thrilled with the news, but then we told our families we didn't think we wanted to go ahead with the pregnancy. "Have the baby," my uncle Perce (my dad's youngest brother) said. "It's your own flesh and blood." We weighed up all the pros and cons and in the end decided the best decision was for Joy to have an abortion. It wasn't an easy decision for either of us and when the day came, we both felt wretched. I drove Joy down to the hospital in

Brighton and the ward sister told us it would take three or four hours, sending me home as I wasn't allowed to stay on the ward.

Returning to my studio, I threw myself into finishing a piece of music I was composing. It helped me so much. I forgot everything as I worked through the scores. In fact, I was so lost in my music that when I eventually glanced up at the clock, I realized I was going to be late picking Joy up.

Joy was waiting for me and the sister told us, "It's a shame you didn't have it—you would have had a lovely baby boy." In hindsight, of course, I have often bitterly regretted this decision. Our son would have been twenty-seven years old today and carried on the Fox name, as there aren't many of us Fox's left. Yes, the remorse is deep within me but above all, my music came first as it always has done. At that time, we couldn't possibly have looked after a young child when so much was going on in our professional lives.

Sometimes, I think that is an excuse–a stupid excuse! It was a decision we both made twenty-seven years ago and sadly, we can't do anything about it now. Yet who knows what life holds for us all? I had a gift and I felt my life was chosen. Metaphorically, I have given 'life' many times. Given life to music and given music to life, and I truly believe this is the path God intended for me.

Talking of lost children, at the bottom of my garden, in the very colourful field where bluebells and other wildflowers grow, is the most beautiful cherry blossom tree. It is such a big gorgeous tree full of blossoms in the spring; in 1991 it was planted in memory of a child. In May of that year, a fair was held in the field. This was an annual event that raised money for charity and there were lots of different stalls including coconut shies, small roundabouts for children, popcorn, candy-floss and fortune tellers. There were also pony rides. This particular morning, as everyone was setting up their stalls, I was taking my dogs for their walk and stopped to talk to a young girl called Joanne Long. Joanne owned the ponies and was excited about giving pony rides to the children throughout the afternoon.

Late in the afternoon, after all the fun was over, when the organizers were packing up and leaving, Joanne's stepfather arrived with a horsebox to pick up the ponies. For some inexplicable reason, as he was quickly pulling away, Joanne jumped on the trailer's running board, but she missed her footing and fell off. She was killed outright.

What a tragic accident and such an awful end to what had been such a wonderful day! Joanne was a lovely, plucky little girl and her mother planted this cherry blossom tree just a few feet high on the spot where Joanne died. Now, nearly seventeen years later, it has grown to be so colourful and that young, lovely little girl would have been twenty-seven years old.

I like to think this beautiful tree is telling us something, that little Joanne is still with us somewhere and she reminds us of this every year when the tree bursts into the most magnificent blossom. Since that horrific day, there has never been a fair in our field again. I wrote a piece of music in Joanne's memory called 'Blossoms in May,' for harp solo performed by Skaila Kanga, which has been played all over the world.

Skaila is one of the United Kingdom's leading harpists and works not only within the classical genre, but also with pop stars including Paul McCartney, Sting, and Cliff Richard. I would always use her as a harpist in my own orchestra when I needed one. She plays this simple little piece so beautifully; it's as if she knew the little girl Joanne personally.

30

Robert Farnon Society and a Popular French Songwriter

At this stage, I'd like to mention the well-known Canadian composer and arranger Robert Farnon. He was a master of light classical music and has composed, amongst many others, very many popular pieces such as 'Portrait of a Flirt,' 'Jumping Bean,' 'Journey into Melody,' and 'Melody Fair.'

Quite a few years ago, a colleague told me Robert had a worldwide fan club and I decided to join. At these meetings, I enjoyed many long chats with Bob until he became very ill and couldn't manage the journey from Guernsey to London. Not only is his music very poetical, as a musician, he was a real genius; he also had a head for business, which is very rare for famous composers.

There is a Robert Farnon Society meeting twice a year at the Bonnington Hotel in London, where we have an evening meal and take the opportunity to get together with other composers to talk shop. Members attend from all over the world, including some celebrity composers such as Debbie Wiseman, who has written music for many feature films and Adam Saunders, who is described as a 'Young Composer of Note.' Adam and I are great friends and I will tell you more about this later.

The society distributes a magazine three times a year called *Journal into Melody* (quite a unique "pun" title!) and at times, I write articles for this magazine. As a special guest, I have been invited on a number of occasions to talk about music and play some of my latest recordings. The secretary, David Ades, is a real gentleman, who has had that job since the Society was founded. Other special guest musicians who have spoken include, Ernest Tomlinson, the late Trevor Duncan, Brian Kay, Gavin Sutherland, the late Angela Morley, Philip Lane and more recently Nigel Hess, the renowned film and television composer.

In the last part of the twentieth century, Bob was one of the greatest composers of light orchestral music in the world. He was a great string writer and lived in Guernsey for many years. Passing away in his sleep in 2005, he was eighty-seven years old. It was just three weeks before the premier of his last symphony, which he dedicated to Edinburgh. He is still called 'The Guv'nor' in musical circles! He was married for over fifty years to Patricia Smith who was a casting director for Herbert Wilcox when they first met. She died in October 2007.

Bob was also a fine arranger, and this leads me to talk about arranging music, which is an important part of an all-rounder musician's profession. Many music publishers including Bonneville USA, WGAY Washington, SRP, USA, Boosey and Hawkes, Chappell's and, of course, the BBC have commissioned me to write many hundreds of arrangements.

You have to be skilful in writing for voices when arranging for choirs, which is something I have done a lot of throughout my career. I find this type of work very enjoyable, especially when arranging folk songs, and throughout the years my commissions have been to arrange many, many songs with or without an accompaniment.

The majority of the easy listening stations in the United States play my arrangements of many popular songs, such as 'This Is My Lovely Day' by Vivian Ellis, 'All the Things You Are' by Jerome Kern, 'And I Love Her' by Lennon and McCartney, 'Misty' by Errol Garner, and 'Desafinado' by Jobin. It would take me hours and hours to count how many arrangements I have written professionally in my long career.

The American listeners love lots of strings, and a couple of my string arrangements, including 'Pieces of Dreams' and 'What Are You Doing the Rest of Your Life?' were recorded for the vast American market. Strings are probably my favourite part of the orchestra and it was my string writing that helped me so much to become a recognized master of orchestral evergreen arrangements. Nevertheless, the whole orchestra is still my cup of tea!

The two songs just mentioned were written by the late Michel Legrand, a French-Armenian composer, arranger and pianist who has performed with orchestras from all over the world. Well-known for his film musical scores, which include *Wuthering Heights, The Go-Between, Yentl,* and *Predator 2,* he won three Oscars and five Grammy's.

I would like to bump into Michel again, as he borrowed a baton of mine years ago that he didn't return! You might think this is churlish, but conductors become very attached to their batons. Choosing which baton to use becomes almost a ritual and most conductors have their favourite, which they get very used to and believe brings them luck.

One morning, I was conducting the full BBC Radio Orchestra and Michel was conducting the afternoon session. When he arrived, he asked me if he could borrow my baton. I was a little incredulous. "What? You don't have a baton?" I said. "Yes, yes, I have a baton but I've forgotten it," he replied in his strong French accent, gesticulating wildly with his hands.

I never saw that baton again and it was rather special to me as it had been my favourite for years. When that session began, I was in the control box and three or four brass players sauntered into the studio about five minutes late. I've never heard a conductor tell them off quite like Michel Legrand did that afternoon!

Mind you, I didn't like latecomers either when conducting sessions as it completely upsets the whole schedule for the rest of the orchestra.

Leaders, as we call them, within the orchestra are very important. Leaders are normally first violinists and you see the whole orchestra at a concert waiting for the Leader who joins the orchestra after everyone else, to tune his or her violin with the 'A' note. This provides a tuning note for the whole orchestra, which the oboe player picks up as the oboe has a perfect 'A' notation. From there, the rest of the orchestra picks up from the oboe, and if there isn't an oboe in the orchestra for some reason, the piano would be used to pitch the note.

The Leader also chooses which direction the bows play, whether up or down, so when playing, all the bows are flowing in unison in the same direction. Because of my experience and expertise in writing for strings, the ability to write the notes for the correct direction of the bow is something that comes very easily to me, especially as my second instrument at college was the violin. Very often, if an inexperienced arranger or composer has written the music, the Leader or the conductor might have to make some adjustments if the notes don't quite match the direction of the bow.

Of course, when an orchestra is playing for broadcasting, it doesn't actually matter too much but when where you actually *see* the performance and not just hear it, correct bowing is very important.

Michael Tomlin was the Leader of the BBC Radio Orchestra for many years, and his wife, June, was the lead cellist. Leaders are very good soloists and are often given a solo within an orchestral piece. Michael was always a perfect gentleman and during the twenty-odd years we worked together, we never had a cross word on or off a session.

George French was the leader of my own orchestra, the John Fox Orchestra, and we have always got on extremely well as our tastes in arranging and composing are so similar. He was an excellent violinist and we would often get together with our wives, Joy and Marion, and have what we called 'listening' sessions as we played and had serious talks about music. During one of these times, George asked me to play over and over again, my arrangement of 'Scarborough Fair,' which is a very pastoral arrangement and is featured on my CD, *Voyage of a Lifetime*. George is very English and just a few years older than me. Sadly, he is going through some very bad times as he has had some sight problems recently and his lovely wife, Marion, is suffering from arthritis.

In the mid-nineties, I received a letter from a young man who was studying composition at the Royal Academy of Music in London. This Academy allows last year students to choose their favourite composer and ask that composer to give them three lessons of advice. From this young man's letter, it sounded as if he had talent, so I wrote back and asked him to come and see me.

Adam Saunders was thrilled to receive my reply and when I asked him how he knew of me, he told me he had been inspired by my music, which he had heard on the radio from an early age. The Academy paid me handsomely for the three lessons I gave Adam and we have been firm friends ever since. He has gone from strength to strength with his music since then, which was almost twelve years ago.

Composing in all the styles, his grounding in music is very similar to my own background. I do believe in those early days, I helped him to recognize that no matter how much he may like the music of different composers, it was important to find his own style and voice. Adam took the trouble to record to a CD twenty-six of my serious works played by the Royal Ballet Sinfonia conducted by Gavin Sutherland for my eighty-fourth birthday. The pieces have been taken from a number of commercial CDs I have made in recent years on various labels. Creating a colourful pastoral scene for the front cover, he called it the *John Fox Concert Music*. What a surprise to receive the best birthday present I have ever had. What a friend indeed! What a genius!

We have a great time when we get together listening to one another's music and discussing the subject until the cows come home, or the whisky runs out! Adam is also a fine pianist and occasionally plays as a solo artist at classy hotels in London. Adam's wife, Clare, is an actress and singer who played Dorothy recently in a local rep production of *The Wizard of Oz*. Adam has written large orchestral works amongst many other types of music including jazz.

Just as I accompanied Joy on the piano, so Adam accompanies his wife on many occasions. Recently, they have been blessed with a lovely baby girl called Rose, but they still find time to visit me and it is wonderful we have remained firm friends from that very first meeting when he idolized me and my music.

Isn't music a marvellous art? It brings so many wonderful people into your life. It can pull at the heartstrings, make you happy, sad, romantic, and it can reach into your very soul. What on earth would we do without music?

31

English Folk Songs and English Pastoral Music

In 1977, Chris Morgan commissioned me to write for a BBC album of English folk songs with the John Fox Singers and a few instruments such as the recorder, harpsichord, flute and harp. The album is called *Fairest Isle,* which is the name of one of the tracks and it features other well-known folk songs originating from all over the British Isles including, 'Greensleeves,' 'Billy Boy,' 'John Peel,' 'Here's to the Maiden' and 'Scarborough Fair.'

Being an Englishman, I am very patriotic and although I have visited many other countries, I don't think anything beats the English countryside, especially in the spring. As I write, my mind reflects to when I walk with my dogs through Banstead Wood in Surrey amongst thousands and thousands of bluebells growing underneath the tall trees. Then stepping over the old five-barred gate and hearing birds singing beautifully, it seems to me time almost stands still during these magical moments.

My walks have helped me paint a picture in music of what I think the English countryside is all about, especially Surrey where I have lived all my long life! These walks and my love of rural life have inspired all my pastoral compositions including 'Pastoral Impressions,' 'Ponies of the Forest,' and many more on nocturnal wildlife.

Titles like 'Melodic Panorama,' 'Dancing Bluebells,' 'Down the Woodland Path,' 'Down by the Crystal Riverside and 'On the Wing

Again,' are all examples of my compositions of rustic music depicting the English countryside. This pastoral library music, which provides me with many good royalties, is played in many countries round the world including South Africa and most of Europe especially Germany, Norway, Sweden, and France.

The haunting provocative sound of the cuckoo perfectly captures Banstead Wood's rustic atmosphere but sadly, I haven't heard it very much lately. I do miss its call very much and often wonder if cuckoos are slowly dying out. Perhaps my best pastoral string writing is my *Countryside Suite* in four movements for strings and harp beginning with 'Morning Air,' and followed by 'Black Clouds Over the Moors,' 'My Village' and 'Country Folk.'

The Royal Ballet Sinfonia conducted by Gavin Sutherland beautifully played this suite, recording it on the White Line Label in 2003. The album also features the music of Sir Edward Elgar's *Sospiri op. 70,* which is a great honour for me.

In 2000, the Internet business musicmaker.com, launched in 1999 by a New York-based company, issued a double CD called *Twilight Time* featuring thirty of my best arranged and conducted stringy evergreens. Chosen from 180 pieces originally written for Bonneville, musicmaker.com recorded the tracks on a number of CDs. The purpose of this Internet site was to allow customers to create customized CDs and provide music in downloadable format but unfortunately the company went into liquidation in 2001.

Some years ago, CTS Studios in Wembley, London originally recorded these popular songs from *Twilight Time.* Unfortunately, the redevelopment of Wembley Stadium saw the end of CTS Studios at this site when, after twenty-eight years,, the doors were closed for the last time in June 2000. CTS relocated their premises to the Colosseum in Watford to become CTS Lansdowne. For me, this was the end of a fantastic era where the best composers and musicians from all over the world would come to record their music and where the world's first comprehensive all digital studio was launched in 1985.

32

The BBC Producers

Today, the BBC is the world's largest broadcasting corporation and historically, it was the only legal radio broadcaster until 1967. Its monopoly on radio services persisted well into the '70s. How immensely proud I am that the BBC was instrumental in the success of my music career with many of the producers commissioning me over a considerable number of years to write arrangements, compositions and broadcasts such as *String Sound*.

Chris Vezey, a composer who lives very close to me in Epsom Downs and is still working, produced *String Sound,* and I composed the signature tune called 'String Magic' for that programme. Of course, the most important executive producer to me was Chris Morgan. He really was the first person at the BBC who believed in my music and discovered my talent, producing all the commercial albums of mine and the various series of broadcasts I conducted and arranged.

Producer Roy Herbert didn't give me much work unless other executive producers told him to give me a commission. I often wondered about this, until one evening I met him at a BBC party, and he came up to me and said, "Hello John, will you have a drink on me?" Completely taken aback and before I could answer, he went on, "I feel very guilty about not using you on broadcasts very much and the simple reason is, I am jealous of your remarkable talent."

I looked him straight in the eye and replied, "I'll have a double scotch please." I explained to him I had no idea he was a composer while also explaining it hadn't mattered too much because I had been so busy and didn't really need his commissions anyway. That evening certainly was an eye-opener and I have to admit it was good of him to confess this to me. It was quite common for producers to think they were composers and perhaps he was a good musician but I only knew him as a producer.

The most musical producer of all and a great pianist was a young man called Graham Belchere. He was the musical director for the show *They're Playing Our Song,* when the show came over from Broadway to the West End London. Marvin Hamlisch, the multi-award winning American composer, wrote the songs, and his first real break was being the rehearsal pianist for Barbara Streisand in *Funny Girl.* Graham commissioned me to be the first composer and arranger on a new series for BBC Radio 2 called *The Radio Orchestra Show,* in the mid- eighties. This show ran for about three hours with Steve Race as the main presenter together with Bob Monkhouse, who was often the guest presenter. Graham and I had always got on very well and it was awful news to me in later years when I heard he had died at a young age some years after BBC made the musicians redundant.

The producer of the BBC transcription service, Neville Rayner, who was rather aristocratic and a very fine concert pianist, produced a series called *John Fox Presents* in the early eighties, which went out to all the British Commonwealth countries. I recorded and announced many of these programmes with my singers and orchestra. I was often very nervous and Neville, who was such a likeable person, would say in his la-de-da accent, "Let's go and have a pint in the canteen, John; it will make you more relaxed." One particular day, we visited the canteen on several occasions and by the time I was ready to talk on the programme, I was slurring my words! It was rather a difficult situation to be in but luckily for me, nobody noticed!

These half-hour, easy listening broadcasts are still being played in many parts of the world and a couple of years ago when I was at the Bonnington Hotel in London for a dinner event, some of my fans and producers who were over from many countries throughout the world including South Africa, China, and Australia queued up for my autograph. What a special moment that was!

Robert Beaumont, often referred to as Bob, is a very good tenor singer and for many years was the producer of *Friday Night is Music Night* and he would often use the John Fox Singers as part of that popular hour's light music show. Additionally, he would play my arrangements and compositions in the many programmes he produced. In the early eighties, he also gave Joy some singing lessons but he was very tough, often reducing her to tears. I heard evidence of this when I played the cassette her lessons were recorded on.

He wasn't the most popular producer as he was sometimes a difficult person to get along with but I shall never forget how kind he was towards me one Christmas when I was very lonely. He used to live very close to Banstead in south Sutton and it was the first Christmas after Jackie died.

The phone rang and Bob asked, "Are you on your own, John? If you are, I would like you to come over and join us." His whole family was so hospitable and made me feel very welcome.

Now a very well-known conductor, Barry Knight used to be the executive producer for BBC Radio 2. One day at the BBC, we met in one of the corridors and he exclaimed, "Ah, John! I've been looking for you. Would you like to do six concerts for me?" Of course, I jumped at this opportunity and recorded these concerts called *The John Fox Concerts* at the Pebble Mill Studios in Birmingham, which involved Joy singing for one of the concerts. He also gave me many other series of programmes to arrange and conduct. These concerts consisted of many wonderful evergreen melodies from the past.

As happens in many walks of life, there was one particular junior producer whom I didn't like at all and he didn't like me either! During a broadcast, after each piece, he would come out of the control box and criticise each arrangement of mine. At one time, I was conducting a piece that had been recorded recently on a commercial BBC record using the John Fox Singers. It was called, 'This Is My Lovely Day,' and he wanted to leave my singers out completely.

I disagreed entirely, and we argued and I made an official complaint to the BBC bosses about this man being against 90 percent of everything I recorded in the Maida Vale Studios. I went through some very hard times with him, but some years later I was sorry to hear the news he had died in an accident. Evidently, soon after he bought a property abroad, he was killed instantly after falling off a ladder.

Probably one of my favourites was Charles Clark-Maxwell, because he was such a character. He was quite the comedian and did enjoy a drink or two. Although he was a very good producer, he was renowned for sometimes falling asleep during the afternoon sessions and after one particular piece I was conducting with the BBC Radio Orchestra, Charles called from the control box through the microphone, "That was marvellous, John! Next one, please!" In fact, he hadn't heard a thing as he had been fast asleep and the engineer had nudged him to wake him up on my last note!

I did become particularly friendly with Ray Harvey who during the eighties was the producer of a programme called *Much More Music* on BBC Radio 2. He often featured my music on this very relaxing, pleasant afternoon programme and we would sometimes have a pint of beer after working together. He was the producer of my first *Musical World* concert on BBC Radio 2. He is a big band lover and now plays in many groups on saxophones and clarinet. Ray and his wife, Barbara, would sometimes meet Joy and me to have Sunday lunches together at The George, in a small village close to Tonbridge in Kent. There are, of course, many more producers, too numerous to mention, whose paths I crossed during my many years at the BBC and I am grateful to each and every one of them for my most memorable and enjoyable times.

33

A Dangerous Week in Belfast

In the late eighties, the BBC commissioned me to conduct the BBC Northern Ireland Orchestra in Belfast. It was to be mostly my own arrangements, with some of my own compositions and the music of other composers such as Robert Farnon, Eric Coates, and Sydney Torch.

Despite the fact it was during the time of Northern Ireland's Troubles, I wasn't too concerned and I decided to take Joy with me. We were due to fly into Belfast Airport and someone from the BBC was meeting us with a car. We landed in the evening and it was already dark. The airport was very small and simple and it was almost as if we had landed in a field with the airport building a barn in the middle of nowhere! We left the main building, but the BBC car was nowhere in sight. We waited and waited. By the time we knew the car just wasn't going to arrive, we had also missed the bus! The airport was some distance from the town and there was nobody about, nor were there any taxis.

While we had been waiting, we noticed in the distance a few searchlights cutting across the dark sky and the sound of muffled bombing, which didn't seem to stop. It suddenly occurred to us the 'Troubles' in Northern Ireland were worse than we thought and we had no idea when we left England that it was so bad. After all, we had heard very little on the radio or television and in the papers, the conflict was mentioned only briefly, which certainly didn't sound very dangerous or even very important.

However, our immediate concern was, 'How on earth could we travel from such a remote area without a car in sight?' Joy didn't panic at all and said something or someone would come along. Eventually, they did. The first vehicle we saw was an old lorry pulling a truck full of hay and Joy very nicely asked the driver and his assistant for a lift. They agreed but said we would have to ride in the hay truck! So we scrambled in the back feeling very relieved.

Five miles down the road, the driver told us it was the end of his journey as he had reached his farm. This was quite an alarming moment for us, as we had our suitcases and I had my bag of music, too, which was quite heavy. Nevertheless, there was nothing we could do, and we began walking very slowly along the road. To make matters worse, it was very dark as there were no street lights. Although neither of us said anything, we were very nervous by this time, especially as we could still hear bombs going off in the distance. Some time later, a lorry came along and we frantically flagged it down. We crammed into the front seat and forty minutes later, we were in the centre of Belfast.

We made that journey in complete silence. Neither Joy nor I felt like talking, and the driver remained silent, too, and only said, "That's okay mate," when we got out and we said thank you. What a frightening experience that was and it occurred to me that when I agreed to go, I really hadn't thought through the situation at all. With a great sense of relief, we found a taxi that took us to the small hotel outside the city, where the BBC had booked us in for our stay because it was safer.

We found out the car hadn't turned up because they weren't expecting us until the following evening. What a BBC blunder, I thought! After such a harrowing experience, we couldn't wait to get to our rooms and rest. However, there was worse to come. The hotel was fully booked. The manager phoned round several other hotels without success but eventually found one of the best hotels in Belfast right in the centre of the city. We had no choice but to get back in a taxi and make our way to this hotel; little did we know it was situated in an area that was constantly bombed. We couldn't believe our eyes because everything was in complete devastation. Even our hotel had suffered bomb damage, and we now realised why the BBC had booked us into a hotel on the outskirts of the city. We spent a sleepless night on the sixth floor with the constant bombing a complete nightmare. As we were so high up, Joy and I spent most of the night watching the searchlights from our bedroom window. Standing there, I was taken back forty years to World War II and it was a very strange feeling. As I watched, I saw the red atmosphere, like a hundred sunsets from the bombs and the guns, light up the night sky. I am not sure why, but it didn't once occur to us we could be bombed. Maybe it was because the action seemed to be taking place so far away.

The next morning, I phoned the BBC and a car was immediately sent round to take us to Broadcasting House in Belfast. When we arrived, the entrances were blocked and we had to prove who we were by showing our passports and my contract with the BBC, even though they were expecting me and the security guards said, "Good Morning, Mr. Fox." They recognized me from my previous visits to conduct the orchestra.

At 10:00 a.m., we began rehearsing and the first thing I noticed was there were quite a few ladies in the orchestra, especially in the string section. Then something amazing happened. As soon as there were a few bars rest, these ladies would put down their fiddles and pick up their knitting needles and knit nineteen to the dozen! More amazingly, you couldn't hear the clicking of the needles as they knitted in complete silence during these tacit bars. I found it a little disconcerting to begin with and even played a little joke. I dropped my baton and said, "Would you like to borrow my baton to knit?" These ladies never missed a note and quick as a flash would pick up their fiddles to come in at precisely the right second! Of course, this only happened during rehearsal and not when the red light was on in the studio indicating we were recording. Over the years, I have often thought of those female musicians knitting their hearts out and have played with the idea of composing 'The Knitting Concerto' or the 'Knitting Symphony'! These Irish players were very talented and played so well throughout that week, I couldn't fault them.

Each day during the lunch break, Joy and I would walk round Belfast and we found a certain silence amongst all the people walking about. If there wasn't any bombing or guns going off, which seemed to happen mostly at night, everywhere was so quiet and if you closed your eyes, you could almost believe you were in a silent city. The shopping centre could have been any shopping centre anywhere in the United Kingdom except for this uncanny quietness and the fact even in supermarkets, there were no chattering women and if anyone did speak, it was in whispers.

For some reason, our hotel didn't sell alcohol. One evening on our way back from the studio, I asked our taxi driver to stop at a wine shop. I simply walked across the road to this rather derelict looking wine shop, which once I was inside was covered in cobwebs. In addition to cobwebs, there were several suspicious looking characters hanging about who all looked very stern and stared very hard at me. I felt the atmosphere was very tense.

The shopkeeper was pleasant enough and I bought a rather expensive bottle of red wine and made a hasty retreat. The taxi driver still had his engine running and as I got into the car, said quietly in his soft Irish accent, "You shouldn't have done that, Sir." Slightly perplexed, I asked why and he replied, "Because the Protestants live on this side and the Catholics on the other side. You could have been shot."

Now I don't like to stereotype, but it occurred to me that it is often said the Irish at times are fairly simple folk and I have to say I couldn't understand why on earth he hadn't said anything to me before I did cross the road! I have laughed many times at this incident, although it wasn't funny at the time.

I often thought during that disturbing week of the Irish song, 'When Irish Eyes Are Smiling,' but I have to say on that particular visit to Belfast, we didn't see many smiling eyes.

The last session of that week ended in what I would term a 'comedy situation.' The very last piece I was conducting happened to be a Robert Farnon composition where the timpanist did not seem able to play the ending properly. It was a 'timpani' solo and he kept making mistakes. We went through this ending so many times and suddenly I became very impatient. Angrily, I threw my baton up in the air and caught it at the same time as shouting to the poor percussionist, *"For Christ's sake get it right!"* There was complete silence in the studio and you could have heard a pin drop. The leader of the orchestra stood up slowly said quietly, "Please, Mr. Fox, no swearing in the studio."

It was the first and last time I ever lost my patience in front of an orchestra! That was the end to an extremely eventful and quite harrowing week and if I was to write some music it will forever go down in my book as *dramatic workshop, emotions, sad occasions, comic selection,* and *comedy situations,* all rolled together as one, in an up and down rhapsody!

John Major was Prime Minister at the time, and he was making big strides in trying to establish the Northern Ireland peace process and I suppose we heard more about this in the United Kingdom than about the actual fighting. This is probably the reason we were so surprised at the level of violence in Belfast. For us, this certainly was 'the week that was.' We got over it, of course, but it left a big impression on me as to the reality of the Northern Ireland conflict and how far removed we were from it in the United Kingdom.

34

Joy's Migraines and a Fantastic Concert

In the early nineties, my composing and arranging were running smoothly and life felt good. Joy's singing career was going well, too, and she was also proficient in looking after the administration side of my music career.

The only downside was Joy's occasional horrific migraines, which she had begun to suffer from in more recent years. When she had one of these attacks, she would feel so unwell with nausea and pain that I would have to leave her alone for two to three hours. Sometimes the attacks would be so bad, I would find her lying on the bedroom carpet with a bucket by her side, too ill to get into bed. Joy didn't like me seeing her like that and would ask me to go back downstairs until she felt better.

When I heard a little tap on the ceiling and Joy calling out, "John, will you make me a cup of tea?" I knew it was over and would feel so relieved. Eventually, she agreed to see a specialist who diagnosed a tumour on the pituitary gland, which is located behind the eyes at the base of the brain. Luckily, the tumour was benign and Joy's migraines disappeared after receiving treatment for a few months with various drugs.

How relieved we were, especially as not long afterwards, I received a telephone call from Dr. Bungart, our German producer. He wanted

Joy and me to perform in Cologne again at some concerts even larger than the previous ones when I had conducted The Köln Concert Orchestra. This time, he also required a male baritone singer together with a choir (the Germans acquired this! Pun!). Once again, Dr. Bungart came over to England to stay at our house for two weeks to discuss and plan the programme with me.

We chose the excellent baritone Lindsay Benson, who Joy had sung with at the BBC and had worked with me as a vocalist. He was to sing solos in addition to a couple of duets with Joy. The three of us chose 'Can't Help Lovin' that Man' and 'Cabaret' for Joy, with 'On the Street Where You Live,' Some Enchanted Evening,' and 'Ol' Man River,' for Lindsay. The two duets I arranged for Joy and Lindsay were, 'Almost Like Being in Love,' and the great Andrew Lloyd Webber hit from *Phantom of the Opera,* 'All I Ask of You,' with added choir.

There was one very special song by Kurt Weill, called 'It Never Was You,' which Joy had sung in a previous concert and had become her main feature with me accompanying her on piano. Kurt Weill was a leading German composer and songwriter who, after fleeing the Nazis, became an American citizen. He went to Hollywood where he quickly learned how to write in the American style, producing a number of musicals for Broadway and becoming famous for his film and theatre music.

One of his all-time favourites, which sold millions, was 'September Song' from *Knickerbocker Holiday* sung by Walter Houston. But probably his greatest and best-known of all was 'Mack the Knife,' originally written in German and becoming a jazz standard through Louis Armstrong and Bobby Darin after his death.

Just as we did the first time, we performed four concerts in the suburbs of Cologne, before the great performance on the Saturday evening in the marvellous Cologne Opera and Philharmonic Concert House, which seats over two thousand people. On that night, it was completely packed. How nervous we were, and how thrilled!

We had been rehearsing hard for a whole week with the orchestra, choir and of course the solo artistes. The rehearsals had been particularly difficult for the choir as they weren't very good sight-singers, but they had practiced so thoroughly, they were very good on the night. This concert, called *Zauber De Melodie,* is without doubt the best concert I have ever composed, arranged and conducted in my whole life. It was fabulous! My publishers, Gerhard and Heidi of Sonoton Music, came all the way from Munich to be there for this great event. I had written a new composition, called 'Music of the Stars' to open the concert and had arranged a massive selection of the late German composer Kunnecke's operetta as the grand finale. The audience also loved Joy's solo with me accompanying her on the piano.

A beautiful Steinway grand piano had been raised on a small stage and Joy looked elegant as she stood in the bell of that grand piano and performed 'It Never Was You.' The two thousand people in the audience were so silent, you could hear a pin drop. How proud I felt of my lovely Joy at that unforgettable moment. To end the first half, with my orchestral backing, Lindsay sang the classic 'Ol' Man River' beautifully and none of us will ever forget when the audience went wild with enthusiasm as we struck the last note of Kunnecke's *Der Vetter Ans Dingsda*. What unbelievable applause and standing ovation we received. It was breathtaking! Perhaps *All I Ask of You* is to believe me!

My German publisher, Gerhard Narholz, and his wife, Heidi, organized a special party after this fabulous concert at a classy restaurant in Cologne. All the people who organised the concert were invited and Dr. Bungart became very drunk! We had to drag him into a taxi to take him home. Gerhard and Heidi made Joy and me guests of honour in that restaurant, insisting on sitting with us to celebrate such a successful evening.

Later, Dr. Bungart commissioned me to rearrange two of my selections from that concert, the *Memories of Robert Stolz,* (a tribute to the last of the Viennese composers) and Kunnecke's operetta *Der Vetter aus Dingsda*. This involved rewriting the original solo singing parts for the impressive Munich Radio Choir accompanied by the magnificent Köln Orchestra. He kindly recorded the broadcast on cassette and sent it to me, which I have now transferred to CD. It was great listening to it again. How impressive it sounds when my selections for a massive ending on both arrangements sound as if the skies are falling in!

35

Good News—Then Bad News

Early in 1996, Joy saw an advertisement offering women a free mammogram at a clinic in Guildford. Deciding to take advantage of this offer to check she was in good health, Joy asked me to take her to this clinic. Several weeks later, we went back and sat in a waiting room packed with husbands and wives waiting for their results.

It soon became apparent it was a slightly uncomfortable situation because we would be watching this door open and close, and sometimes the woman who came out was very happy and sometimes it would be a woman in tears. By the time they called out, "Mrs. Fox," we had become very apprehensive. I sat watching that door with my heart in my mouth. The instant I saw Joy's face, I knew the results. She was smiling happily. Everything was okay! We both felt so relieved.

About a year later, a mobile mammogram caravan was stationary for a few days in the Horseshoe at Banstead, once again offering women scans. I am not sure why Joy wanted to go again, especially as she had only been very recently, but she did. Not long afterwards, Joy received a letter telling her she needed to go in to see them again for the results.

It was then a specialist at Epsom Hospital diagnosed her with cancer in her left breast. We were stunned. We just couldn't believe it and why hadn't this tumour shown up the year before? We clung to one another and cried our eyes out. At home, the family together with a couple of close friends were waiting for us in the kitchen. Everyone was very solemn and tearful. It seemed for a long while afterwards, our days were filled with friends and family in tears at this cruel news.

The events of this day are firmly embedded in my mind. It was the Thursday just before I was due in Budapest for some sessions for Sonoton Music. The specialist told Joy it would be good therapy for her if she went with me. I managed to get her a seat on the plane and we flew out that weekend for my recordings. I don't know how we struggled through the next few days. Joy was being very brave but I knew she was frightened and eventually one evening, she broke down. After that, she recovered quickly and kept telling me not to worry; she was sure everything would be okay.

The music I was composing and recording in Budapest Hungary was about animal lovers and nature studies called *Animals and Landscapes*. It didn't help that some of these compositions were sad in nature and it was very difficult to concentrate, as I was worrying so much about Joy. Although theses sessions did come out very well considering the circumstances, when I listen to them now, it takes me back to those first few traumatic days when we were trying to come to terms with the dreadful news. On the Monday morning after we returned home, we went to the Royal Marsden Cancer Hospital in south Sutton for Joy to begin her chemotherapy treatment.

Fortunately, this hospital is only a couple of miles or so from our house in Banstead and each time over the next six months I took Joy for her treatment, waiting and waiting through the long hours, I silently prayed for her recovery.

For the first time in my life, music took second place and I stopped working. I told my publishers and agents I wasn't available; I turned down a number of commissions and I stayed at home with Joy. My publishers were wonderful, telling me it was fine and they would wait until I could return to my music when Joy was better. Joy was very popular and well-loved by my publishers and they were deeply saddened and shocked to hear our news.

This period of our lives was very, very hard. We spent our time between the hospital and home when the effects of the chemotherapy would kick in and Joy would feel terribly ill. Then the specialist told us the tumour, which had been very big, was gradually shrinking away and they admitted they found it quite amazing. After continuing with the chemotherapy for a while, they put Joy on radiotherapy. Then we had some wonderful news. The specialist told us that although she had to take tamoxifen for five years, Joy wouldn't have to have her breast removed. For the first time in many months, feeling as happy as sandboys, we had some brief moments of peace.

One very sad morning at home, Joy's beautiful fair hair began to come out in big handfuls and this upset her terribly. I was devastated, too, to see my lovely Joy in such a state. It wasn't long before she was almost bald and I immediately took her to the department at the Royal Marsden where they supplied wigs and after some considerable time searching, we managed to find a long and silky hairpiece just like her own hair. Joy was so courageous during this awful period, which lasted about ten months. She was a tremendous fighter who vowed she would never give in.

Gradually, Joy became her old self again with her hair growing back very quickly and lovelier than ever. I once more returned to my music, safe in the knowledge Joy was through the worst of her ordeal. We began to attend social events and Joy again accompanied me to my sessions. We went away on holiday to our favourite resort, Puerto Pollensa, staying of course at the Illa d'Or Hotel. Yes, life had become normal for us again and how sweet those days were after our struggles through the long dark months of illness and uncertainty.

36
Composing for Piano—Bill— and All Saints Church

Meanwhile, I was still composing for Sonoton Music and for Ian Dale of Amphonic Music. Ian is the son of the renowned late Syd Dale and he commissioned me to write for him after his father's death. Syd founded Amphonic Music in 1971 to produce compositions for television, radio and films. He quickly became Britain's major supplier of library music. Although I wrote a few arrangements for Syd in the early seventies, he became my rival in New York where he arranged Muzak while I was arranging for Bonneville in New Jersey.

Once we spent quite an amusing evening together when Joy and I happened to be in New York at the same time as Syd. He rang my room saying, "Is that John Fox?" and I replied, "It is," and before I could say anything else he said, "Let's meet in the bar."

We had quite a few gin and tonics, which went straight to our heads as we hadn't eaten. Before the evening was out, Joy had to retire to the room, leaving Syd and me to chat. A while later, I also began to feel very intoxicated and staggering away, left Syd to pay the bill! The next morning, I remembered I had abandoned Syd but didn't feel too bad about it because over the years I had known him, he had very rarely bought anyone, or me, a drink!

Syd lived very close to Banstead in Kingswood, where he had a recording studio, and he hired a full-size Steinway grand piano to record my piano pieces for two albums on CD. For *Piano Pieces,* I wrote 'Water Colours,' 'Lullaby of the Brook' and 'Impressionist,' while for *Classical and Romantic Piano,* my pieces were 'Rendez-vous' and 'The Time that Was.' At this particular time, I was quite out of practice with playing the piano because I had been so busy composing, arranging and conducting, so I had to work hard on these pieces.

The results were certainly worth it and Syd was very pleased particularly as the album quickly became popular. It was great for me, too, because it wasn't long before the royalties began to come in particularly for my piece 'Impressionist.'

Just to name a few ivory tinklers, my pieces on those two CDs sit alongside those of other well-known names including Johnny Pearson, Ronnie Price, Steve Gray, and Geoff Eales. Johnny was the Musical Director of *Top of the Pops* on BBC television for many years and also composed the Big Ben *News at Ten* score, together with the theme tune for the famous televisions series *All Creatures Great and Small.*

I don't think there is anything quite as intimate as the sound of a well-played piano. 'A tinkling piano in the next apartment,' says it all in the Jack Strachey song, 'These Foolish Things.' This very melodic tune reminds me of many years ago when stationed at the RAF Camp in Weeton; I was tinkling romantic tunes in the pub to that lovely blonde girl whose boyfriend punched and knocked me out!

Do you remember my good friend Geoff Barham who came to me for piano lessons at the tender age of six? He is now the choirmaster of All Saints, our church in Banstead, which is over eight hundred years old. In the mid-nineties, Geoff decided to produce and direct a film on the history of the church and of the village. He called it *Son et Lumiere* and asked me to compose the music, with Guy Michemore (the son of Cliff Michemore) as the narrator. Geoff researched eight hundred years of history up to the present day with fascinating results and I composed the music in an early style using some Medieval instruments such as the Carsack, viol, gambas, harpsichords, recorders, bowed psaltery, crumhorn, bass racket, virginal, lute and oboe d'amore. It proved to be a very interesting and different experience writing music for these types of instruments.

I asked Paul Arden Taylor, the oboist in the BBC Midland Radio Orchestra, to play these instruments for me. It was intriguing when he arrived with all these rather strange-looking instruments in the back of his car.

When Geoff completed the whole production, he showed the actual premiere in the church. There were quite a number of small television screens set up around this magnificent old church with the main big film shown close to the altar. It was quite an occasion! With the church packed with many reporters from the local press, the vicar Reverend Tom was thrilled with the whole project.

Not so long ago, the current vicar, Rev. David Chance, asked me to talk to the congregation one evening about my life as a composer and arranger. I was very pleased to be asked, so set about writing down the important milestones in my musical career from way back in the early days to current times. From throughout the years, I also selected examples of my music and recorded them on a cassette to play during my talk.

My good friend, The Rev. Peter Naylor, kindly came over from his Parish in Nork near Banstead to introduce me to the packed congregation. It was thrilling for me that so many local people were interested in my music and amongst the audience, there were many friends and relatives including my two sisters, Judy and Maureen. My presentation included playing pieces on the church upright piano. Not far away from where I was talking, Joy was out of sight behind a pillar ready to follow my script and play the various pieces of music where appropriate.

Joy sang a few songs herself on this occasion. I hadn't heard her sing since she had fallen ill and seeing her there with her hair almost back to normal, listening to her amazing rendition of 'Send in the Clowns' was a poignant, special moment for me.

We also had one or two comedy moments when we played some of the tracks in the wrong order! This didn't matter at all as Joy and I made everyone laugh with our natural banter going backwards and forwards. It was particularly amusing as the audience couldn't see Joy; they just heard this voice coming from behind the pillar! It was hilarious and we had the Rev. David in stitches. What an enjoyable and successful time we had that evening.

The programme was called *The Musical World of John Fox* and not so long ago, Rev. David did ask me if I would prepare another 'Musical World' because he said he wanted to have a good laugh again! It has often occurred to me over the years with all the comedy situations I have been in, I should have perhaps been a comedian rather than a musician—I'm only joking!

37

The Tragic Death of Maureen

In the late nineties, my sister Maureen fell and fractured her hip in Oaks Park close to Banstead. Maureen's fall was serious and the ambulance took her to St. Helier Hospital in Carshalton where our mother was born. Maureen spent quite a number of weeks there, during which there was a sudden outbreak of a serious disease that today we believe is MRSA. When she came out, she was never quite the same again. Maureen was also suffering from terrible arthritis so had to move downstairs to sleep, as she could no longer walk up so many stairs to her bedroom.

Maureen and her husband, Tom, had been sharing Judy and Roy's house in Fir Tree Road for some thirty years. I don't think it was a very successful arrangement as over the years there were often rows and I do think wives dislike sharing a kitchen.

Judy had bought the house after she returned from Toronto where she had been living for seven years and she had come home because she found out Roy was having an affair. He followed her several months later and they remained married and I have often suspected they were never really happy after that episode.

Maureen originally rented a property in Banstead. However, because they didn't have much money and it would also be financially helpful to Judy and Roy, they decided to live together under one roof. When Tom died in his mid-seventies, Maureen continued to live there but over the years, the friction between the three of them was often obvious. Roy seemed an unhappy man. He loved his garden and was never without his pipe. He often worked in our garden, too, and the day he died, he was gardening for our next door neighbour when he had a massive heart attack.

As a teenager, Maureen had worked in Croydon in a milk factory where she had the job of putting the milk into milk bottles and it was there she first met Tom. She would have to get up very early to be at work at four in the morning, as she had a half-an-hour walk to reach the depot because there weren't any buses at that time of the day. Later, she worked for the Co-op in Sutton for a few years before becoming a secretary at Prospect Garage, which used to be situated on the A217.

Soon after her fall, she was admitted to a nursing home where she became ill with a severe chest infection. One day when I visited her, she couldn't seem to breathe and she just stared at me with open eyes while repeatedly pointing at her throat. I spoke to the Matron who told me Maureen was dying. I felt in total shock. "Why?" I asked. "She was perfectly okay a couple of days ago." I was numb, but I couldn't stay any longer and watch her suffer. In a way, I felt a bit of a coward because I had a session to attend at Ian Dale's place and I just wanted to go and get away from the distressing sight of Maureen.

She was such a good-looking bubbly girl with lots of personality and a wonderful smile. I have many fond memories of our times together. Maureen and Joy always got on very well and were quite close. At one time, Maureen gave Joy a Bond worth quite a lot of money, which Tom's brother had left her when he died.

Sadly, Judy and Maureen didn't always see eye to eye and it seemed to me they were often arguing. I put this down to the fact they were living together. Strangely enough, just before Maureen died in that nursing home, Judy also suffered from a massive stroke. I wasn't as close to Maureen as I was to Judy but she was very proud of her 'little brother' and loved listening to my music throughout her life. She always made a big effort not to miss any of my broadcasts and although she was eighty-six years old when she died, I miss her very much.

38
Jamie—Sophie—and Our Neighbours

I'd like to tell you about how our little terrier, Jamie, came into our lives in the early nineties. Joy and I were walking our dog Robbie one morning in Banstead Wood when she saw a little terrier puppy without a lead looking completely hungry and lost. We both felt very sorry for this little terrier but when Joy tried to approach it, the little dog ran away. We went after him and luckily, we managed to catch him just before he reached the main road.

Joy scooped him up and we took him home. He seemed to be very happy to be with us and we fed him, then set about trying to find who his owners were. We advertised in our local shops and asked around but nobody came forward. We decided to adopt this lovely little terrier who begs for everything and is never on the lead!

At the time, our next-door neighbour had a puppy golden retriever called Sophie who constantly looked through our fence in the back garden whenever Jamie was outside. These two dogs, one large and one small, have grown up together for the last ten to twelve years and they both have lovely characters. They have given us such a lot of pleasure over the years and they mean the world to us.

I would like to mention our next-door neighbours, the Harveys, including the father, Malcolm, who owns Sophie and who sometimes comes over to listen to my music and enjoys in particular *The Magic of Joy Devon* album. During the day, we have looked after Sophie for many years while Malcolm is at work. When Sophie goes back home at the weekend, Jamie really misses her and looks forward to Monday mornings when she returns for the rest of the week. If we have to go out for any length of time, Malcolm looks after Jamie and is so fond of him.

Malcolm and I have quite a few chats over a glass or two of whisky and ginger ale as we try to put the world right! Friends indeed! In my opinion, these two dogs, Jamie and Sophie, are like Jack and Jill, two wonderful characters and quite honestly, we don't know what we would do without them.

39

Redundancy of the BBC Orchestras—Librarians and Copyists

My time at the BBC was very special as I made many excellent friends and had such exciting times working with the many fine orchestras that helped to make the BBC great.

Years ago, it was very formal at the BBC and nobody called one another by their first names. However, I struck up such a good relationship with the orchestra that after only a few broadcasts, I arrived one morning and announced, "You have played so well for me and now I would like you to call me John. But be warned: never Johnny!"

For many years, I had the pleasure of working with these excellent musicians. Writing and conducting for them, there was always something rather special to play and broadcast on BBC Radio 2. To me, it seemed no matter how many times I heard this orchestra on the radio, there was always something magical about their broadcasts.

These idyllic days continued until 31 March 1991 when the Radio Orchestra broadcast for the last time. The BBC began to disband many of their regional orchestras, making most of the talented and dedicated musicians I worked with, redundant. How deeply saddened I was, even though we all knew it had been on the cards for some while. We had noticed in the previous month the presence of accountants called over from the United States by the BBC to streamline the corporation.

One morning, I was conducting a session with the BBC Radio Orchestra when the senior producer arrived and handed out white envelopes to every member of the orchestra. He left giving strict instructions that nobody could open the envelopes until the break. Everyone suspected the news the envelopes contained and although we carried on that morning, getting through three or four more pieces, I could feel the spirit had gone out of their playing. The same producer of this session told me to leave the studio during that break. This was probably because I was working on contract and not employed by the BBC. I walked out with a heavy heart because I knew it was the end of an era for that marvellous orchestra.

It was such a popular orchestra and it was so difficult for everybody to accept its demise. What upset me most of all was there were all these fantastic musicians and nobody at the BBC had the decency to face them and explain what was happening. After that day, the orchestra stayed on for about three months and how fortunate I felt to be the one who conducted the last broadcast at the Maida Vale 3 recording studios. We were all very emotional, with some of the musicians in tears. It was such a distressing occasion for everyone involved.

In a roundabout way, it turned out that this rather troublesome episode benefited me professionally. Some of the musicians made redundant consequently came to play in my own orchestra, the John Fox Orchestra, with the loss of the BBC Radio Orchestra resulting in more work for me on broadcasts.

It isn't easy to select individuals from an orchestra when they are all so talented. There were, of course, a chosen few who were outstanding, not just because of a professional bond formed through a mutual love of music, but because of the friendships we had formed.

In particular, I would like to mention the late Bobby Harrison who was a tremendous trumpet player and who doubled on the flugelhorn. At the time we were working together, I had developed what I thought was a magical sound that I called 'The Blend.' It included using the alto flute, alto sax, cor anglais and flugelhorn for my arrangements and was my technique of blending all the sounds of the instruments to create a smooth unison sound.

Chatting to Bobby during one particular session, I coaxed him to produce a soft sound on his flugelhorn to blend effortlessly with the other three instruments. He made an unusual mute for his flugelhorn, especially for me, in order to create the right auditory effect for my 'Blend.' It certainly was an original combination creating this different sound, which at the time many listeners recognized by as the 'John Fox Sound.'

Bobby unfortunately died not long afterwards, and his wife, Audrey, sometimes rings me even now, to talk about music and her late husband, Bobby. He really was a tremendous man. Then there is Tony Arnopp, who is a first-class musician. He came to see me in the BBC Studios one day telling me he had bought a bass flute, which I have to say, is a rather awkward-looking instrument.

I wrote some arrangements where I added this unfamiliar instrument as a solo to create a deep original sound. One in particular is Kurt Weill's song, 'Speak Low,' where you will hear this bass flute playing beautifully in the low register.

Besides taking up the bass flute, Tony also doubled up on musical instruments such as the piccolo, flute, alto flute, all the five saxes, clarinet, and bass clarinet. He was truly a good friend of mine, and the most decent man you could ever wish to meet.

Another talented member of the BBC Radio Orchestra was the leader of the second violins, Sally Brooke-Pike. Despite the fact Sally would often arrive late to the Radio Orchestra's regular sessions, which I conducted, somehow she always seemed to be *on time* for my first down beat with my baton at ten o'clock in the morning! A wonderful violinist, she was a lovely lady and quite a character. She still lives in the famous fishing village of Hallsands, South Devon, which was originally swept away by the sea in 1917 as a result of dredging in the bay. A new village was built further up the hill and Sally has a lovely cottage on the cliff top overlooking the remains of the ruined village.

She often invited Joy and me to stay and we spent many wonderful holidays there, taking our collie dog Robbie with us on that long car journey. From the cottage where we would often sit eating breakfast on the old doorstep, the views of the unspoiled cove, the sea and coastline were magnificent. It is not surprising that this quiet place in the middle of nature inspired many of my composing ideas.

In recent years, Sally has asked me to visit a number of times, but I am not so sprightly these days and there are too many steep steps leading up and down to the cottage. Robbie loved the magic of the place, too, and would run swiftly down those steep steps alone for a swim in the sea, returning drenched and happy!

We used to go on the never-to-be-forgotten 'butterfly' walk across the cliffs, watching out for all the amazing rare species of butterflies. What lovely memories I have of those happy days!

Included in this special group of musicians was Gordon Langford, yet another talented pianist, who played in many of my sessions. A highly regarded composer and arranger, too, he had a natural ability to sight-read, which he did with great ease for my arrangements of *The Warsaw Concerto* and Gershwin's *Rhapsody in Blue*. He also had a certain cheeky side, which he displayed if any of the musicians came in late to the studio. He would tinkle a tune on the piano he knew they liked, in a certain sarcastic way! Then we have the late Ronnie Price, a pianist of high repute with a remarkable talent for filling in behind vocalists. How I remember the many magical moments he created to help my music to sound that little bit extra special!

We mustn't forget Harold Rich, who is retired now. A member of the Robert Farnon Society, he played in the BBC Midland Radio Orchestra as the regular pianist. He was a well-accomplished pianist who often helped my wife, Joy, when she was rehearsing for broadcasts at Pebble Mill, the BBC recording studios in Birmingham. Like Gordon, he played my arrangement of *Warsaw Concerto* skillfully, which would take place during my conducting of the hourly concerts in Birmingham.

Another fantastic musician from Pebble Mill, who I mentioned earlier, is Paul Arden Taylor. He played the oboe and the cor anglais in the BBC Midland Radio Orchestra. Paul also played all the recorders and the fascinating oboe d'amore, (the oboe of love), a Baroque woodwind instrument that largely fell into disuse after the eighteenth century until musicians such as Frederick Delius, Richard Strauss and Maurice Ravel rediscovered it. It is slightly larger than the normal oboe and has an enchanting tender sound. Paul did, at times, record for my sessions in London, playing all those unusual ancient instruments.

At this point, I would like to mention the very important task of the librarian, as conductors and composers rely heavily on their skills. The librarian is responsible for putting all the various parts for the musicians to play on the stands and this includes, of course, the conductor's score. After a concert or a recording, it is essential these music sheets are returned to the correct folder.

My good friend Reg Arthur, who lives close to Banstead Wood, had the very important job as the BBC Radio Orchestra's senior librarian. A noteworthy player of the piano, he is also a fine musician and even today, still plays at a few gigs.

In addition to the librarians, there were the equally important copyists, although today you hardly hear about real music copyists. In my heyday, they were the unsung heroes in the background who supported the work of composers and arrangers. Their work comprised of copying out from original musical scores, writing the individual parts carefully on separate sheets of manuscript paper for the various instrumentalists to read and play from. It is very important for a composer and arranger to engage a good copyist, as accuracy is vital. If a copyist makes one mistake, it takes many precious minutes away from sessions and rehearsals to correct it. If there are more than one or two mistakes, it has a real impact on the length of the session.

Professional copyists having first learned one of the top notoriously difficult Finale or Sibelius programmes would settle to their slow and arduous job writing with special pens and black ink. There isn't so much work now for copyists as much of it is copied directly to the computer. For the past few years, my own compositions and arrangements have been copied in this very neat and tidy way that appears as if the actual music publishers have printed them.

In many ways, this method takes away what we called the old 'session times' when the majority of first-class musicians sight-read and interpreted their parts from a real copyist in his musical handwriting. I nearly always used the copyist Steve Cairns, who was brilliant! He retired a long time ago and settled in Cornwall.

In Tadworth, quite close to Banstead, lives my friend Vic Fraser, who is a wonderful copyist and also an arranger. He has all the modern equipment with very many copyists working for him as a team. Vic actually has the important task of copying for the famous Harry Potter films, written by the composer John Williams, and an even bigger task to copy for 'The Lord of the Rings' films, composed by Howard Shore. This musical score involves using very large orchestras and all kinds of synthesizers as well as huge choirs.

Looking back, I think what a wonderful combination of talent and expertise!

All those lovely people were so generous with their time and their musical professionalism helped me produce so many defining musical moments in my arrangements and broadcasts at the BBC.

40

Farewell to Maida Vale 3

I used to drive from Banstead to Maida Vale Studios where all those fabulous BBC sessions were recorded. I would leave very early in the morning so I could get to the studios in plenty of time. This gave me time to have a cup of tea and bun at the canteen while greeting everybody as they came in. It was important and very pleasant to relax before the session, whether it was the morning or afternoon.

We would record in Maida Vale 3 Studio, which wasn't very large and if it were the large orchestra it would be difficult to move! Then if my choir, *The John Fox Singers,* was involved in the recording session, too, it really was quite a feat fitting everyone in! Getting organized, we would have a good laugh with everyone being very helpful and congenial.

If I close my eyes now, I can see all the musicians coming into that studio carrying their various instruments. All those familiar faces, all those hellos and goodbyes and I can hear all those magical sounds we made! It feels like yesterday; my tears of pride and joy are never far away when I think of those never-to-be-forgotten days!

It is particularly sad, as we don't hear much of this type of light music anymore, especially in the United Kingdom. If we hear it playing at all, it seems now to be music to see by and not to listen by! The radio no longer plays such a big role in entertainment as it used to when the whole family would sit round it in the evenings and listen. Television has replaced most of these special personal listening times with everyone dreaming the night away with their very own special thoughts.

Of course, I am able still to listen to this type of music as I have my studio full of my own music, together with many albums and CDs of light music of all the great and good who brought hours of entertainment to radio and concert audiences. So it remains for me to say once again, *"If music be the food of love, play on—again—John!"*

41

Musicals Here and in the United States

One of my greatest pleasures over the past few years is using my music for charities. Joy and I became involved in many charity concerts at the Community Hall in Banstead. One of our proudest moments was presenting a large cheque about six feet long and three feet wide, to the Royal Marsden Cancer Hospital for one thousands pounds!

I would now like to talk about the early days of some of the most famous songwriters and composers of Great Britain. Probably one of the most popular songwriters and composers of the early twentieth century, forever linked with the golden era of the British stage musical, is Ivor Novello, who was born in Wales. His 'Dancing Years,' 'Glamorous Night' and 'Perchance to Dream,' are among his most famous and he was highly acclaimed for his wonderful and highly romantic melodies. Only recently, the Strand Theatre in London, refurbished in 2005, was renamed the Novello Theatre after Ivor. He lived above the theatre in one of the flats for thirty-eight years, where he wrote many of his best musicals.

He died at the age of fifty-eight from coronary thrombosis, just hours after he appeared in his own production of *Kings Rhapsody*. Over seven thousand mourners attended his funeral in London and he is the only non-royal to ever have had a state funeral. There is renewed interest in his music since the recent release of the movie *Gosford Park,* which featured several of his songs on the soundtrack and where Jeremy Northam, who is a pianist, plays his character.

It was often thought in musical circles, Novello failed to reach the acclaims in his lifetime that Noel Coward achieved, because he was overshadowed by Coward. Coward, of course, was a genius who wrote all his own lyrics and music. Wherever he travelled throughout the world, he took with him a pianist and wrote the famous 'Mrs. Worthington' or 'Don't Put Your Daughter on the Stage, Mrs. Worthington,' 'Someday I'll Find You,' and 'I'll See You Again' amongst many others, too numerous to mention.

The musical comedy composer Vivian Ellis was well-known in London's West End from 1925 to 1958, gaining recognition for 'Spread a Little Happiness,' 'She's My Lovely,' 'This is my Lovely Day' and 'Coronation Scot.' A fine songwriter, he wrote the delightful 'Bless the Bride' and he was President of the Performing Rights Society (PRS) for many years. His musical, *Mr. Cinders,* was revived in the late eighties, at the King's Head Theatre in London.

I wrote a selection called *A Tribute to Vivian Ellis* and *Ivor Novello's Waltzes* and how very pleased I was to have this opportunity to arrange those prolific musical comedy writers' melodic selections.

The BBC Midland Radio Orchestra recorded these arrangements, which included well-known male and female singers, and broadcasted from two of *The John Fox Concerts* at Pebble Mill in Birmingham. There were eight in total of these concerts and Joy sang some of her favourite songs in the fifth concert, including 'You Go to My Head,' 'Crazy,' 'A Lady Loves' and 'The Glory of Love.'

Another prolific composer was Richard Addinsell, who wrote much of the British Film music in the 1940s and 1950s. He is probably best remembered for *Warsaw Concerto* in the 1941 film *Dangerous Moonlight.* This is a great piano piece and although not easy, nevertheless, it is a piece that every pianist loves to play! He wrote the score for Noel Coward's *Blythe Spirit* and also the music for *Goodbye Mr. Chips* and *Tom Brown's Schooldays.* It appears millions of people have heard his music, yet don't know who he is nor who wrote the music that is so familiar to them!

I have arranged for the BBC Concert Orchestra quite a number of popular songs as classical arrangements including, 'Fool on the Hill,' 'Michelle,' and 'Here, There and Everywhere,' composed by two of the most recent talented songwriters, Lennon and McCarthy. One of my favourite songs by these two is 'And I Love Her.' What a gorgeous melody; I have arranged and played this many times, using mainly strings to bring out a very lush and romantic sound.

Our most contemporary composer, of course, is the Rt. Hon. Andrew Lloyd Webber, famous for his West End and Broadway musicals including, *Cats, Jesus Christ Superstar, Joseph and the Amazing Technicolor Dreamcoat, Evita,* which won an Academy Award for Best Music, Original Song, *Sunset Boulevard* and *Phantom of the Opera.* Of course, my own personal favourite is 'All I Ask of You' from *Phantom of the Opera,* because of the concerts in Cologne when Joy sang it with Lindsay Benson and brought the house down (but not the chandelier!).

Richard Rodney Bennett is another super composer who wrote many scores for British films such as many Agatha Christie movies and a beautiful score for *Nicolas & Alexander.*

What was happening at this time over the pond in the United States? Well, the first show that springs to mind is Bernstein's *West Side Story.* If anything hit the ordinary man in the street, it was most certainly *West Side Story,* with words by Stephen Sondheim. I personally think this is the most original musical I've ever seen and listened to. Pure genius!

Then of course, there was Rodgers and Hart who worked together until Hart's death of alcoholism in 1943. Their breakthrough came with the musical *Garrick Gaities* with the hit song 'Manhattan' and they worked together on about thirty musicals, including *Spring is Here,* which features 'With a Song in my Heart.' Further famous songs include, 'The Lady Is a Tramp,' 'My Funny Valentine,' 'Blue Moon' and 'There's a Small Hotel.'

I wrote an arrangement of 'With a Song in my Heart' with the John Fox Orchestra and voices that became the signature tune for *Family Favourites* on Sunday lunchtime on Radio 2 for many years. It was recorded on a commercial LP called *Candler by Candlelight!* Rodgers is probably better known for his partnership with Hammerstein as they became renowned for their Broadway musicals such as *South Pacific, The King and I, Carousel, Oklahoma,* and *The Sound of Music,* which are delightful shows and reproduced again and again over the years for the stage, both in the States and the United Kingdom. It wouldn't be right not to mention *My Fair Lady* written by Lerner and Lowe, who were the American team of lyricist and librettist and based of course on George Bernard Shaw's play *Pygmalion.*

Such wonderful original songs as 'Get Me to the Church on Time,' 'On the Street Where You Live,' and 'Wouldn't It Be Loverly?.'

Despite the fact these two were originally European songwriters, how they could write such typically 'English' songs I'll never know.

How happy it makes me knowing these marvellous shows have also been made into movies, which is proof enough this kind of music is universally popular. Regrettably, I also feel there are very few, if any, talented composers today who can write such wonderful lyrics and tunes for people of all ages.

I shall never forget what joy it has been listening to such shows over the years. It is a great part of a composer and arranger's wonderful profession to enjoy other composers' and songwriters' music. I am now going to let you in on a little secret. Anything that is sad—whether it's music, a film, a play or a book—I cry.

Most of us have a film that stands out in our minds as one that affects us deeply. For me, it is *Carousel,* particularly when the main star, Gordon MacRae, has been murdered and is then some years later allowed down from heaven by his guardian angel for a very short time to look through the window at his wife and daughter, whom he loved dearly, and singing from the middle of the song, 'If I Loved You':

"Longing to tell you, but afraid and shy.

I'd let my golden chances pass me by.

Soon you'd leave me, off you would go in the mist of day.

Never, never, to know, how I loved you—

If I loved you."

Gordon MacRae beautifully and softly sang that song with very little accompaniment from the orchestra. That magical scene always touches me deeply. Another very emotional film with a wonderful musical score by John Williams is *E.T.*

I'll tell you something about that ending. When Joy and I first went to see this remarkable film in the cinema, it was completely packed and after the scene where the little boy, Elliot, and E.T. say their goodbyes, when the cinema lights went up, I have never seen in my long life so many of the people in the audience with their handkerchiefs out trying desperately to wipe away their tears, which of course included us, too!

I wrote an arrangement combining *E.T.* with *Close Encounters of the Third Kind,* using a large orchestra which I conducted as well. It is an arranger's dream to have such wonderful music to work with and I really enjoyed writing this combination from the music of these two fantastic films. I interweaved the two themes and many times BBC producers of various programmes have asked me to add my *E.T.* and *Close Encounters* arrangement in their particular programmes. I also recorded it for the American market, which proved to be very popular there, too.

42

The 100-Year-Old Concert Pianist and Marion

I would now like to tell you about one very charming musical incident that happened to me quite a few years ago. Joy and I were visiting her daughter, Marion, in New York who had emigrated there in the early nineties, where she lives in a suburb not too dissimilar to Banstead, called Mount Kisco.

While we were there, a friend of Marion's asked if I would have time to visit her grandmother Clara, who was 100 years old and a well-known retired concert pianist. Apparently her grandmother had often heard my music on the radio and when she knew I was in New York said she would love to meet me.

The granddaughter picked Joy and me up in a large, vintage, luxury American car with beautiful leather seats and although the journey took some while, we were so comfortable we didn't mind at all. We arrived at this small country village and it was as if we had stepped back in time to the previous century. It was a delightful place with the houses made out of clapboard and verandas fronting the properties. Clara's house was completely wooden inside and we sat round a fire in the kitchen, where she poured tea from an old-fashioned teapot and fed us delicious muffins.

Clara was a delightful lady, and noticing she had a full-size Steinway Grand, I asked her if she still played. Well, Clara was most indignant! Sauntering over to the piano—remember she was

100 years old—she sat down and played the most wonderful music. Not only did she play from memory, she chose some very difficult pieces, too, from Chopin, Beethoven, Mozart, Debussy and Ravel.

We noticed photographs on the walls of Clara playing at the world famous Carnegie Hall in New York. Since its opening in 1891, every great performer's ambition is to play at Carnegie Hall. Dvorak's *New World Symphony* made its world premier there in 1893, the twenty-six-year-old Winston Churchill made a speech about the Boer War in 1901, and in 1934 the house manager lent the hall to George Gershwin for a dress rehearsal of *Porgy and Bess*. Musicians from Benny Goodman, Count Basie, Duke Ellington, Leonard Bernstein, and The Beatles to Judy Garland, Maria Callas and many other famous names have played and sang in that great hall alongside orchestras, pianists, soloists, operas and ballets from all over the world.

Listening to Clara play, we were both speechless as her nimble fingers flew lightly over the keys of that wonderful Steinway without any music to read by! When she finished, I felt very humble, particularly when she asked me to play some of my own music. Firstly, I chose 'Send in the Clowns,' because Joy sang that song so beautifully. Then 'Cabaret' and 'People,' the well-known song written by Jules Styne and Bob Merrill for the Broadway musical *Funny Girl*. Lastly, I put some music I had composed together with a piano piece called 'A Touch of Spring,' which she particularly liked.

Clara was equally thrilled by our performance and I had also brought along some of my CDs, which she listened to with great pleasure. What a great musical evening we had and one I shall never forget. Not only meeting such a wonderful pianist such as Clara, but also the thrill of playing on that marvellous Steinway grand.

Marion still lives in New York and now has two lovely daughters called Montana and Christiana. I have written compositions for both these girls, which have been published and played in many countries. They are called 'Montana's Little Dance' and 'Young and Innocent,' from a CD of short pieces named *Interludes*.

Although I haven't actually met those two lovely girls in person yet, I have spoken to them on the telephone many times and have photographs, which Marion sends to me. I haven't visited the United States for years as I do not enjoy flying long distances because it tends to upset me physically. Of course as a younger man, I went to New

York many times on business. I do miss seeing my friends, publishers and of course Joy's daughter, Marion, and her daughters. I wonder if that fantastic 100-year-old pianist Clara is still alive. Having such remarkable talent, I certainly hope so!

James, Marion, and Christiana—all smiles.

Emily and Jenny as young lovely girls—Andrew and Jill's daughters.

Joy holding Ginger our kitten.

John with Bob Farnon, the president of The Robert Farnon Society (for light music).

John and Joy before conducting a concert.

Alex and William—Richard and Tracy's two good looking sons.

Tracy and Richard relaxing at their home.

Montana and Christiana Marion—Richard's beautiful daughters.

John, Joy, and Dr. Bungart just before the concert in Cologne Germany.

The Hotel Illador in Majorca where Joy and I spent many relaxing holidays.

Group of important people at John's 80th birthday party.

David and Moira Ades, special guests at my 80th birthday party.

John with Roy and Pat Fox, his cousin and wife who live in Canada.

Robbie, John's lovely border collie dog.

Lady—a gorgeous dog.

Sophie (on the left) and Jamie (on the right).

John's favourite photo when he was at the height of his career.

John with Marian Foster who presented the six Musical World of John Fox concerts.

Next to me is Janet Brown who used to appear on television and radio imitating Margaret Thatcher.

Rosemary Squires who was a famous vocalist especially in her earlier years.

With Debbie Wiseman, who is one of the best composers of films in today's world.

My Musical World

John with Brian Kay, the choir master at the Leith Hill choir festival at Dorking Halls.

Bronte, John, Tarenda, and swan at Walton On the Hill, Surrey.

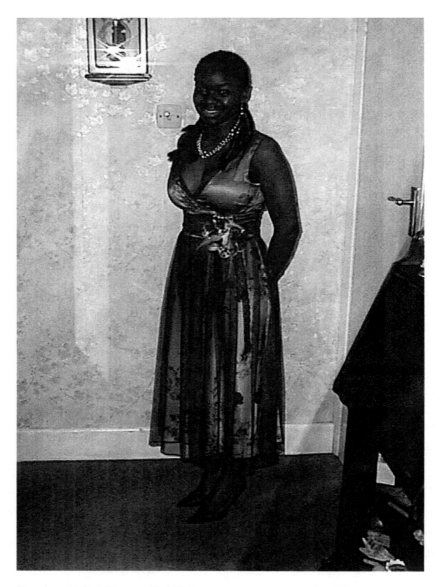

Beverley at John's Voyage of a Lifetime party—one extra special girl.

John with his best man Adam Saunders on his wedding day to Perpetua.

43
Changes in the Turn of the Century

We all know many things change as we pass from one century to another. As we enter into the new millennium from the twentieth century, the era of light classical music seems to have passed, too. Also the state of the world in this new century is so precarious with the advent of terrorists, suicide bombing of innocent people, including the terrible twin towers disaster in New York seen live on television, and global warming. Or should it be global warning?

I also think society appears to be breaking down with more married couples both working for extra money rather than the mother staying at home to look after the children. It seems this is a contributing factor to many marriages ending in divorce, with a large number of separations resulting in a society full of single mothers. The news on television, radio and in the newspapers seems to be nothing but bad news, which seems to be good news to the media, which is a great pity! What is happening to us?

When shopping today, there are all sorts of what I call 'awful pop sounds' being pumped out over the speakers that youngsters seem to love so much. As far as I am concerned, these loud banging noises are the most unmusical sounds I have ever had the misfortune to listen to. Of course, it is very difficult for me to like such sounds when in my musical profession we have been brought up on the beauty of melody.

Today there seems to be a constant loud boring sound, which I feel must affect the eardrums in time. Very often, it's the same with television adverts, and I am sure 90 percent of viewers must turn the sound down. It is of great comfort to me my own music is often played in adverts, knowing that my type of music is still universally appealing, although I do accept it is a new world out there with very little time for what I would call *real* music.

I am not very popular with the younger generation when I express views such as these because they believe I'm an old-fashioned fuddy-duddy. Perhaps I am, but I have been through the most magical times, writing the kind of music that has emphasis on melody, which I have always believed in and luckily over the past sixty years, so have my many listeners from around the world.

Many times during composing, I have written non-melodic music to achieve what I have been commissioned to compose, which might include an atmospheric style with orchestral sounds that lead up to a certain climax and I have also enjoyed this style of writing.

However much of my composing contains pure sounds such as the 'Ethereal Sphere' from the *Earth and Space* album, which is recorded on the CD *Voyage of a Lifetime.* This type of music requires an excellent orchestra, together with good session players who can sight-read music and these are few and far between in our modern world.

Light music probably had its heyday in the middle of the last century, however there is still considerable interest in this genre, despite the fact the last light music programme on BBC radio was discontinued in 2007. Additionally, there is a young conductor, composer and arranger in his mid-thirties who has a considerable reputation in light music. John Wilson is recognised internationally as an expert in light music, jazz and music for film and I do hope he is successful in helping this generation hold on to the fine art of orchestration.

Also, I do know my young friend Gavin Sutherland, known as a recognized worldwide conductor, composer and arranger, is in that category. We certainly need these kinds of musicians to help keep light music from being neglected and forgotten. I have been through the many magical years when light music was in its prime and as I am now in my eighties, I have to leave the younger composers who are interested, to continue to fight the light music battle and never let go.

In the year 2000, my old favourite friend and publisher in Munich, Gerhard Narholz, of Sonoton Music commissioned me to compose a very interesting subject for library music called *Politics*. The CD is called *Winning in Politics,* and the compositions I wrote were very powerful pieces, including 'Man of Liberty.' In this piece, I felt I wanted to bring all the different notes from various patriotic American songs together in the middle of the piece, before returning to the main theme. The second one is called 'Summit Conference,' where I used quite a bit of heavy brass to depict political music suitable for any country.

When Gerhard called me to commission these two pieces, I told him I was right in the middle of writing *Surrey Rhapsody* and he replied, "I know you John—you can do it—please do me this favour." I felt after all the work he had given me over the years, I couldn't let him down so setting aside *Surrey Rhapsody,* I began work on his pieces. When composing, I have a habit of always taking manuscript paper with me when I am out walking and writing down notes and ideas so my studio becomes littered with these bits of paper. I have to say, I had quite a lot of trouble finding them again for *Surrey Rhapsody* after I had stopped writing for Gerhard!

I also arranged two pieces from the CD called 'A True Patriot' and 'Victory and Emotions,' which Gerhard composed himself. Incidentally, he is a great musician and composer who often requires a good arranger and I am often his first choice when he wants arrangements for a large orchestra.

Played by the Sonoton Orchestra, which I have conducted many times, this CD was recorded in Budapest, Hungary. It is a fabulous eighty- to ninety-piece orchestra, and I know recording in places like Budapest and Prague is preferred to Germany and England simply because the orchestras in these two places cost less money. Nevertheless, they are as good as any orchestra I have had the privilege to write and conduct for, except perhaps the BBC Radio Orchestra!

44

Another John Fox Connected with Harold Turner's Niece!

As with most people, there have been some amazing coincidences in my life. One Sunday afternoon in June 2003, Joy and I visited my sister Judy who was a resident at Parkside Nursing Home in Banstead. As usual at the weekends, there were quite a number of visitors with the visiting room buzzing. Halfway through our visit, one of the nurses came up to me and said, "Do you know there's another John Fox visiting here today?" I was incredulous. "No!" I replied. "Go and fetch the impostor!"

The nurse returned with quite a youngish, good-looking chap and a young girl who was his wife. We laughed at this strange coincidence and as 'John Fox the younger' turned to introduce me to his wife, she asked me, "Are you John Fox the composer and pianist?" and when I replied, "Yes," she kept saying, "But you can't be; you can't be."

It was then that a second coincidence of the day happened. I was thinking if you read this in a book, you wouldn't believe it because you would think it was being made up. Isn't it said that fact is stranger than fiction? This young girl turned out to be Harold Turner's niece!

What a moment that was, as I was immediately taken back to the evening forty years previously, when Harold was killed in that awful car accident on the way back from Eastbourne. We had quite a chat that afternoon and I was glad to be able to tell her about my happy times working with Harold. I learned they lived quite close to Banstead and were visiting their grandmother. For a long time afterwards, Joy and I couldn't stop talking about this amazing coincidence. After that day, we never saw them again but I found the whole experience extremely spiritual. Wouldn't you?

45

Philip Lane and Gavin Sutherland

In the early months of the new century, I received a telephone call from a charming man called Philip Lane. A well-known composer, arranger and producer, who is about six feet two inches tall, he is a great believer in light music. He worked as a music teacher at Cheltenham Ladies College for twenty-three years in addition to composing for London publishers as a freelance.

Latterly, he became involved in looking after the musical interest of Richard Addinsell's estate and with great patience, Philip re-created the scores to Richard's film music, including one of his most famous, *Goodbye Mr. Chips*. Many of these original film manuscripts were lost as nobody during those early days had any inkling these scores would be sought after in years to come. Since then, he has been involved in many reconstructions of lost scores including some of Sir Alfred Hitchcock's most famous films, *The Thirty-Nine Steps* and *The Lady Vanishes*.

This type of work is very difficult when you need to copy the whole score from a film soundtrack, with nothing to go by apart from a pair of good ears and a piano! To copy musical notes from a large orchestra is highly skilful work and requires great patience. Philip asked me if I was the composer who had written many pieces he had heard on BBC Radio 2 over a number of years, and in particular,

Jovial Knights Overture and *Summer Overture*. When I confirmed I was, he wanted to know if I was interested in having one of my compositions recorded by The Royal Ballet Sinphonia, conducted by Gavin Sutherland, the well-known conductor, pianist and composer.

This was my first meeting with Gavin and the three of us hit it off straight away, becoming immediate friends. I was thrilled with Philip's suggestion and *Summer Overture* was recorded on CD by the White Line Label under, *British Light Overtures*. Gavin had begun his career working as a conductor and pianist for the Northern Ballet Theatre and he first worked with the Royal Ballet Sinphonia in 1998 on a CD called *British Light Music Discoveries*. Through his many recordings, Gavin has been instrumental in the revival of interest in British Light Music. He also conducts regularly for the BBC Concert Orchestra in addition to the Bournemouth Symphony Orchestra.

A couple of years later, Joy and I were invited to Gavin's wedding to the well-known clarinettist Verity Butler. Unfortunately, Joy couldn't attend the wedding because she was so unwell and I went on my own to the very lovely old church in Ashlead for the service. I was so happy to be there for my friend Gavin, but little did anyone know I was also very worried about Joy at this time, as she wasn't well at all.

46

Country Talk

Early June is a fantastic time of year in Ruffetts Wood, which is a half mile from my house. If ever I am feeling a little low, a morning walk through this wood with my two dogs and I find my spirits once more begin to soar.

There is a wooded, winding path where at this time of year, the most gorgeous wildlife lives and grows, but you need to tread carefully and as Jamie, Sophie and I are getting on a little now, there is definitely no running involved! Then you come to a five-barred gate, years and years old, when suddenly you behold the most wonderful, breathtaking pastoral scene. Stretching out before you is a field filled with thousands and thousands of poppies and wildflowers. It's difficult to convey just how exquisite this scene of the English countryside is to the naked eye.

After walking through this wonderful field, you can walk back through a wooded tunnel made up entirely of intertwined trees and shrubs embracing one another to make a rounded, arched, natural tunnel. In the spring, the ground is littered with primroses and this walk inspired me to write a piece of chamber music with Joy humming without any words, called 'Pathway to Paradise' because that's exactly what it is.

A piece I composed, 'A Pastoral Reflection,' was greatly influenced by the beautiful countryside in this part of Surrey. This was included on the CD called *British Light Music Discoveries No. 5,* on the White Line Label. It was originally called 'A Pastoral Impression,' but Philip Lane said 'A Pastoral Reflection' sounded better and I agreed with him. In addition, there is an early suite called *Three Shades of Green* for piano solo (one of my early titles) as for me this perfectly explains the various hues of green I see all about me when on my walks.

During the summer months, the big field is left entirely to grow wild, encouraging butterflies and many other insects to come back to nature again. I never fail to stop and stare at the sheer beauty of this magnificent scene with the many different coloured shrubs along the edge of this field covered with layers of thick, white, rather tall and beautiful daisies. I always feel so refreshed after walking there and on my return home, enjoy a cup of coffee with Jamie and Sophie chomping on their bonios, as I sit quietly reflecting on my magical walk.

My friend Peter Atkins, the artist, recently painted a magnificent picture of this scene with me and the dogs with of course my walking stick, strolling through Ruffetts Wood. So at any time, I can look at this painting and immediately be back in that beautiful place, breathing in the fresh clean air and walking that pastoral paradise.

My work on the many pastoral compositions I have written, demonstrates how enthusiastically I want to convey these images to music. Some of the following are just a few of the titles I have written on the subject.

Countryside Suite for strings and harp in four movements.

1. *Morning Air.* If you have ever been on a walk in the country very early in the morning, you will feel the wonder and freshness of the air. It is so exhilarating, exciting and overwhelming, you feel as if you could jump over the sun! This piece has an upbeat tempo with a beautiful melody in the middle section, which then slows right down to depict the love for every blade of grass and then picks up again to have you jumping for joy.
2. *Black Clouds Over the Moors.* Experiencing the dramatic and dark clouds is a sight to behold. The air is dismal with the threat of rain, thunder and lightening and as I wrote the music for this, I chose notes to make the strings sound gloomy and nasty. The middle section opens with a solo violin, and then I introduce the viola and the cello increasing the tension of the music to reflect the countryside's bleak and sinister mood.

3. *My Village.* It is immensely pleasurable living in Banstead village and here the music is moderately slow, easy and happy to reflect the pace of village life.
4. *Country Folk.* I love this, too, with the strings of the violins sending out light notes to represent the gossipy and chatty tones of charming village folk.

Those four movements are available on CD on the White Line Label called *British String Miniatures No. 3* played beautifully by the Royal Ballet Sinphonia and conducted by my friend Gavin Sunderland. Once again my music is in very good company as far as famous English composers are concerned as this CD also contains music by Sir Edward Elgar, Gilbert Vinter and Peter Warlock.

This *Countryside Suite* was only recently played in June 2008 on Classic FM in an evening programme called *The Full Works*. I felt it stood out as a typical English piece amongst the other pieces played. I love writing for strings as I feel I can express my deepest feelings, thoughts, joys and happiness. Writing for strings is quite a special talent, as it requires a deeper understanding of how to write for each individual instrument, in order to reflect the notes in the correct pitch and chord structure.

Writing a piece for piano is totally different from writing the same type of piece for the harp, but many composers, especially pianists, are not able to do this as it is very difficult to fully understand that the sounds a piano and harp produce are completely different. Sometimes the harp in a full orchestral piece is only required once or twice, which requires a good deal of patience from a good harpist.

Invariably, many pianists write for the harp using the notes from the piano rather than being able to write the notes that best suit this fantastic instrument, which needs to be used sparingly to achieve the best results. For example, many composers rely on *glissandos* where the cascade of notes is the most influential part; however, a good composer knows the harp can cleverly fit into a piece with many different and unusual sounds.

A string quartet is always written for two violins, one viola and one cello. It is an essential part of being a good composer knowing how to write for this small, popular combination of string instruments, which most great composers have written for very successfully. Probably the best way to explain it is that good, all-round composers will think about how a piece can be written so each instrument has something interesting to play. This involves using playable double stops, which means 'going over four strings' and this takes quite a lot of composing. Putting it all together with the correct timing in order to know what the ultimate scores will produce in terms of sounds, makes the real difference between a mediocre sound and something that we can say sounds 'gorgeous.'

Going back to the subject of the countryside, when I described those lovely colourful views earlier and all the wonderful things that our eyes allow us to see, how sad I feel when many people I come across when out walking, whether in the countryside or the village, seem to have mobile telephones to keep them company. Talk! Talk! Talk! How can you see what is all around you? Seeing is very much believing, but I doubt these people see very much. Not all of us are mobile 'phoneys' or sorry, 'phoners'! Thank goodness. Yes, I must admit these contraptions are very useful at times, yet I do feel there is a generation who is missing out on the wonderful sights all around them.

There doesn't seem any time to breathe in today's world. The pace is so enormously fast and technology is making it faster still. As the poet W. H. Davies famously wrote:[1]

What is this life, if, full of care,
We have no time to stand and stare.

No time to stand beneath the boughs
And stare as long as sheep or cows.

No time to see, when woods we pass,
Where squirrels hide their nuts in grass.

No time to see, in broad daylight,
Streams full of stars, like skies at night.

No time to turn at Beauty's glance,
And watch her feet, how they can dance.

No time to wait till her mouth can
Enrich that smile her eyes began.

A poor life this, if, full of care,
We have no time to stand and stare.

For me the poem depicts perfectly how much beauty there is to see in the country and yes, indeed how poor life is if we don't have time to stop and stare.

---

[1] Reprinted by kind permission of Kieron Griffin as Trustee of the Mrs. H. M. Davies Will Trust.

47

"Comedy Situations"

Over the years, I have also composed many comedy pieces, which I have enjoyed hugely as I always believe it's important to be able to have a good laugh in life.

One of the first musical comedy situations happened many years ago during World War II, when playing at a local dance hall. Our band was playing at a local function and at the end of the dance after the last waltz, the drummer, Willy, didn't seem to be particularly with it so we all shouted, "The Queen! The Queen!"

We were always supposed to play the National Anthem, which began with a drum roll and we had intended to jolt him a little. The drummer leapt to his feet and looking round the hall frantically said, "The Queen? Here? I can't see any Queen!" We had such a good laugh at his day-dreaming or better still his night dreaming! It was very funny, although the audience didn't seem to have noticed a thing!

One of the double bass players who played in a group at the Grand Hotel, Eastbourne, was well-known for constantly passing wind. One evening we were playing some very good jazz music and when we almost reached the end of that jazz piece he shouted, "Leave the last note for me!" This note was in the key of B-flat and it ended on the B-flat above middle C. He actually "passed wind" on that note and it was perfectly in tune and as clear as a bell! At the time some of us thought it was rather in bad taste, although, I must admit it was also very funny and musical!

On another occasion, I was driving back from Eastbourne after an evening playing at the Grand Hotel when a police car stopped me. It was a very cold night and the car windows were closed. When the police approach a stationary car, they seem as if they are on a small march, and the truth is on that particular night all the boys had been drinking, as many of our well known clientele had bought us drinks. A police sergeant and a policeman in training came over and asked me to open my window and as I did the smell of alcohol hit the two policemen!

This young rookie policeman asked me to get out of the car and take the Breathalyzer test. He tested me once but it didn't register anything. He turned to the sergeant saying, "Look sergeant it isn't registering. It must have broken down." The sergeant replied, "So, idiot, try it again; you must be doing something wrong!" The trainee tried again and still it didn't work! The

Sergeant became increasingly impatient, then he suddenly realized something. "You blithering idiot! This man has obviously not been drinking!"

It was true; I had not touched a drop simply because I was driving. However, I did drive away in 'high spirits' that evening and we couldn't stop laughing all the way home!

Another funny incident with the police occurred when Joy and I stopped in a country lay-by one evening. A policeman on a bicycle saw us and leaving his bicycle by the side of the road, he marched very slowly over to our car. Looking through the window he asked, "Is this man molesting you in any way miss?"

At that time, we were both listening intensely to a night programme on the radio of my music, with Joy singing. I said "This is my orchestra and my girlfriend here is singing this lovely song!" Of course, he didn't believe a word replying, "Tell that one to the cleaners; you can't be in two places at the same time!" and he walked indignantly away, riding his bike slowly back into oblivion!

Joy and I had also had a 'funny' incident when we went to a midweek concert at Fairfield Halls in Croydon, a few years ago. It was a sixty- or seventy-piece orchestra and we were the only two in the audience! It turned out to be a marvellous concert with much clapping from the two of us and the orchestra playing a couple of encores at our request.

We felt very privileged as the orchestra played to us as if we were royalty. We were given free tickets in the end and the orchestra didn't seem to mind about the situation at all, saying they had other concerts to perform and this was a good rehearsal for them.

I have spoken at length about Geraldo, the bandleader who was very popular during World War II, and long before we became known to one another, I went to one of his concerts where he played the popular piano piece, *The Warsaw Concerto*. Gerry, as he is known by his friends, played every note wrong in that introduction! It must have been extremely embarrassing for him, but I don't think many people in the audience realized. If I make a mistake when I'm playing the piano to an audience, I feel it stands out so much and it almost gives me a heart attack! At the time, I felt very sorry for such a great bandleader to make those mistakes, although in retrospect, I thought it was really quite a 'comedy situation.'

Probably one of my most favourite of these 'Comedy Situations' is the night dear Joy sang a gorgeous song called, 'Why Did I Choose You,' which contains very personal lyrics from the film, *The Yearling*. She sang this song so intimately for the recording on a lovely CD called, *The Magic of Joy Devon*.

We were both entertaining as a husband-and-wife act at a local concert, which was packed. I played the introduction on this lovely grand piano and because Joy choose this moment to sing the lyrics to me personally, she leaned very close to the piano and looking at me in a very romantic way began singing, "Why did I choose you? What could I see in you?" She was looking at me straight in the eyes and I suddenly winked at her. Totally throwing her, she completely forgot the rest of the words to the song! Joy spent the remainder of the song making up the words, which didn't make any sense with a swimming pool coming into it somewhere, which had nothing to do with the original song! Can you believe the audience didn't notice a thing? Not even the words Joy made up as she sang along! When she finished, the audience clapped, clapped and clapped to a standing ovation! We never forgot that time in our musical lives and we laughed so much!

Joy was indeed a very good sport and she looked dazzling that night as she always did. Perhaps that's why they applauded with so much enthusiasm. Sometimes when she sang, 'Why Did I Choose You,' and I would often reply jokingly, "God only knows why!" But I can tell you, I never again winked at Joy when I was accompanying her on piano!

I do enjoy very much composing funny items, although it's not all that easy to write music to laugh by. To name a few, my own musical contributions in this field are, 'Comedy Situations,' 'Comic Collection,' 'Pizzicato Whimsy,' and 'Slapsticks.'

One time when Joy had organized our holiday at the Illa d'Or Hotel in Puerto Pollensa, I honestly acted just like a zombie! I had been working very hard and was totally exhausted. During this holiday, we met another couple staying at the hotel, a Portuguese chap and his wife, who had been noticing that I seem to be rather accident prone! Almost everything I touched seemed to go wrong! For example, I put the sunshade umbrella up to keep us out of the sun, which kept falling down on top of us and had me struggling several times to put it back up again! I would keep dropping my cutlery at meal times. Sometimes the knife, sometimes the fork, and on some occasions, both! I also managed to knock over my beer, swim in my underpants and drive on the wrong side of the road. This went on for days with this Portuguese chap looking on in astonishment, probably wondering what a lovely girl like Joy was doing with an idiot like me!

Gradually as the days passed, I became more rested and managed to 'conduct' myself in a more normal manner! Towards the end of the holiday, I was in the lounge one afternoon tinkling on the grand piano and quite a large number of people began to gather round to listen. Then lo and behold, the Portuguese fellow came in as well, looking absolutely amazed when he saw it was me playing the piano!

He told me afterwards, he was very sorry he had thought there was something a little odd about me, but he had no idea I was such a talented musician! Joy also sang a few songs, which surprised him even more. On the plane journey home, this Portuguese man came up to our seat and he was so humble and apologetic, while insisting on buying us both a drink. I have to admit, Joy and I had quite a chuckle about our holiday comedy situation and confusing our Portuguese connection!

48

Classical Arrangements and Holiday Disaster!

One of the most interesting and musical sessions I have arranged in recent years is on a CD called *Classical Arrangements* for Amphonic Music, run by Ian Dale. It contains classical arrangements taken from piano works of the great masters, from the earliest of time up to the present date. It begins with early keyboard music written by William Byrd and Henry Purcell, and then follows with Handel, Bach, Mozart, Beethoven, Chopin and Greig. Featuring pieces such as Bach's 'Minuet in G,' Beethoven's 'Moonlight Sonata,' and Chopin's 'Prelude in B Minor,' it finishes with two tracks of my own compositions, 'Monet's Garden' and 'Impressionist.'

I arranged and orchestrated all the pieces for a chamber orchestra. It was quite a challenge, but I enjoyed the work tremendously, particularly when I reached the point where I felt I had mastered the beautiful music of those influential and honoured composers to produce some original and haunting melody landscapes in popular slow movements.

I used a chamber ensemble and harp, while Galina Solodchin led with her wonderful string quartet and the woodwind. Galina has played for the well-known 'Delme Quartet' for the past forty years, which has performed at most music festivals including Salzburg and the Dvorak Birthday Concert in Prague.

Formed by Granville Delme Jones, Jurgen Hess, John Underwood and Joy Hall in 1962, the quartet celebrated forty years in 2002 with a concert at Wigmore Hall that received rave reviews from the critics. Galina joined the quartet on the death of Granville Jones, in the late sixties.

The young men and women students who had recently been studying at music colleges played the pieces beautifully, while also doubling on other woodwind instruments. Also, I used the French horn, a trumpet and a very good harp player called Jean Price. I was very surprised and impressed with the standard of these young talented musicians, who played so very well during these sessions. We recorded the sessions at Kerchesters in Kingswood, a lovely country spot just a few miles from Banstead. We were all very thrilled with the results and for me, it was especially enjoyable working with music that will never date!

This leads to the last time Joy and I went on holiday to our favourite place, the Illa d'Or Hotel in Puerto Pollensa. At the last minute, Joy tried to book a room at this luxury hotel, but it was completely full for the dates we wanted. Our alternative was to book one of the hotel's apartments, situated opposite the hotel with a swimming pool just off the sea front.

On reaching the airport, we made our way to the taxi ranks to take our usual taxi ride to the hotel. Halfway through our journey, a storm began to brew up that became steadily worse the further north we travelled. Our taxi driver told us there had been quite a few bad storms recently; however, we didn't feel particularly concerned.

By the time we reached our hotel, it was dark, and the storm had become a deadly hurricane. The taxi driver had to leave us a short distance away from our apartment because the whole area was flooded. We paddled with our suitcases through the deep floods and walked up the two flights of stairs to our apartment, breathing a sigh of relief we weren't booked on the ground floor! How we managed to find our rooms, I shall never know, because there were no lights anywhere! Fortunately, we met a waiter coming through the darkened corridor with a couple of lit candles and he gave these to us so we could see what we were doing in the apartment.

We eventually plucked up courage to walk across the flooded road to the main hotel. The whole of the ground floor of the hotel was flooded and we could see the shadows of many of the holidaymakers milling about in the main lounge lit up by hundreds of candles. People were slightly panicky as there was no electricity or hot meals, water everywhere and nobody knew what to do or where to go. The lovely grand piano, which I had played many times before during my previous trips, was out of harm's way on the stage. The atmosphere was very tense, as it felt very dangerous with the torrential rain and such loud thunder and lightning. I had never before, or since, witnessed such a frightening storm.

Joy spoke to these scared holidaymakers in a quiet serene voice, telling them not to worry and in her quiet way calmed everyone down with the suggestion of a singsong. I managed to scramble through the people to the piano and accompanied Joy on some very well-known songs, with the holidaymakers joining in on the choruses. It took me back to those days during the war when people were sheltering in Charing Cross Underground Station and singing their hearts out in the darkness, as the sirens shrieked out around London.

Most people were British, middle-aged and some were quite elderly. I felt very proud of Joy's courage as she helped those frightened people forget their worries and troubles. Music really is wonderful for this type of situation, especially if Joy is around, too.

It was a dreadful storm, yet the next morning the sun was shining as bright as ever, as if nothing had happened! However, awful damage greeted us in the morning. Most of the lovely palm trees had blown down along the sea front and there were upturned boats in the harbour, with rubbish littered everywhere. We were devastated to find that overnight, the storm had completely wrecked this beautiful place. Even more devastating—we didn't know at the time—we would never again visit this lovely resort. However, the glorious memories of those balmy, happy days will never die. Joy and I would forget time, never wanting our precious moments in Puerto Pollensa that became so personal to us to end.

Musically, this reminds me of the great song by Leonard Bernstein, 'Somewhere,' with the lines, 'there's a place for us, a time and place for us' from the musical *West Side Story*. That 'somewhere' for Joy and I will forever remain Puerto Pollensa.

We are very lucky that when we go on holiday, we have someone rather special to look after our dogs, Jamie and Sophie, and the house. Sandra Longhurst who lives in Banstead has been looking after us for over twenty years. Every week she comes to the house and cleans and when we go on holiday, she moves in to look after our dogs and our home. She is a lovely, bubbly character who loves dogs and we have no worries when she takes care of our pets. When Sandra is around, somehow everywhere comes alive and the world seems a much better place.

49

The Saddest Occasion—The Loss of Joy

Despite the many unhappy times in my life, nothing prepared me for what was yet to come. It was late in 2003, and we were coming up to quite a major event in my life, that of my eightieth birthday. After beating breast cancer over a period of ten months, Joy had been taking a course of drugs called tamoxifen for six years. This is the usual course for any woman who has suffered from breast cancer. Every year she underwent a test and was given a clean bill of health.

Joy had not been feeling quite right for a few months when the time came for her to have her yearly check. It was then we learned the most devastating news. It wasn't her breast cancer that had returned; no, it was far, far worse. Joy was diagnosed with a very rare kind of cancer, the deadly sarcoma of the uterus, for which there is no known cure.

It is very difficult to convey just how awful those first few moments were when we received this news. We were both in shock and felt completely stunned. I suppose we just couldn't believe it after all we had been through and, yes, we did both pray for a miracle.

Two incidents stick in my mind, one being Joy's courageous attitude and her determination she would beat this dreadful disease. Two was the way the specialist told me the news. He said, "She won't survive, she won't survive," and carried on with his business as if he was saying, 'Isn't it a nice day today." He probably didn't mean to appear callous, yet for me, that's exactly how it felt.

Joy was admitted to St. George's Hospital in London for a full hysterectomy, where a top surgeon was to perform the operation. He told us the cancer had been spreading very slowly, warning us the operation was very serious. On the day, my cousin, Tony Slaymaker, and his wife, Joyce, took us both to the hospital in their car in the mid-afternoon. It was heartrending saying goodbye because although Joy and I had not spoken about it, we both knew there was a possibility she might not survive the operation. Silently we hugged one another and she simply said, "I love you."

I sat in that hospital trying to remain positive through the long agonizing four hours, while she was in surgery. Late in the evening, they wheeled her into her private room where I was waiting. She was very weak, yet she opened her eyes to whisper, "Hello love." You can't imagine what this meant to me and the sense of sweet relief flooded through me, after hearing those two little endearing words. I should never have doubted my brave little Scot, particularly as she had said to me the week before, "I'll come through this, whatever."

The next morning, the nurses told me how Joy was determined to walk a few yards and they were astonished when she walked with a crutch halfway down the corridor! What a great spirit she had and despite the fact she was very ill, she loved being on the top floor of the hospital where she could enjoy the wonderful view right across London, including the great London Eye.

We had a visit from the surgeon who was Irish and he said to us, "Would you like to hear the good news first, or the bad news?" We decided to hear the good news first and he told us the operation had been very successful. However, the surgeon had been unable to remove the cancerous lymph gland because this would have killed Joy.

Joy said, "Don't worry, love. I have the strength and will power to get through this." In my heart, I couldn't help feeling deeply troubled. She recuperated for about ten days in St. George's, during which time I chauffeured as many friends and family as I could get in my car every day to the hospital and home again. For the first time in my life, my music faded into the background as I spent every possible hour of the day at Joy's bedside.

Everybody loved and adored Joy. She had no enemies because nobody could possibly dislike her gentle and kind disposition. When the time came for her to be discharged from hospital, I felt it was such an honour to pick her up from St. George's and bring her back to her lovely home which she loved so dearly.

Once Joy was back home in Banstead, we were inseparable and for several weeks we lived almost twenty-four hours a day at the Royal Marsden Hospital in Sutton. They even ordered a car for us so we could go back to St. George's in London to see various specialists who could decide what the best treatment for Joy was.

Despite everything and although there were many days when Joy was feeling well, she still felt very weak. However, she was determined to take on the birthday preparations for my eightieth on 30 April 2004. It was important to her my birthday was a success and she worked very hard organising the party to take place at the Horse Shoe in Banstead on a Sunday afternoon and throughout the evening.

We invited well over one hundred fifty family and friends, including my publisher from Germany, Gerhard, and his wife, Heidi. Don Lusher, the famous trombonist, attended (who died soon after in 2006), as did Adam Saunders and his wife, together with David Ades, the editor of the Robert Farnan Society, and his wife, Moira.

Many of Joy's family also came from long distances, with her half-sister Jackie and her husband, Winston, together with her half-brother George and his son travelling from Australia. Joy's father's second wife's sister, known as Aunt Betty, came down from Wakefield in West Yorkshire with another half-brother David.

We were both thrilled that nobody turned down our invitation. My sister Judy was picked up from Parkside Nursing Home and brought to the party in her wheelchair, and I personally wheeled her in with everyone clapping. It made my birthday to see Judy enjoying herself so much that evening; it was also great watching Joy and Judy chatting and laughing together.

There were musicians, composers, publishers and celebrities from the music world, together with a string quartet led by Sally Brooke-Pike, who had been the lead second violinist in the BBC Radio Orchestra. Many of my friends from this orchestra were present and this wonderful quartet played the most appropriate and charming salon music to celebrate this special birthday of mine. Firstly, Gerhard made a wonderful speech and then David Ades said some lovely words.

Finally, I stood up and spoke at some length about my life, making quite a few jokes and thanking everyone who had supported me over the years and in particular during Joy's illness. A big cake was wheeled into the room with a miniature orchestra decorating the top with me as the conductor and Joy in her favourite red sparkling dress, while beside us sat our two dogs, Jamie and Sophie. What an amazing sight that was! We had a few jokes about the cake as I attempted to cut it amidst lots of laughter, while pretending to almost cut off my finger! What a marvellous job our close friend Sylvia had made of this most original and fantastic cake.

Another dear friend, Ralph Thompson, made a complete video with clips of my music playing in the background of the whole occasion, taking the time and patience to prepare it as a special eightieth birthday present for me. Joy had also organized a couple of display boards and pinned up many family photographs together with photographs of me as a child, up to present day photographs with many of my work as a conductor and composer, too.

It was thrilling when my cousin Tony announced a specially recorded message, which my publisher, Marlin Taylor, had sent over from Washington, D.C. This personal message was recorded on a cassette and the whole room was quiet as we listened to Marlin and his wife, Alicia, wishing me well. Alicia, who was a well-known opera singer, sang 'Happy Birthday' to me totally unaccompanied, and also 'I've Got You under my Skin.' Everyone was enthralled.

It was wonderful to celebrate my eightieth birthday party with Joy looking so well. She wore a pretty blue dress I bought for her in a beautiful little village called Shere, close to the Surrey Hills, and this blue dress matched her blue eyes. She really did look stunning. Seeing her that evening, if you didn't know, you couldn't possibly believe she had been, and was still, so ill.

Soon after that wonderful event, Joy's health seemed to deteriorate very quickly and she returned to the Royal Marsden in Sutton to a small ward of about six women, all with incurable diseases.

At the Royal Marsden, they have a hospital radio station to play requests for patients and visitors. I took a CD of *The Magic of Joy Devon* and requested the disc jockey to play some of Joy's songs. I was there when she heard some of those songs coming through the loud speakers in her ward and throughout the hospital and she was as pleased as Punch! There were some poignant moments when many of the other patients came to visit her in her ward to say how much they enjoyed her singing and by golly what a voice she had!

During this time, our friends Sylvia and Peter had a blessing in the lovely old church at Headley, which is a typical Surrey village close to Banstead, and Joy was determined to make it to this important occasion. I picked her up from the Royal Marsden to travel about eight miles to the church. I had to back the car right up to the church door, as Joy couldn't walk far, and only just avoided hitting some gravestones on the way.

She was on crutches and I thought how courageous she was to make such a journey as it was obviously a big, big effort, which was very difficult for her. Once more, some of the songs from *The Magic of Joy Devon* were played at the end of the blessing and they sounded so beautiful echoing throughout that magnificent church. We all felt so proud of Joy and I could see by her face, it was a very special moment for her, too.

Joy managed to chat to quite a number of people including the vicar and I have always felt it was a very 'special occasion' because of the determination of my Scottish Lass to attend that special occasion against all odds. Sylvia and Peter asked me to open the blessing with a composition of mine called 'Let's Dream of Tomorrow,' as it was their favourite tune. I played this on a keyboard in the church and in retrospect, it was a very poignant tune for Joy and me, too, especially since it was so awful to return Joy to the hospital at the end of the day.

Some weeks later, Joy phoned in tears from the Royal Marsden to tell me yet more terrible news. She said in an almost inaudible voice (she was so upset she could hardly speak) "I've got a brain tumour—I've got a brain tumour." I couldn't believe what I was hearing. Feeling devastated, I drove the short distance to the hospital like a maniac, my head whirling with the enormity of Joy's words. I hurried to her ward and saw her walking towards me with the help of a stick. She seemed a long way away down the long corridor at first, but we both rushed towards one another with Joy falling into my arms saying, "It can't be true." We clung to each other in that corridor for a long, long time unable to utter another word.

Once again, I experienced the matter-of-fact attitude so many of these consultants seem to have. I was told, "She will be lucky to live three months. It could be less it could be more." How angry I felt and said, "Thank you for telling me in this way. I suppose you have to say this many times, but this happens to be my wife you are talking about."

The consultant told me the cancer had spread to her lungs and to her brain. There was nothing more they could do and I was to take her home and make her as comfortable as possible for however long she still had on this earth. I cannot describe our despair and distress. How can anyone take this news without shedding a million tears? We were inconsolable.

The day I brought Joy home from the Royal Marsden, our friend Ralph was there with his video camera. To try to cheer Joy up, I said I would play some of her favourite tunes on the piano. Joy decided she wanted to get into her special red evening dress that she wore to sing in and I tried to stop her telling there was no need for all that, with her feeling so unwell. I couldn't put Joy off and she said, "I would like to do this as a last bow." I couldn't believe it when I saw her walking down the stairs in that dress looking as lovely as ever, with her hair and make-up done to perfection.

Joy stood in our conservatory and mimed four songs from her CD *The Magic of Joy Devon:* 'Send in the Clowns,' 'I Fall to Pieces,' 'The Glory of Love' and 'People.' Looking at Joy at that time, nobody would have believed she was on the verge of death. It is a lovely memory to have, although now, when watching the video, I am reminded of how tormented I was by my grief for Joy. The look of distress is clearly etched on my face. She was so very brave to even think of doing such a thing. On the few occasions when I have watched that video, I have felt so sad and it's difficult to stop my tears from flowing. Singing was Joy's whole life and she wanted to sing that last time for the video camera to make sure I had something to remember her by. In the old song 'Love Is the Sweetest Thing,' this line is lovely, but it's not so sweet when you lose love. Although in spirit, I know in my heart we haven't lost the love of Joy.

The nurses came twice a day to give Joy her tablets, as there were so many to take and it was a very difficult task for even the nurses to deal with. She had to take drugs the whole time and with her body constantly in pain, she was also taking many pain killers. I knew Joy was putting up a tremendous fight against shocking odds, yet every time she had company, she would make a big effort to put on a little make-up and look good for her visitors.

One morning, Joy spoke on the phone to her new friend, Perpetua, who was the senior nurse at Parkside Nursing home, where my sister Judy was staying. They had become friendly when Joy was still well during our many visits to see Judy and they would often talk for so long, I confess at times it would slightly irritate me!

Joy knew her time was short and just like the lovely caring person she was, her worries were more about me than herself. She asked Perpetua, "Could you please look after John for me, because I know he cannot look after himself and I'm very worried," and then she cried, heartbroken she wouldn't be here for me.

I didn't know any of this until much later, when Perpetua told me.

Soon the stairs became too much for Joy, so Malcolm, our friend and neighbour from next door, carried the single bed downstairs on his own to our sitting room. Many friends and relatives came every day including our Reverend David Chance of All Saints Church. At times, they were as many as twelve people sitting around the room chatting and this really helped to keep Joy cheerful as she enjoyed listening to everyone talking.

At night, after everyone had left and I had to leave Joy and go upstairs to bed, we would talk for a short while to each other over the phone and as the popular song says: "I Just Called to Say I Love You," and that's just what we did.

Early one Sunday morning, I was making a cup of tea when Joy shouted from the sitting room, "John, I've fallen over and can't get up." I rushed in and saw her plight. I rang for the ambulance to take her to casualty at Epsom Hospital. Marion, her daughter, was over here from New York and because it was a Sunday morning, we had to wait a long time before anyone came to attend to Joy.

While we were waiting in the casualty ward, Marion and I saw an X-ray taken of Joy, pinned up on the wall in the distance. It was black all over. Marion said to me, "Look," and I replied, "Yes, I'm afraid there doesn't seem to be any hope." The dreadful realization of what this meant really hit me at that moment, as I suppose up until then I had still been hoping against hope and praying that Joy would somehow pull through.

An ambulance took Joy straight from casualty to a hospice in Esher, while I followed in my car with Marion. The hospice was in a pretty place with a small river running though the grounds and lots of wildlife. Her sons, Andrew, Richard, their wives, and of course Marion, plus many friends went to see her each day. I always visited in the afternoon but gradually she became weaker and weaker. One day near the end, she whispered to me "I love you."

Four or five days after Joy had been admitted, the phone rang at 1:30 in the morning. It was Saturday 14 August and the night nurse told me to come quickly to the hospice. I knew what that meant, and telephoning Joy's children I rushed over to the hospice with Marion. It was agony to see my Joy in this state of barely being conscious and I went to the chapel to pray.

Later, there were nine of us around Joy's bed when the telephone rang and a nurse said, "There is a call for you, Mr. Fox. It is from the United States. Would you like to take it?"

Weakly I whispered, "Yes," even though I had no idea who it could be. It was my publisher in Washington, D.C., Marlin Taylor. He was so very fond of Joy and being a religious man with a firm belief in God, he said a sermon over the phone. It was a wonderful spiritual message to Joy and I noticed she briefly raised her eyebrows. A few minutes later, she passed away peacefully.

My heart was so full of pain and I was sobbing my heart out. Then the most magical incident occurred. Marion exclaimed, "Look! John, there are two white doves looking in," and as I looked up at the window, a third white dove flew in the middle of the other two doves!

That moment was unbelievable—to see these three white doves appear at the window just as Joy left this world! Nobody could really believe it, however, all nine of us, including our good friends Sylvia and Peter saw this miracle. We were all incredulous, and for a brief moment this miracle took the pain away as we all marvelled at this sight. For me, the doves symbolized Joy was at last in peace. They were telling me, while I had been constantly at her side through those long harrowing months praying for her recovery, my time with her was no more on this earth.

The loss of Joy has affected many people from near and far because everyone who had the pleasure of knowing her adored and cherished her. 'The Magic of Joy Devon' says it all. There was an article in a magazine that sums up everything about Joy, written by David Ades, which he has kindly allowed me to use in my book.

Joy Fox: A Lovely Lady is Sadly Missed

> Those of us, who were privileged to know Joy, will remember her as a very special person who always displayed a magical charm of her own. In her presence, the world seemed a better place: she had that rare ability of being able to make everyone she met feel important to her—even for just a few moments. Sadly, on Saturday, August 14, 2004, we received the news that Joy's brave fight against ill health had finally come to an end. A lesser person would probably have given up the battle much sooner, but Joy's strength of character had sustained her through many periods of painful treatment. Incredibly, less than four months earlier, she had been at her husband's eightieth birthday celebration looking as bright and vivacious as she always did.
>
> Joy's real name was Joyce, but she was known to her adoring public as the singer Joy Devon. RFS members who attended our London meetings will know that Joy was often with us at the Bonnington Hotel, alongside her devoted husband. John Fox is one of our finest composers and conductors, and there have been many happy

instances where their careers have intertwined from large lush orchestrations, to sensitive accompaniments with John on piano. Joy has created some memorable performances of popular songs, which we can still enjoy today, through the miracle of recorded sound.

Joy always looked lovely and she sang beautifully. At her memorial service in All Saint's Church, Banstead on Thursday, August 24, we heard her voice sounding almost ethereal alongside John's sensitive music in one of the most moving tributes that many in the congregation could recall. One of Joy's favourites was 'Send in the Clowns' and fittingly the opening notes were captured on one of the family wreaths.

The obituary notice in the Daily Telegraph simply stated that Joyce Marion Fox, beloved wife of the composer John Fox, had died on August 14, aged sixty-three, after a brave fight against cancer. What mere words cannot convey is the real sense of loss that so many of us feel.

However, Joy will never be forgotten. When the time seems right, John is planning to compose a special work in her honour, and we feel certain that it will be one of his finest creations. The deep love they shared with each other will surely result in something quite magnificent.

To John and his family, we send our sincere and affectionate condolences. We know that Joy lives on in his heart, as she does in all of ours.

David Ades

The retired Rev. Peter Naylor travelled from the south of France accompanied by his charming wife, Wendy, to take the funeral service at All Saint's Church. When the moment came, I was too distressed to speak to the congregation, so Tony Slaymaker, my cousin, spoke in my place but I promised to compose an orchestral suite for Joy and call it *Love of Joy*.

The church was crammed with people of all ages and I chose two songs to play during the service from one of Joy's cherished CDs, 'The Glory of Love' and 'Send in the Clowns.' After the service, the family and I followed the hearse to Randall's Park crematorium where Joy was cremated.

I had invited everyone back to Coniston including her two step brothers, not to celebrate, but to remember Joy forever, as David Ades so aptly said. Joy's ashes are buried in the cemetery at All Saint's Church in remembrance. She loved Banstead, where we spent very happy memories in 'togetherness' which is the title of one of 'our' CDs. Some of her lovely songs and my compositions and arrangements can be heard on the album *Togetherness*.

We are told 'life must go on.' At times, I have found this very difficult. Bereavement is such a feeling of despair, unhappiness and loneliness, a gut-wrenching physical feeling, which doesn't go away for a very long time. Memories sometimes come flooding back to me, some of which I thought would never ever come back and there are many times when my grief at losing Joy is unbearable and I cry so much it worries me. I have managed to capture many of these emotional times in my music and I call them *Sad Occasions*.

When you lose someone you love there are many lonely times. The heartache stays with you day after day, month after month, and it takes a long time to heal, if ever. Yes, the initial physical pain dulls, however, the ache is always there and sometimes at unexpected moments, my grief overwhelms me.

Since my awful loss, it's a long healing process; somehow though, I know Joy is still around. In the early days after her death, a number of funny incidences happened in the house that I cannot explain logically. One such incident was when I lost my watch. I searched for it high and low all through the house. As evening approached, I gave up and settled down to watch the television.

The next morning, I walked into the sitting room and there was my watch lying in the middle of the room looking up at me. I was astounded! I had searched the sitting room from top to bottom. It just wasn't possible that I could have missed it the day before. I felt Joy was close by me, helping me and at times, I even felt with certain little things, she was pulling my leg a little in the way she might have done had she still been alive.

As the months passed I felt her presence a little less. I believe this is because she knows I am now being well looked after by Perpetua and she doesn't have to worry about me anymore. However, I know for certain, she is near me in spirit and that is the truth.

50

The Light Blue Estate Car—
The Colour of Joy's Eyes

One Sunday morning a couple of years before Joy's terrible illness, we decided to go to one of our favourite places to walk our dogs. Oaks Park is a short distance from Banstead with wonderful opens spaces and woodlands covered with wildflowers. The car park there has a pretty formal garden with a pond and we had just arrived, when a man in a large light blue estate car drove up beside us. We watched as he opened his boot to let out three lovely dogs.

For some reason, Joy immediately took to this light blue vehicle, prompting her to say it was about time we had a new car and perhaps we could consider buying something similar. I liked the car; it was a Rover 75 and Joy talked about it for some while after that day. Somehow, other things took over our life, including Joy's bad health, and it was forgotten. Then a couple of months after Joy's tragic death, something strange happened.

In an effort to cheer myself up a little, I had been toying with the idea of changing my car and visited a local garage in Epsom. There didn't seem to be anything there that interested me and I put that down to my state of mind. The salesman was very helpful and promised to let me know when a new batch of cars was expected. Feeling very disappointed, I was just about to leave when I suddenly noticed a large light blue car parked alone, some way from the forecourt.

I called to the salesman and pointed it out to him. He was puzzled, telling me he knew nothing about a blue estate car. He enquired at his office to find out it had only just come in and it was for sale. I felt amazed because even if it wasn't the same car we saw in Oaks Park that day, it was the exact model and colour and at that moment, I felt as if it had just been dropped down from heaven.

Everything was right about this car. It was almost new and had only three thousand miles on the clock, a beautiful interior with leather seats and a large boot for the dogs. For more reasons than one, I knew I had to buy it.

As I drove away from the garage, I couldn't get that day in Oaks Park with Joy out of my mind and most of all how the colour reminded me of her lovely blue eyes. I really felt Joy wasn't very far away from me that day and I felt better than I had for a long while. Now if you are a cynic, you will think this is a trivial story, yet for me this incident had a deep spiritual meaning and one that is difficult to explain. Could you honestly say this wasn't some sort of amazing coincidence? Even now, I often smile to myself thinking, "Well, love, you got your own way after all!"

Perpetua and John's colourful wedding with Rev. David Chance at All Saints Church Banstead Surrey.

John and Perpetua's wedding day with all the composers: (from left) Philip Lane, Gavin Sutherland, John, Perpetua, Gerhard Narholz and Adam Saunders.

Gavin and Verity Sutherland, Philip Lane, Peter and Alice Taylor from Spain Thiyiwe and Grace.

Gerhard, me, Perpetua, Judy, (in wheelchair) Heidi, Monica, and Edward on far right.

Perpetua's family (left) Selina, Edward, me, Perpertua, Monica, Miriam, and Nyasha.,

Perpetua with her bridesmaids, Miriam and Maureen.

The two of us with ladies at wedding: Charity, Heidi, Abigail, Miriam, Zanele, and Daisy, the flower girl.

John and Perpetua with Peter and Sylvia—two very good friends of ours.

Charming Heidi Narholz and John posing happily.

Top table at the wedding reception at Bridge House Hotel Reigate Surrey.

John and his friend Peter Atkins, the artist. Peter Taylor in the background.

Me with closest and lovely sister Judy at Parkside Home where she spent her last years of life.

Sally, Tarenda, Perpetua, Bronte, Milly (singer) and John.

John with Bronte, Tarenda, and baby Rose Saunders—a happy gathering.

John and Perpetua's house in Banstead.

Gerhard, John and Heidie viewing the hills in Salzburg during our holidays.

John admiring Beethoven's grave monument at cemetry in Vienna Austria.

John and Perpetua at Beverley's Graduation ceremony in Capetown South Africa.

Masimba, Perpetua, Beverley, me, and Nyasha at Cape town University after Beverly's graduation.

John playing piano at a Stellenbosch restaurant in South Africa.

John, Perpertua and Masimba with the Indian Ocean in the background.

John and Perpetua at the Cape of Good Hope—the most south western point of the African cont.

John and Perpetua with Nyasha and her lovely children.

John with a giraffe at a wild life park on the outskirts of Johannesburg.

John with Nyasha's lovely baby, Veneka Thea.

John composing at his desk where he wrote hundreds and hundreds of his works.

John at his piano for composing in his studio.

John's Grand Gaveau piano.

A look into John's studio. What a sight! So many records tapes and CD's over the years.

Perpetua and John's house in Zimbabwe.

Jamie relaxing—John's favourite pet who is now sixteen plus years of age!

John seriously conducting at a concert in earlier days.

Cherry Blossom tree planted in the field in memory of Joy.

Joyce, Tony, a favourite cousin, and Tanya on the way to a surprise birthday party.

Perpetua (middle) with first daughter, Pamela (left) and Tina (right) at the park in Chicago.

Sam on John's computer helping with the book—a wonderful friend of ours.

51

"Love of Joy"—My Promised Suite for Full Orchestra

Somehow, I struggled through the months after Joy's untimely death, mostly because of the unfailing support I received from my family and friends. Everyone was so kind and in particular, Peter and Sylvia, Adam Saunders and his wife, Clare, Philip and Anne Cakebread, Peter Atkins and Pam, David Ades, Gavin Sutherland, Philip Lane, Rosemary Tames, Tony and Joyce, and my stepsons: Andrew and his two girls, Richard and Tracy with their two boys. There are many more friends and neighbours far too numerous to mention, but without them I couldn't have gotten through those early painful days.

Also, not forgetting her promise to Joy, Perpetua kept in constant contact with me. There weren't many days when she didn't call me to make sure I was okay. My friends came and went, urging me to compose the suite I had promised everyone at Joy's funeral I would write. I had made a solemn promise and somehow I had to carry it out; however in those early days I honestly did not have the will or the energy to write anything.

Where do I begin? Each day, I just could not think about it and it just wasn't possible to write about my Joy so soon after her passing. My emotions were still so terribly raw. Then one precious day, an idea just popped into my head. I thought about the very first time we met, our walks with the dogs, her fast driving, her wonderful voice, her lovely nature and how everyone who had ever known her, loved her.

I began to look for my score paper, notebooks, good pencils and good rubbers, manuscript paper, Sellotape, and everything I needed to begin composing. On my long country walks with Sophie and Jamie, my two faithful dogs who I knew missed their mistress very much, I set to thinking about something that would last forever. One day it came to me; an idea dropped from heaven just like my blue car did. A suite! That's it! The idea was brilliantly clear. How had I not thought of it before? A suite in eight movements to portray my life with Joy from our first meeting, through all our years together, to the time she left this unsettled world. What should I call it? That came easily, *Love of Joy*. What a magical word 'joy' is and so aptly describes what Joy's presence meant to anyone who met her, 'Joy to the world.'

I believe 'thinking' is an essential component of composing. My thoughts went back to our first meeting. I was stunned by her charm, her looks, her quiet relaxing speaking voice, her sereneness, her presence and last but not least, her beautiful blue eyes!

I called the first piece 'First Meeting,' followed by 'Those Warm Summer Days' remembering our walks in Surrey with the dogs. The third piece is 'In a Mad Rush' describing Joy's driving style, then 'Waltz for Joy' because she was such an excellent dancer and would often dance around the house for fun. Afterwards when the suite was finished, many listeners said this was their favourite piece. The fifth movement is 'Siesta in Puerto Pollensa' for obvious reasons, followed by 'The Blue-Eyed Mackenzie Lass' as Joy was born in Edinburgh Scotland. Next is 'Our Garden of Memories' as we both loved our garden so much and the last piece is the sad and spiritual 'Three White Doves' describing Joy in peace forever.

During the time I wrote this eight-movement suite, many of my friends requested to hear some of the themes with bits and pieces of the titles as I think they wanted to encourage me to keep going. Unfortunately, it is almost impossible to play a piece on a piano if it has been written specifically for a large orchestra; however, on this occasion I did my best and although it didn't really work, I enjoyed playing what I could, which delighted my friends.

I don't often use the piano in an orchestra with the exception of using it for deep sombre notes, such as in the beginning of the last movement in my suite *Love of Joy*. I do use the celesta, which looks like a small upright piano with hammers that strike metal bars giving it a bell-like sound. Tchaikovsky was the first composer to use this instrument in his famous *The Nutcracker* for the piece 'Dance of the

Sugar Plum Fairy.' In the last movement of my suite, 'Three White Doves,' you can hear some of this delightful instrument's ethereal sounds and it is most appropriate as celesta means 'heavenly' in French.

Considering how painful it was at the time to think about my life with Joy, I wrote those eight movements quite quickly. One person in particular helped me tremendously through this time, especially when I couldn't sleep and would be feeling very low. We spoke on the telephone for very long periods of time, and she always had the ability to calm me with her sensible talk. Yes, it was Perpetua. Her name has a lovely meaning to it as well: everlasting.

Perpetua comes from Zimbabwe, which is a country going through some dreadful times as I am writing these memoirs. The strangest thing is she is almost the same age as Joy was, just six months younger, the same height and is the same size in shoes. Can you believe that? Some more very strange coincidences—or was it meant to be, do you think?

Adam Saunders adored Joy and in her memory, he offered to copy the whole eight movements of the suite onto the computer for me. Not long after we had checked the music, the actual date of recording came through, which felt very exciting. Life had begun to have meaning once more. Philip Lane was the producer and organized everything including the orchestra, the Royal Sinphonia, conducted by my friend Gavin Sutherland and the balancing engineer Richard Scott, who was a wizard at mixing music. Tony Slaymaker and his wife drove me to Whitfield Street Studios London, on 22 February 2005 and as we walked into the control room, to my utter surprise the whole place was packed with familiar faces including my step-children with their children.

I had, of course, been talking about this suite for some while, yet had no idea that everyone had planned to get together and be there for the event. They wanted to surprise me while also witnessing the recording of Joy's suite by a large orchestra. How very thrilled I was to see so many friends and family present to support me at such a crucial and painful period in my life.

Whilst this major recording took place, everyone in the control room was very quiet and listened intently, even the children! I sat beside Philip Lane in the control box to help sort out certain sections and when I wanted Gavin to interpret bars in a certain way, Philip would phone through to Gavin in the studio to instruct him. It was a truly memorable occasion even, though at times very emotional, with many of my family and friends in tears as they listened to the suite.

Everyone in the orchestra played so well that day and at the end of the sessions, I thanked them all from the bottom of my heart. The suite turned out exactly as I wanted, something to remember forever and a day, in loving memory of Joy. After the recording, Philip sent a copy of the suite for me to change or amend. I listened carefully to the recording and in parts I changed the strings to sound more positive and in other places to sound softer, I brought the harp to the fore a little more and made all sorts of changes that helped to improve the actual balance of the piece in general. It took lots of patience reaching the point where I felt I had achieved the very best out of the suite. When I finally heard the finished recording, it sounded perfect!

This suite was included on my CD called *Voyage of a Lifetime,* which is the name of the first powerful piece on this album that also consists of other compositions and arrangements of mine together with a couple of Joy's songs such as 'Love Walked In' and 'Danny Boy.' It also features a couple of folk songs sung by The John Fox singers, 'Billy Boy' and a cappella version of 'She Moved Through the Fair.'

Philip Lane wrote some charming words for the CD sleeve, which also features a colour photograph of Joy and me, taken at one of our London concerts. When this CD first became commercially available, Brian Kay played the whole eight-movement suite *Love of Joy* on BBC Radio 3. Featured as the last item during his Thursday afternoon programme, he took the time and the trouble to carefully explain each movement. It was a wonderful moment as it meant so much to me that I had finally been able to fulfil my promise.

The end product was certainly worth all the trouble, worry, and my loss of sleep. And, to paraphrase Winston Churchill, I truly felt, 'This was my finest hour.' I am so thankful I am able to compose, arrange and conduct in this wonderful profession, and I just have to say it once more, *"If music be the food of love, play on John—for Joy's sake!"*

52

Loneliness—Perpetua—Spongebob Squarepants!

After completing Joy's suite, the loneliness seemed to hit me even harder than ever. Even though it had been almost unbearable during those first few months, at least I had been able to concentrate on doing something positive working on *The Love of Joy*. Keeping my mind occupied on two subjects that meant more to me than anything else in this world had helped me so much.

It was a lonely life and I found it very difficult to adjust. I am not a great lover of television and during those long days, I would resign myself to watching it more than I had ever done in my life. I even watched programmes I actively abhor such as pop shows! I also listened to my music at all times of the day. Still the hours and days dragged endlessly. The mornings were the worst, when I first woke up and remembered that Joy was no longer with me. These were very painful moments.

It doesn't help that I am not very practical with regards to the house and garden. I dislike housework of any kind and although I love the garden, I am not a gardener. I suppose I had always been looked after one way or another, firstly by my parents and sisters, then Jackie and Joy. I have never had to think about these kinds of things and had probably been more than a little pampered over the years.

I coped by going out for lunch most days. It got me out of the house, away from all the painful memories, and also meant I didn't have to worry about cooking for myself in the evenings. I had never even cooked a sausage and could only just about manage to boil myself an egg or have soup out of a tin or packet! Sometimes I went for lunch on my own but mostly with friends and family who understood what I was going through.

On many occasions, I felt so destitute I simply burst into tears at my own misery. It was a long time before I even felt a little normal again. Little did I know my salvation was only just round the corner.

When I was organizing Joy's funeral, I called in to Parkside Nursing Home to see Judy and found Perpetua looking after her. Talking through the service with them both, I didn't know which Bible reading to put in and Perpetua helped me choose one. She also drove Judy to the funeral and a few days later, I rang to say thank you. I had often seen her at the nursing home when I visited Judy, but we rarely spoke more than a few words and if I am honest, at times I was probably a little off-hand.

The morning after Joy had died, Perpetua had telephoned to see how Joy was, not realizing what had happened. Marion told Perpetua that Joy had fallen out of bed the Sunday before and broken quite a few bones. Nothing could be done for her and she had died just five days later. Perpetua had visited Joy on a regular basis during her illness and they had also spoken extensively over the phone. They had become very good friends and the news that Joy had passed away was quite a shock to her.

Later that same day, Perpetua called in to give her condolences as is the custom in her own country, Zimbabwe. This is something everyone does, even if they have not got on with the person who died or their family. Later, Perpetua told me she hadn't really taken to me at all, as on the occasions she had met me she thought me rather arrogant. She remembers one incident when visiting Joy, she had asked me for some nail scissors so she could give Joy a pedicure.

Apparently, I didn't respond very well to this request saying, "Oh I wouldn't know where they are." I went off and found several pairs of scissors, which I ungracefully gave to her. Also, that very same day Joy had been talking to Perpetua, as she was very concerned about me, and asked Perpetua to explain to me I would have to begin shopping for groceries, because Joy could no longer go out. Perpetua asked me, 'Is it true you can't even shop?' I brushed this off, as I didn't think at the time it had come to that and at that moment she didn't really like me at all.

As a qualified nurse, Perpetua was given leave to stay for five years when she arrived in the United Kingdom in 2002. Later, she told me even though she had said to Joy not to worry and she would make sure I was okay, deep in her heart she thought, "I won't be able to help this man. I come from another country, I'm black and I didn't come here to stay." At this time Perpetua wasn't even aware I was a musician and only heard Joy sing for the first time at her funeral.

A couple of weeks after the funeral, I telephoned Perpetua because I felt so terribly lonely and I remembered how kind she had been to Joy. She was very sweet to me when I told her I couldn't sleep and I needed someone to talk to. She told me I could call her at any time for a chat if it helped me. Perpetua gave me so much comfort at that time. She was so kind and talked to me in such a wise and wonderful way, giving me practical advice and listening to me so patiently. I believe she should have been a psychiatrist.

I began to call her more and more because we seemed to have such good intelligent and stimulating conversations, talking for hours on end about everything. Perpetua was happy to talk to me because she believed this was a phase I would pass through, and I would soon be gone from her life. It wasn't long before we were speaking two or three times a week and when I bought my new car, I decided to ask Perpetua if she would like to go for a drive.

From then on, we spoke almost every day. Six months later, we went out on our first date when I took her for a meal and before too long, we were enjoying meals together at Perpetua's flat in Sutton. One day I said to her, "I am not coping very well. I have been spoiled; I even have to ask the staff at the supermarkets to help me." Perpetua replied, "You have to learn to do things for yourself," and she promptly showed me how to make porridge!

The days rolled into about fifteen months and we were becoming increasingly close and fond of one another. We enjoyed each other's company and sense of humour, having many laughs together. One day I decided that I had to stop this relationship from going any further, because I didn't believe it could work. It troubled me that my friends and family wouldn't accept Perpetua as she was Zimbabwean and also because it hadn't been long since Joy died.

I was very practical about the whole situation, explaining all my concerns to Perpetua. She understood saying she accepted my decision and we parted. Two weeks went by and I felt so terribly miserable without her. I had no idea I would miss her so much and just how much she had come to mean to me. One day I couldn't stand it anymore, so I called Perpetua telling her I didn't want to go on without her.

I was so happy when she told me she had been equally miserable. She had not shown it at the time we said our goodbyes because she was trying to be brave, but she had felt a deep vacuum inside because she realized she had come to love me. We knew at that moment, we couldn't live without each other.

I then suggested we should go on holiday together to see if we could get along twenty-four hours a day. I suppose you could say it was some sort of test to see if our relationship was just infatuation or something deeper, which would enable us to live comfortably together under the same roof. We went to Calafel in northern Spain about fifty miles from Barcelona for ten days and had a wonderful time. On our return, I decided it was time to introduce Peps (as I had begun to call her) to my friends and musicians, so we organized a party that also coincided with the launching of my *Voyage of a Lifetime* CD.

It was a great success and everyone liked Peps immensely. She was more than welcomed into my circle, which made me very happy. The companionship between Perpetua and me has made life worth living again for an eighty plus year old! I have met many of her Zimbabwean friends who are so friendly, extremely likable, kind and caring people.

Perpetua's daughter Beverley, who is in her early twenties and studying at Cape Town University, was also in England at this time and we hit it off immediately. She has now returned to university and sadly, is presently unable to obtain a visa from the Home Office to visit us again.

On the work front, my publisher, Gerhard, had been in contact with me regarding some slapstick and comedy library music I had been writing over the years. Writing this type of music requires a good sense of humour and the ability to understand what makes people laugh.

If you remember, I had great success with the comedian Sally Barnes in the early fifties and the comedy acts with my sister Maureen's husband, Tom, when our family and friends would fall about in tears of laughter at our antics! Ability to interpret humorous situations seems to come naturally to me and little did I know my comedy pieces would one day be used in a worldwide popular animated television series.

I had heard quite a bit about the television half-hour series *Spongebob Squarepants* and now Gerhard was telling me my pieces representing *slap sticks, emotions, gags, links* and whimsy effects from the Sonoton Music Library had been selected for use in the series. This was very exciting for me especially as it also meant I would receive many royalties. *Spongebob Squarepants* struggled in its early years and only began to gain recognition in 2000, when eventually its ratings overtook the other very popular animated series *The Rugrats*.

It has received many awards, including five Emmy Awards over four consecutive years from 2002 to 2005 and in 2007, for 'Outstanding Animated Programme' (for programmes less than an hour long). It has proved to have broad appeal to children and adults all over the world with its quirky humorous style and in 2007, Time magazine named it as one of the greatest television shows of all time.

Spongebob Squarepants—The Movie was released in 2004, and most of the music for that film was written by Gregor Narholz, Gerhard's second son, who has told me on many occasions he was influenced by my music in his earlier years. We got on so well, he even invited me to his wedding in Austria in 2005, which was a most enjoyable and lavish occasion, taking place in Gmundun near the lakes that were featured in the film *The Sound of Music*. Gregor, who is an extremely talented and likable young man just like his father, has lived in Hollywood for sometime now and composes music for quite a number of feature films.

A *Spongebob Squarepants* television movie was also released in late 2007, called *Atlantis Square Pantis* and the television series is currently in its fifth season. There is even a 'Spongebob' Monopoly game along with other merchandising products including the ever popular, McDonalds Happy Meals.

It's such enjoyable work, too, as the ability to make any instrument 'talk' in a comic way seems to be my second nature. I might, for instance, use the piccolo for producing high squeaky notes or mute a trumpet with a hand over the bell to make all manner of strange sounds, while using the bass drum and timpani for a quick succession of notes or drum rolls.

Although I am of the generation who think Walt Disney takes some beating, every time I receive pages and pages detailing the royalties for my music contributions to the series played all over the world, I am very glad 'Spongebob' is so universally popular!

53

"A Surrey Rhapsody"

To the people of Surrey, its countryside is the best in the United Kingdom and if you are born there, your bias is even worse! So when Philip Lane asked me if I would write a musical piece about Surrey, I was thrilled. There is so much to inspire me with its hills and downs, the woods and tiny country lanes flanked by tall and impressive trees together with the famous Epsom Derby horse race, the Oxford and Cambridge boat race, sanctuaries and folk dancing.

I knew there was much to talk and write music about, so I put pencil to paper and decided to call this piece, *A Surrey Rhapsody.* I open it with a dawn chorus, birds singing, the breeze gently blowing the corn and building up to a bigger theme, which I composed to suggest some of the Surrey Hills such as Collie Hill, Box Hill and Leith Hill. It follows with melodies to depict dog walks, serene pastoral scenes, the Derby, the parks, the sanctuary, the folk dancing; then finally, I return to the main theme to end the piece.

A rhapsody is a composition containing different moods, generally written in one continuous movement, which is less structured than a more classical piece and more spontaneous. This type of music most appealed to the Romantic composers, yet surprisingly there are very few famous rhapsodies, apart from Gershwin's *Rhapsody in Blue,* in comparison to overtures and symphonies. My best attempt at explaining a rhapsody in terms of composing is to say it is like having to think a multitude of things in a single thought, and perhaps for many composers this doesn't come easily.

Just as a point of interest in this composition, there is a serene part 'the joy of love, remembering the lovely walks we used to have' that in my mind portrays Oaks Park, where Joy and I walked our lovely dogs. Under the trees in the woodland part where we would often stop and feed our dogs with a snack or two, I had a bench specially made in memory of Joy with her name inscribed on it.

While I was composing this rhapsody, a friend of Peps' visited us and gazing out of our conservatory, she suddenly exclaimed, "Oh look, an English country garden!" This chance remark gave me the idea to include the folk song, 'English Country Garden.' If you listen carefully, you will hear it alongside the pastoral theme which is playing 'above' the main theme, meaning lower and higher notes are playing simultaneously, yet in different rhythms. It isn't always easy to hear two themes played together, which is a method of composing known as a counterpoint.

Halfway through composing this piece, Gerhard interrupted me in a great panic. He urgently required me to compose two panoramic pieces for a large orchestra to record in Budapest, Hungary. I told him that I was in the middle of an important piece of work, but he wouldn't take "no!" for an answer! Finally, I gave in and carefully put my unfinished rhapsody aside for a while.

I wrote the two panoramic pieces and sent them off for copying in Germany to Gerhard. His son Gregor went over to Budapest from Hollywood to conduct these pieces of mine together with other composers' work, which was then recorded by the Sonoton Orchestra. In the circumstances, I am pleased to say the two compositions came out very well!

I had to get back to writing my own half-written rhapsody and it took me ages to find the little bits of paper I had written my notes on! I had thought of some good ideas whilst walking the dogs and had written rough little bits and pieces down on sheets of manuscript paper. When composing a large work, it's important to write ideas down straight away, which is similar to shorthand only in sketches. Good ideas are easily lost and even if what you have written down doesn't seem to fit at first, it's amazing how simply it all seems to fit together later, just like a jigsaw puzzle. This is the exciting part, when everything begins to take shape and the careful orchestration of the composition begins. At times, it can be very frustrating and I have learned that you have to be very patient in this line of work.

During the writing of this rhapsody, there were times when I would get up in the middle of the night and quietly orchestrate for a few hours in my studio. Time stands still in the middle of the night. It is so tranquil, the air is beautiful and in a strange way, you feel the whole world is yours alone. At times, it was the pressure of completing a piece that drove me to get up; under such peaceful conditions, the compositions would flow from my pen. Many, many times, in the past I have done this very thing, not really worrying about my lack of sleep, which I knew I could catch up on at any time.

I managed to begin again where I had left off and I completed my 'unfinished rhapsody' in just a few weeks! Perpetua didn't disturb me at all during the time I was writing it. The house was quiet; she didn't have the radio or the television on because she completely understands what makes me tick as a composer, leaving me alone to carry on my important work.

I do believe most composers need almost complete silence to write well. Any unnecessary sounds will interrupt important thoughts and it can be very frustrating to try to work under these conditions. However, Perpetua did keep me going with many cups of coffee, thank goodness!

Philip Lane produced this piece, which is nine minutes long, and recorded it at the Angel Studios, Islington, with Gavin conducting the wonderful Royal Ballet Sinphonia. I oversaw the whole recording in the control room with Philip. This new CD was released in 2007 under the Dutton label, called *British Light Music Premiers* and soon after its release, Brian Kay broadcast it on BBC Radio 3.

I certainly found this episode very challenging, writing and composing for two entirely different publishers. However, I am lucky to be able to put my hand to any kind of composing. I really believe I am blessed with real talent, which I think in any form, is a pure gift. If you do have such a gift, don't waste it, because you are one of the lucky ones in this world of ours.

54

Marriage to Perpetua

It was about the time I was composing *A Surrey Rhapsody* that life was about to take on another change for the better. Many of my friends and family were very surprised, but also very happy for me, when I announced I had asked Perpetua to marry me. I suppose after Joy, they thought I wouldn't want to be married again; however, Peps and I had developed a deep attachment to one another and unlike many other people, I am hopeless at looking after myself.

Our love cannot be compared with my love for Joy, and Pepsi, being such a wonderful person, understands that we both share equally in a loving relationship. We have a great fondness and gentle love for each other based on intelligent companionship and mutual respect. It is marvellous that a man at my age can find this kind of friendship and love; in my heart, I know Joy would be happy for me. Also, I am a hard man to live with and I don't have much patience, so to find someone like Peps who loves and cares for me in the way she does, I feel I couldn't be more blessed.

Peps has done so much for me over these past couple of years and first encouraged me to write this autobiography because she thought my life was so full of fascinating, interesting and unusual events, both privately and professionally.

We had been out to lunch at the Kingswood Arms and when we returned home, we were relaxing in the sitting room; suddenly, I knew what I wanted to do. I got on my knees to Peps and said, "I want to ask you something—would you marry me?" She looked very surprised and for what seemed the longest time, she didn't answer and I stayed there holding her hand. I knew it was a big undertaking for Peps as she had been very badly hurt over her first marriage. She had vowed never to marry again as she never wanted to find herself in a similar situation ever again. In fact, Peps had once told me she felt very bitter towards men.

Finally, she said, "Yes!" We hugged each other with both of us having tears of emotion in our eyes. Peps was quite overwhelmed and told me, "After ten years of being on my own I thought nobody will ever love me again."

How happy we felt with this unplanned moment! It just felt like it was the right time even though I didn't even have a ring to give to Peps! However, I bought the ring a couple of days later and we began to make our wedding plans.

On Wednesday, 4 October 2006, we married at the Registry Office in Weybridge, Surrey. We didn't have any celebrations that day because we were having a blessing the following Saturday at All Saint's Church in Banstead. Our blessing was a wonderful affair, although we did have a couple of little hiccups that added a little spice to our day!

On the morning, I got dressed in my white dinner jacket made by Harry Secombe's tailor and the one I always wear for conducting. Leaving Peps to get ready, I left for the church travelling in the special limousine we had hired. Our friend Sylvia had asked her if she wanted to stay at her house the night before, as it was a tradition the bride and bridegroom do not see each other before the ceremony. Peps didn't want to leave me on my own, so compromising she decided to sleep in our spare room.

I reached the church in plenty of time and helped to show everyone to their seats. With the bells chiming, there was a great atmosphere in the lovely old church as it buzzed with the voices of family, friends and musicians. Everything was perfect. Then the minutes began ticking by and there was no sign of Peps. I began to glance behind me rather anxiously thinking, "Late as usual!"

Fifteen minutes doesn't seem like a long time, but when you are waiting in a church in full view of everyone, it feels like two hours! It didn't help that the bell ringers had also given up and the congregation was becoming a little restless. I decided to go back outside to search for any signs of my bride.

After I had left the house, Peps waited in our spare room for the limo to return and pick her up. She waited and waited and waited. Finally, she went downstairs to the sitting room to her sister, brother and bridesmaids to find out what was happening. Nobody could understand what had delayed the limo, because the church was only a few minutes away.

Eventually a message came through that it had broken down and Peps had to travel to the church in the same car as the bridesmaids, Monica, her sister, and her brother, Edward. Luckily, there was a bottle of champagne in the limo to calm everyone's nerves.

For five long minutes, I waited outside the church with my best man, Adam Saunders, when finally I saw the white limo appear. Poor Peps, she certainly looked a little fraught when she emerged. Still, it was all soon forgotten with the bells chiming once more and Peps walking down the aisle looking radiant in her off-the-shoulder, oyster coloured, satin wedding dress and veil accompanied by her brother, Edward, the bridesmaids and flower girl. All was well!

The bell ringers rang us into this lovely old church to the strains of my pastoral piece 'Safe Grazing,' and on the piano Adam accompanied his lovely wife, Clare, as she sang a beautiful rendering of 'Over the Rainbow.' Our blessing took place in the middle of Harvest Festival and the whole church was full of flowers. My friend Geoff Barham led the All Saint's choir (he has been the conductor for a good many years now) and they sang an anthem of mine called 'The Haven of Thy Peace' for a cappella voices (meaning without instrument), followed by lovely words by the late Rev. Kenneth Tames, whose wife, Rosemary, was also present.

After the prayers, another one of my compositions called 'My Village' was played on CD and everyone was so quiet you could hear a pin drop! Peps' 31-year-old daughter, Nyasha, recited the beautiful words from the Bible, 1 Corinthians, Chapter 13, called 'The Theme of Love.' The Rev. David Chance, whose parents knew Zimbabwe very well, took the splendid service and he asked the many Zimbabweans present to stand up and sing. What an inspiring event that was!

They sang their hearts out and clapped in time as well as harmonising and ululating. This is a form of singing technique to express a celebration, particularly weddings, where it represents welcoming the bride and groom. The whole congregation also clapped their hearts out and joined in the fun. Singing my personal favourite hymn 'Jerusalem' was such a rousing performance, it nearly brought the church down! For me, it epitomised a very special English moment.

My favourite cousin on the Fox side of the family, Maureen, was one of the bridesmaids at the ripe age of seventy-eight! She did look lovely and certainly didn't look her age. The other bridesmaid was a young Zimbabwean girl called Miriam who is a relative of Peps and lives in the United Kingdom, and Daisy, a friend's granddaughter, was our pretty flower girl. Originally my stepson Andrew's children were going to be the flower girls, however two weeks before the wedding, Andrew called me to explain he couldn't go through with being at the church because it would remind him too much of his mother. Obviously, we were both very disappointed but we understood how he felt and were very glad they felt able to attend our wedding breakfast.

A South African friend of Peps called Zanele, a dazzling looking lady, flew in from her country on her own and arrived just an hour or so before the wedding ceremony. Both Peps' brother, Edward, and his sister, Monica, travelled from Zimbabwe to the United Kingdom for the very first time and they, too, only just arrived in time for the wedding ceremony.

It had taken some arranging to get them here for our wedding, as I had to appeal to the British Embassy in Zimbabwe to issue them both with a visa to allow them to come to the United Kingdom. My sister Judy was brought from Parkside Nursing Home to the church in a wheel chair and she looked very elegant dressed in a lovely frock and a gorgeous looking hat, all chosen by Peps. Judy joined in the singing of the well-known hymns enthusiastically and we were both very happy to see her enjoying herself so much, as we knew it wasn't much fun for her in the nursing home.

After the service, most of our guests had their photographs taken outside the church. There is a lovely pampas grass growing in the grounds of All Saint's Church and it was in front of these magnificent grasses that the Zimbabweans met the English with lots of hugging and kissing. This was probably one of my favourite moments, seeing our guests looking so happy and colourful. Yes, for me it was a most magical and very emotional moment.

Photographs were taken amidst laughter and a few tears of joy with my music playing in the background. Many groups of wonderful friends with many musicians and well-known composers including Philip Lane, Gavin Sutherland with his wife, Verity, the famous clarinettist, Gerhard and Heidi are all captured on film against the entrance to the church, with Pepsi's choice of pink roses and lilies surrounding the arched door. One photograph we particularly liked was of Peps and me together with all the lovely ladies. As you can imagine, I liked that very much!

Gerhard and Heidi, as usual, had travelled from Munich to be with us on this day with our friends Peter Taylor and his Spanish wife, Alice, also travelling from Calafell in Northern Spain. Brian Allgar, who is a fellow musician, came over from Paris with his bubbly attractive wife, Francoise. There were many more guests from all walks of life who had made a big effort to make our big day such a special event. I thank God it was such a blessed occasion with the sun shining brightly upon us.

After the ceremony, all the guests made their way to the Bridge House Hotel on Reigate Hill, about seven miles from the church. There is a wonderful view of the Surrey countryside at the top of that hill, called Collie Hill, and on that lovely sunny afternoon, the wonderful pastoral view was crystal clear.

On our arrival, everyone was sitting down, and then as we entered, Clare, Adam's wife, went to the door and said, "Welcome and congratulations to John and Peps." Everyone stood up and clapped and I replied, "Thank you one and all." It was a wonderful moment. The room was full of genial noise with lots of drinking and talking: snatches of conversation, such as, "I haven't seen you for ages!"—"How are you?"—"You don't look a day older!"—gossip, gossip, gossip, but very happy gossip. Everyone was so happy, and they talked the afternoon away.

We had a most delicious wedding breakfast with many of our guests commenting pleasantly about the abundance of champagne and wine. Our guests were all seated on seven or eight large long tables with the top table consisting of Peps and me, Gerhard and Heidi, Adam and Clare Saunders, the bridesmaids and a few other very close friends.

Gerhard and I chatted about the Zimbabwean music sung at the blessing, which he had enjoyed so much, and he asked me to think about composing some of this type of music. He told me it would certainly add something special to his Sonoton Music Library.

Then we had the speeches. Adam opened with a wonderful tribute to me, speaking about my achievements and how much pleasure my music has given to so many people all over the world, helping to make their lives a little extra special. He told our guests he grew up with my music, listening to it almost every day and night because he so enjoyed my arrangement and composition styles. I am very fond of

Adam and he is almost like a son to me. In my own speech I said, "Adam regards me as a great-great-grandfather!" which brought great peals of laughter throughout the room! Adam even showed some of my LPs to the guests including, *Gershwin, Here There and Everywhere, Memory, Colours in Rhythm, Tinkling Piano, Unforgettable Melodies* and *Fairest Isle.*

Adam also has great affection for Peps and he asked everyone to raise their glasses and drink a toast to the bride and the bridegroom. Then a good friend of Peps, Abigail, sang a very sad song, unaccompanied, about saying goodbye to Africa. She had left there a long time ago and now lives permanently in the United Kingdom. Abigail is also a great character with a wonderful ability to make everyone laugh. Perpetua's eldest brother, Edward, made an emotional speech as he talked about his rural life in Zimbabwe and how grateful and honoured he was to be at our wedding and what a great day it was for him. He said he would never forget the welcome he received and in fact, many of our guests were quite tearful after his speech.

He has been a headmaster in several schools in Zimbabwe for well over twenty years and had never travelled by air anywhere! Edward and I had some very good conversations during the time he was here for three weeks. He really is a true gentleman and everyone liked him very much.

Another special friend, Peter Rix, also made a speech. He has one tremendous library of very old records through to the CD era and is a great fan of mine. He is also one hell of a handyman when I need his help! After Peter, came his very talented wife, Sylvia, with a spark! She began her speech by saying, emotionally, "I'd like to say hello to Africa." Sylvia is a lovely person, who is extremely kind and has lots of personality. Now I call this lady talented because she is so very artistic at arranging flowers and she arranged most of the flowers at our wedding, both at the church and the reception at the Bridge House.

She also made the wedding cake, which was delicious, to say the least. The subject of her speech to both of us was about the ingredients of the special wedding cake that was mixed with one pound of love, half a pound of this and that, and she talked through the many special ways she made the cake, mixing it thoroughly so it would last forever!

It was in three tiers, the same colour as Pepsi's dress with pink roses and lilies decorating the sides. On each tier, it had a set of words with the top layer saying, 'To Have,' the middle layer, 'To Hold,' and the bottom layer saying, 'To Cherish.'

Gerhard also made a most splendid speech. He has known me since 1973 and has been with me through all my ups and downs in my life. Heidi also stood up with her husband and she calls me "chohn." Finally, it was my turn and I thanked everyone who had helped me over the years and friends who have come into our lives quite recently.

After the speeches came the music with the Adam Saunders Trio, with lovely Clare singing. Philip Lane and I were requested to play on the keyboard and he played one piece, 'As Time Goes By' and I played my favourite piano piece, 'Misty.' The end of a perfect day and evening!

Perpetua and I stayed at the Bridge House in a special bridal suite. How spoiled we were! However, we had a very funny situation the next morning. We had brought a suitcase with us and without realizing it, had left our day clothes at home. When we woke, we didn't have anything to get dressed into! We asked Nyasha to take Pepsi's car and return to Coniston to collect our clothes. Unfortunately, she took a wrong turn just before the Bridge House and found herself driving on the M25 in the wrong direction!

Once more that weekend, we were waiting and waiting. Eventually, our guests who had also stayed at the hotel came to say goodbye to us in our bridal suite and we had to greet them dressed only in pyjamas and dressing gowns! At last, Nyasha made her way back to Coniston and to our hotel three hours later. What a comedy situation, and we all laughed about it afterwards!

Peter Taylor from Spain wrote a wonderful article about this wedding of ours in the magazine *Journal into Melody,* which featured two colour photographs, one with all the composers and Perpetua, the only woman in the picture, and one with Perpetua and me outside the church with the pampas grass in the background. We are both so thankful to Peter and his wife, Alice, for taking the trouble to write this fabulous article.

We of course have some marvellous photographs and a video of the day and many of our guests called us later congratulating us on such a wonderful event. This was indeed a very, very special day for us and one we shall never forget.

55

Conductors and Special Musicians

At this point, I would like to talk about conducting, as it is an important part of a musician's life. Conducting music has been about for longer than many may believe, with hand gestures being used as far back as the Middle Ages; then during the seventeenth century, rolled up sheets of paper were used or small sticks. Felix Mendelssohn claimed to be the first conductor to use a wooden baton to direct musical beat.

During the 1968 election campaign in the United States, someone asked Eugene McCarthy what qualified him to be president of the United States. He replied that neither he, nor anyone, was probably qualified. Apparently, the same has been said about conducting, and it is widely accepted there are not many conductors who have the versatility, or possess the complete set of skills required to conduct any style of music. Some only know how to conduct classical music or specialize in jazz and I wonder if an out-and-out classical musician could conduct a jazz orientated piece like, 'Take the A Train.'

I class myself as a versatile all-rounder and seem to have the ability to adapt the different styles required to compose, conduct or arrange a wide range of music. This includes classical, jazz, light music, musicals for shows or film, popular songs and comedy pieces.

I began my conducting life through the music of Eric Coates, together with other light music composers. I was very lucky to conduct mostly my own music over the years, whether as compositions, arrangements or accompanying a singer or a choir. Although I did have a few lessons at one time, this is a skill I acquired through the actual 'doing' together with trial and error, rather than through any traditional training.

One vital lesson I learned about conducting is how important it is the orchestra likes and relates to the conductor, as this makes a real difference to the quality of the music being played. In my own experience, I believe each conductor has his or her own style and I always achieved the results I wanted with my own methods from the many orchestras I have conducted over sixty years. This is mostly because I can 'feel' the music and the art of conducting comes as naturally to me as composing or arranging. One other important factor is being able to judge your performers, which requires tact and empathy.

In addition to being a superb pianist, Gavin Sutherland is a very likable and very good conductor who is a composer and arranger. In recent years, he has often conducted my compositions and arrangements in exactly the way I like it! Being a worldwide conductor, he is very much in demand and has often said to me sadly, he hasn't much time for composing these days.

In the early days when the BBC played a lot of light classical, easy listening music, they used arrangers and composers to conduct their own styles, which of course included me. We would tend to conduct our own music arrangements together with a few original compositions thrown in and although I have conducted well-known classical music such as Chopin, Beethoven and Ravel, composing and arranging is more important to me than conducting.

Gavin came to see me in 2006, when we were going over a composition of mine that he was preparing to conduct when he asked, "Have you got anything for clarinet and piano?" I have to mention that the clarinet is one of my favourite instruments and straightaway I said there is a file in my studio with all my old compositions and there might be something in it. To my great relief, I found some sketches! I remembered it was recorded to tape and after listening to the piece, Gavin said he would consider it for an album he was about to make with Verity.

The composition in question is simply called, *Six Sketches for Clarinet and Piano,* which I wrote for my clarinet friend Alan Hartwell, who has been recording sessions with some of the biggest names in jazz since 1958. As well as teaching and playing in military bands, interestingly, in his early years, Alan also taught Verity on the clarinet. I wrote these six sketches with myself on the piano when we were both students at the Royal College of Music many moons ago! Gavin decided he really liked my sketches and he recorded these for his album produced with Verity on a CD called *Clarinet Kaleidoscope* on the Campion Cameo Label in 2007, where he accompanies Verity on the piano.

This album also contains the works of well-known English composers such as the composer and symphonist Sir Malcolm Arnold, who died in 2006, Philip Lane, Ernest Tomlinson, who founded 'The Library of Light Orchestral Music' in 1984, after he found out the BBC were disposing of their light music archive, and Gordon Jacob, best known for his wind instrumental compositions.

Sometime later, I wrote a *Sonata for Clarinet and Piano,* which Gavin wants to record on the next *Clarinet Kaleidoscope Vol. 3.* As there appears to be quite a shortage of this type of music, I think these six sketches for clarinet and piano would fit very well into the Associated Board Exams for Grade 6 or 7, but it is doubtful this will happen as the Board has a tradition of using the classical composers—they tend to be intellectual 'snobs.' This is a real shame, as there are a number of contemporary composers who have much to offer that is entirely suitable for a wide range of age groups from young people upwards.

Early in February 2007, I organized an evening at home with a piano recital by Juliet Chaplin. Playing beautifully on my French Gaveau grand piano, she recited the most intricate and highly technical pieces you could imagine including Bach, Mozart, Beethoven, Chopin, Brahms and Ravel. The house was packed with musical friends and it proved to be a very successful evening with Peps providing the finishing touches, with a fine buffet and drinks for our guests after the recital.

While talking about famous musicians, it is important to mention Don Lusher, who in most people's opinions, including mine, was one of the finest trombonists in the world. He was well-known for his association with the Ted Heath Jazz Band where he was the leading trombonist for nine years. He received an OBE in 2002 for his services to the music industry and died in 2006 in his early eighties. He came with his wife, Diana, to my eightieth birthday party and also the launching party for my CD *Voyage of a Lifetime.*

Sadly, Diana died very soon after him. Don truly was one of the *greats* and what a gentleman! Our kind of music will never be the same without him. He played many times on my sessions and concerts with the BBC Big Band at Maida Vale and at the Golders Green Hippodrome.

Another guest at my eightieth was the popular journalist and broadcaster, the likeable Sheila Tracy, who for many years was one of the trombonists in the Ivy Benson All Girls Band. She then formed a vocal and trombone duo called 'The Tracy Sisters' appearing in radio and TV. Sheila was the first female News Reader on BBC Radio 4 and introduced the *BBC Big Band Special* for twelve years in its heyday. She later became presenter of the BBC Radio Big Band conducted by Barry Forgie, while also compiling an extremely interesting book called *Who's Who in Popular Music* in 1984.

It includes the most popular British artists, singers and groups and I appear with my photograph in the second section, which lists composers, arrangers and conductors. In more recent years, Sheila has been giving lectures on the P&O Liners about swing time and jazz, together with presenting on Prime Time and Saga Radio Stations. We have known each other for many years and we are almost neighbours as she lives in Kingswood, just a short distance from Banstead.

An outstanding musician who died quite young many years ago and whose wife died very soon afterwards was Bernard George. He played the clarinet and the saxophone beautifully and we were great friends. In my early years, Bernard used to play in the Harold Turner Quartet when I was the pianist at the Jacaranda Club in Chelsea, London. We played some wonderful jazz at that club before we eventually went our separate ways. Later, Bernard joined the BBC Radio Big Band where he played baritone saxophone and bass clarinet and in my days as conductor and arranger for the BBC, I also worked with the Big Band combined with the whole Radio Orchestra. So once again we played together.

He particularly admired the introduction of my arrangement of 'I Feel a Song Comin' On,' which begins very softly and gradually crescendos using modern harmonies, which means I was adapting the music in an extra special way. For instance, making three-note chords and adding six more notes to produce richer harmonic sounds and I used this method to lead into the chorus.

Before we began this piece, Bernard would throw me a special look full of pride and whenever I play that arrangement, which has been recorded from our broadcasts on CD and is often aired in the United States on the radio, I think of Bernard and his special glance of admiration and approval. When he died, I found it difficult to accept the loss of such a great musician and friend.

56

Classical Composers

As the years move on with my music career, one of the issues that come frequently to mind is a musician's rights to royalties today. When I began composing seriously nearly seventy years ago, the fact I might be financially rewarded for my music composed at that time was the last thing on my mind. I am blessed with a gift and I wouldn't choose my life any differently even if this wasn't the case.

As with any art form, musicians like myself bring so much enjoyment to people all over the world and this giving of pleasure it's something we love and enjoy ourselves. It helps to bring happiness to people's lives in the midst of all the angst and sadness humanity faces on this imperfect planet and it is only right we are paid for our creativity. This has not always been the case with the Performing Rights Society (PRS) only coming into existence in 1914.

The PRS ensures we are properly paid through collecting fees on behalf of composers, songwriters and music publishers for music played in any public place outside the home, from all over the world. This brings me to the subject of our classical composers, most of whom had very hard lives.

A certain English genius largely self-taught was Sir Edward Elgar, who struggled for recognition in class-conscious Victorian England. He was the son of a piano tuner and music dealer and married one of his pupils, Caroline Alice Roberts, who was eight years older than her husband. His wife's family was against the marriage as he was seen to belong to another class and she was the daughter of a major-general. She also became his business manager, supporting him endlessly and it is generally accepted he did little work of importance after her death. Knighted in 1904, at forty-six years old by King Edward VII, he was the first composer to make extensive recordings of his music through 'His Master's Voice' insisting his music should be paid for when it was performed in public. Between 1901 and 1930, Elgar composed the five *Pomp and Circumstance Marches,* for which he is probably best remembered.

I was commissioned to arrange Elgar's work including 'Nimrod' from the *Enigma Variations,* and make them shorter in length. I recorded these works at CTS Studios in London with a 90-piece orchestra and was the first composer in 1987 to have my music recorded digitally at these famous studios.

The music of the prolific German composer Johann Sebastian Bach was not particularly popular during his lifetime as he was better known as an organist. He composed more than one thousand works and today is considered one of the great masters of music. At the beginning of his career, he was a court musician, and then spent his last thirty years working for St. Thomas' Church and School in Leipzig, where he died in 1750 at age sixty-five.

When I was recording one of my big sessions in Leipzig, I visited this large church, which is quite magnificent. There was a young organist playing Bach's organ works beautifully on the original organ that Bach had played on. Bach had twenty children, ten of whom died in infancy and he became blind in the last year of his life.

Mozart, born in 1756, greatly admired Bach and began composing at five years old and playing in piano concerts when he was just eight years old. At this young age, he even performed at concerts in London with his older sister playing piano duets. How amused and thrilled I was to learn that just as I did from an early age, Mozart began his music career by imitating music instruments! Throughout his life, he wrote a dozen operas, including *Cosi Fan Tutte, The Marriage of Figaro* and *Don Giovanni.* He wrote in almost every music genre, including symphony, opera, concerto, chamber, piano concerto and sonatas. The Pope knighted him at fourteen years and in childhood, he played with Marie Antoinette. Yet, when he died at age thirty-five, nobody was at his funeral and he was placed in an unmarked grave! Can you believe this?

Three years before his death, he wrote three symphonies and these are considered amongst the finest ever written. He rightly predicted his last work, *Requiem,* was an omen and only just managed to conduct the premier of *The Magic Flute,* two months before he died. It is believed he was poisoned by his rival composer, Salieri, who envied him.

In 1770, Ludwig van Beethoven, who is often referred to as the 'Shakespeare of music,' was born into a musical but poor family. He was a great composer and virtuoso pianist, who in 1814, began to experience the first signs of deafness, becoming completely deaf by the time he was thirty. At one time, his affliction distressed him so much he thought about committing suicide. On his brother's death, despite the fact his brother's wife was still living, he became obsessed with a custody row over his nine-year-old nephew. This took its toll on his music and during this time, he stopped composing completely.

He composed his famous *Ninth Symphony* and five string quartets before he died in 1827, at age fifty-six during a terrific thunderstorm in Vienna. How often I have thought of this great man and I personally cannot begin to comprehend what it is like being completely deaf and composing something that you cannot hear. I can only think he must have had perfect pitch in his mind and his brain heard it in notation.

I have orchestrated and recorded Beethoven's *Moonlight Sonata,* a piece he composed for the piano and one I have also arranged for a chamber ensemble, on an album called *Classical Arrangements* for the Sounds Stage Music Library recorded at the Ian Dale studios. His pieces that are popular throughout the world today still sound original and quite unique, which is testament his compositions were first class. Whatever the original composition might be, if it has been written in the purest music forms, it will always sound wonderful even if it is played on a mouth organ.

He never married but had affairs with his female pupils and at one time fell into debt. What would we music lovers do without Beethoven! Beethoven is the only composer whose work began with the Classical and ended with the Romantic Movement, resulting in his enormous influence on future generations of composers.

Franz Schubert, born in 1797 in Vienna, was Beethoven's contemporary and he would often see Beethoven sitting alone in the coffeehouse he visited, but Schubert never plucked up the courage to go over and speak to him. Schubert wrote nine symphonies including the famous *Unfinished Symphony,* sonatas, string quartets, composed chamber and solo piano music and was almost as prolific as Bach, writing 998 works!

In 1827, he was a torchbearer at Beethoven's funeral, dying just one year later, at the young age of thirty-one. During his lifetime, his music was not widely appreciated and he didn't seem to be able to find suitable employment resulting in relying on friends and family to financially support him. Since the age of twenty-five, he had battled syphilis and was treated with mercury, which was the popular remedy for this condition at the time. Although he died of typhoid fever some of the symptoms match mercury poisoning. At one time, he was admitted to an asylum when he was seriously ill. A piano was brought in to enable Schubert to continue composing and playing, so he would often be heard playing to the very unfortunate sick people incarcerated in the place. Schubert requested to be buried in a grave next to Beethoven.

Moving from Germany and Austria to Russia, during the great Romantic era we have Tchaikovsky. What a composer! It was his mother's death in 1854 from cholera that drove him to music and within a few weeks of her death, he was composing serious works. He began life as a civil servant, when told by one of his music teachers he had nothing much to offer in the way of musical talent! He married one of his students briefly; however, it didn't work out, probably because he was homosexual. His works include his famous three ballets *Romeo and Juliet, The Nutcracker* and *Swan Lake,* alongside his many symphonies and piano concertos of the Romantic era.

I have arranged *Romeo and Juliet,* which in my opinion is one of the best melodies of all and one of the best ballets. I didn't look at the score because I thought I would write a better arrangement by just listening to the music on a CD. My arrangement consisted of taking the main theme and bringing out the melody, concentrating on what I believed would be enjoyable to listen to, rather than reproducing it as a ballet piece and perhaps also to look at the music in the same way Tchaikovsky might have done in today's world. It was a condensed arrangement, using a full symphony orchestra and recorded on the *Heart Strings* album by Sonoton.

Despite warnings by friends who were present at the time, in 1893 during a cholera outbreak in St. Petersburg, he drank non-boiled water and died a week later of cholera, nine days after the premier of his *Sixth Symphony.* Many at the time wondered if it was a deliberate attempt at suicide.

The one I regard as the 'poet of the piano' is of course the most famous of Polish composers, Chopin. His preludes have so much feeling and I find them delightful to play. Born in 1810, in a small village on the outskirts of Warsaw, Chopin suffered throughout his short life with ill health. He was friends with the Hungarian composer Liszt, who greatly admired his work and all his compositions involved solo piano or piano with other instruments. He was also responsible for creating a new musical form called the 'ballade.'

He left Warsaw just before the 'November Uprising' in 1830, travelling first to Vienna then on to Paris, unsure of where he wanted to settle. However, he made a comfortable living as a composer and piano teacher in Paris until he fled from the Revolution to England.

While in Paris, he had a romantic liaison for over ten years with George Sand the famous female French Romantic writer, but he never married. There was a time when he went on holiday in Mallorca not far from the special place Joy and I stayed at in Puerto Pollensa. Apparently, he went there to convalesce at a monastery with George Sand and we visited this place during one of our holidays and saw the plaque stating his visit.

Chopin stayed just a year in London, hurrying back to Paris when he knew he was dying. Suffering from tuberculosis, he died at the age of thirty-nine in 1849. He requested Mozart's *Requiem* together with his own *Funeral March* at his funeral, which was attended by over three thousand mourners. He is buried at the Père-Lachaise in Paris, which is one of the most famous cemeteries in the world. I orchestrated one of his nocturnes, the popular one in E-flat that was originally written for piano and one hell of a melodic piano piece.

Brahms wrote many wonderful piano pieces; however I have found it difficult to play his music, which is the case with many pianists. He had a close friendship with Schumann and was a lifelong friend of Johann Strauss. Born in Hamburg, he was one of the most influential composers of the early twentieth century with the wide variety of styles he used in his music. He didn't marry and lived in furnished rooms for much of his life, despite the fact in later years he became quite wealthy and could afford to change his lifestyle.

Instead, he would help finance promising young musicians and give his money away to help others. Brahms was a perfectionist and destroyed much of his earlier work. Like Beethoven, he loved nature and was very fond of walking, often taking long walks in the woods around Vienna. He died in Vienna in 1897 of cirrhosis of the liver at age sixty-three.

The founder of the French Impressionist School (which is my favourite school of music) was Debussy. His most popular pieces are *Clair de Lune* for piano and a prelude for orchestra called *L'Apres-*

midi d'un Faune (Afternoon of a Fawn), a most beautiful piece of French impressionistic music for orchestra. Developing his own style, particularly in harmonies, Debussy certainly brought new and fresh sounds to music, which I think took a few years to catch on with the listening public at that time. He was born in 1862 and died in 1918, towards the end of World War I of colorectal cancer, having survived one of the earliest known colostomy operations a couple of years previously.

Shortly after Debussy, comes my very favourite composer, Maurice Ravel, who was born in the Basque country and studied at the Paris Conservatoire at the age of fourteen. He was a progressive composer, whose *Bolero* is probably the most popular piece he composed because it was used in a film called *10* featuring Dudley Moore and Bo Derek. If you have never listened to his fantastic ballet *Daphnis and Chloe,* then I suggest you get a copy of a CD to hear this great work for yourself immediately! Especially, the *Dawn Suite.*

The orchestration and added wordless choir of this wonderful work, absolutely takes your breath away. Hearing it takes one into a different, magical world. The daybreak part of this great work, when gradually the world comes alive, is very emotional and pastoral, with the sounds of wildlife bringing tears to the eyes because of the greatness and wonder of this phenomenal piece. That is Ravel's music at its very best. It has not often been performed as a ballet, only purely as a suite.

He wrote *Pavane for a Dead Infanta,* a very sad piece that began as a piano solo and then later orchestrated. I have arranged this *Pavane* for orchestra and soprano saxophone and it was beautifully played by Lara James and recorded on a CD. This instrument is quite uncommon and it sounds so lovely in its low register.

Ravel took a blow to the head in a taxi accident in Paris and soon after began to suffer from a brain disorder similar to 'Pick's Disease.' He died after an unsuccessful operation for a brain tumour in 1937 at age sixty-two. Ravel's music will always remain in my heart and I could go on forever about this French genius.

This brief summary of some of the most famous composers leaves many unmentioned but it does give you a taste of what musicians over the centuries have endured particularly financial and personal hardship in their quest to bring music to the ears of the people.

57

English Composers, American Jazz and Musicals

I am proud to be an Englishman through and through, with no 'ifs or buts'! How sad I feel that it seems we rarely use the word 'English' these days and yet we still hear about the Welsh, the Scottish and the Irish. Each country has its own special anthem which the people are proud of and I don't blame them! Many great functions in England play 'Jerusalem,' which in my opinion is worthy enough to be our National Anthem, especially with the last words ending 'in England's green and pleasant land.'

At football matches and many other sporting events, thousands of people join in this rousing emotional song and it brings tears to the eyes of many who take part in these great occasions. 'Jerusalem' is an extremely patriotic song and it spells out in huge letters— *ENGLAND!*

Returning to the subject of great composers, we had a big gap in England from 1695 to 1848. Henry Purcell died in 1695, at age thirty-six, and the next notable composer did not come along until Sir Hubert Parry, who was born in 1848. He wrote the glorious music of 'Jerusalem,' to the magical words by the wonderful poet William Blake. Born in Bournemouth, Dorset, Parry was greatly influenced by Bach and Brahms and one of his finest achievements at the time was 'Blest Pair of Sirens,' which established him as a leading composer. He became a knight in 1898.

I have already mentioned the most popular of all English composers, Sir Edward Elgar, and my personal favourites of his are *Cockaigne Overture, The Cello Concerto, Enigma Variations,* with especially *Nimrod* and *Pomp and Circumstances.*

The next composer was Albert Delius, born in Bradford England and of German parentage. Later in life, possibly suffering from the symptoms of syphilis, he went blind. His 'On Hearing the First Cuckoo in Spring' is a typically beautiful and extremely pastoral English piece. Studying music in Leipzig, he became a lifelong friend of Grieg and when he died he was originally buried in Grez, a small French village near Fontainebleau. Despite the fact he spent most of his life living in France, he left express wishes to be buried in 'a quiet country churchyard in a south of England village.' His remains were subsequently exhumed and he was buried at Church of Saint Peter, in Limpsfield Surrey, quite close to the grave of the great lady pianist, Eileen Joyce.

Other popular composers include Sir William Walton, who wrote film scores in addition to his other work, Rodger Quilter, who was known for his light music as well as his songs, and Benjamin Britton, with probably the best known work of his career being *War Requiem.* He wrote this in 1962 for the consecration of Coventry Cathedral, which had just been built. Original in his style, Vaughan Williams was famous for composing and film scores in addition to being a prolific collector of English folk songs and music and a great teacher. He was a lecturer in music and he founded the Leith Hill Festivals in Surrey. He lived near Dorking in Surrey all his life and died at the age of eighty-six.

John Ireland, a lifelong bachelor, was a frequent visitor to the Channel Islands where the landscape inspired much of his work. He was a wonderful composer and I met him when I was a student at the Royal College of Music, where one of his past pupils was Benjamin Britton. While I was there, he gave an interesting talk to about 150 students about his life as a composer and because there where no CDs in those days, he played his music live or from LPs on a record player. I particularly remember he had very large hands and at times seemed a little heavy-handed as a pianist.

All these composers had the lyrical, melodic and nostalgic English style, which is also often referred to as romantic and timeless. About this time in America, the black composers of jazz such as Duke Ellington, Louis Armstrong, the wonderful trumpet player, and Oscar Peterson, the great jazz pianist, came to the foreground. They contributed to the world of jazz in a big way. It was Scott Joplin, the American composer of ragtime music who also wrote the famous 'The Entertainer,' who began it all and it progressed into that scene with jazz singers including Billie Holiday, Ella Fitzgerald, Sarah Vaughan and Nat King Cole.

In the United Kingdom before World War II, we had big bands such as Tommy Dorsey, Robert Farnon and Glen Miller, who all produced a different type of dance and jazzy music, generally with added strings, which quickly became very popular.

The great songwriter at this time was George Gershwin, who actually went over to France to visit Ravel as he wanted to learn more about orchestration. However, the great French composer said to Gershwin, "You are so famous in the States—*you* should teach *me!*"

Then the terrific film scene came to Hollywood with the silent movie period with the never to be forgotten English comedian, Charlie Chaplin, who never ceases to make me laugh and sometimes cry. A year after I was born in 1925, *Phantom of the Opera* with Lon Chaney came on the scene—or screen!

Then along came talking pictures with the first musical ever made as a 'talkie' with Al Jolson in *The Jazz Singer*. Other magical musicals include the *Gold Digger,* with the famous dancing pair Fred Astaire and Ginger Rodgers, featuring such wonderful lyrical songs by Irving Berlin, Cole Porter, and Jerome Kern.

The talent in Hollywood at that time was unbelievable and what about Walt Disney's Mickey Mouse, Donald Duck and Goofy cartoons? I think they were called Silly Symphonies. Just before World War II came the first full-length Disney cartoon, *Snow White and the Seven Dwarfs* in wonderful Technicolor.

I'm still inclined to think this film is the best of the bunch with such a wonderful array of tuneful songs. Such talents! The next Disney movie was *Bambi,* a film which still makes me shed a tear or two at my age! A great genius Walt Disney was to say the least! Around about the same time as 'Snow White,' the film of *all* films came out. The mighty, *Gone with the Wind.* What a film!

What a story! And what a wonderful score by Max Steiner! The stars Vivien Leigh, Clark Gable, Olivia de Havilland and Leslie Howard are unforgettable, too. Also, to my great delight in 2008, for the first time, it became a stage play, which was wonderful news that this timeless classic still appears to have appeal today. Sadly, this joy was short-lived with the play closing down after only two months.

Most people who went to see it raved about it, yet the critics were so harsh in savaging it again and again. A real pity.

The theme tune to this film is called 'Tara's Theme' and I was commissioned quite a number of years ago to write an arrangement of this music. A short while ago, I received a CD of the Film Philharmonic Orchestra playing concert music and being conducted by Frank Strobel in Hamburg. How thrilling it was to see that the very first piece was my arrangement of 'Tara's Theme.'

It sounds magnificent and it makes me feel so proud because judging by their applause, the audience seemed to love it, too. Over the years, it certainly seems to be an immensely popular piece as it is regularly selected for playing at concerts. I can honestly say that despite the fact I have conducted this piece myself a number of times, none of them have been as excellent as this performance and it certainly is a remarkable rendering of my arrangement.

This arrangement of it has proved to be very popular as I've received quite a number of royalties for the hiring of this piece. Many of my other big orchestral arrangements of popular film themes have also been played abroad from time to time, but for me nothing is as good as 'Tara's Theme' played at that Hamburg concert.

Mickey Rooney and Judy Garland also starred in fabulous musical films, including *Babes in Arms* and *Strike up the Band,* which are two of my favourites. Mickey Rooney is still alive in his late eighties at this time and still going strong! Another of my favourites is *The Wizard of Oz,* with Judy Garland's wonderful interpretation of Dorothy and her heartfelt rendering of the great emotional song 'Over the Rainbow.' In my opinion, this is one of the most touching moments in the history of musical films and always manages to bring tears to my eyes, no matter how many times I hear it sung.

Quite recently, a young English girl, age six, was in a talent show on TV and she sang 'Over the Rainbow' beautifully and with so much emotion. How talented I thought for a very young pretty girl to sing such an old song and I can honestly tell you, Peps and I were both in tears at that wonderful rendering. Musical talent is always around, but I feel at times you have to look very hard and listen for it! 'Pop' is not music to my ears; it is a means of letting yourself go in the loudest possible, uncreative way!

Of course, that doesn't apply to all our contemporary musicians and it is wonderful to learn Sir Andrew Lloyd Webber is trying desperately to get easy listening classical music back with his series on television for a 'Maria' in *The Sound of Music* and *Joseph and the*

Technicolor Dreamcoat. My favourite of all Lord Lloyd Webber's masterpieces is *Phantom of the Opera,* especially the film version.

Watching it recently reminded me how I could watch it over and over again! The array of songs, both lyrics and music are so melodic. Sir Andrew was quite original in writing the lovely song from *The Phantom* called 'All I Ask of You,' which of course was one of Joy's favourite songs. When the actual chorus comes in, 'Then say you'll love me every waking moment,' the key it is sung in is Db major and it jumps from the top E-flat down to the D-flat, a semitone above middle C. This is quite difficult to pitch, and the many times I've heard this song live, there seems to be that slightly out of tune feel. It is actually a ninth distance between the top E-flat down to the low D-flat, but to me, this is pure magic when it is sung in tune by both the soprano and the tenor voices.

Many of us hope and pray for some producer to come up with something exciting, for example a full symphony orchestra playing light classical music in a well-known hall while being televised or broadcast. I accept that this type of music is not as mainstream as it used to be, yet there are still millions of people out there who love listening to it and don't often have the opportunity, especially in the United Kingdom. Fashions, of course, change and I pray it won't be too long before the light music era comes trip, trip, tripping from our radios once more.

58

Hugh's Courage and Jam Sessions

Now I would like to tell you about a very tall, courageous friend—Hugh. He has been suffering from Leukaemia for about five years now and has been through the most shocking times. This includes many blood transfusions and confinement to an isolated care unit where he was unconscious for quite a while. His will to live is amazing and he simply will not give in to this dreadful disease.

Only recently, I was so surprised to see him strolling slowly around the field at the bottom of my garden with his precious apricot coloured poodle. He calmly said, "Good morning John," as if nothing had happened in between. Do you know what he said to me? "The only thing that has pulled me through this awful period in my life is walking my dog round this wonderful, magnificent field." I can tell his dog really loves him and they seem to share a special relationship. I can quite understand how this simple pleasure means so much to him.

To reach our field from his house, there is quite a steep hill and generally, he uses his car to come here. However, the last few times I've seen him, he has walked all the way here and back! His determination and courage are quite remarkable and I've promised I will write a composition about him. This gesture touched him deeply and he told me he felt highly honoured.

I feel I need to write this tribute to Hugh in a *Nimrod* sort of way, from Elgar's *Enigma Variations,* which has very strong overtures and is very English. It is wonderful to still be composing music at my age, although it's something I love so much I would never dream of stopping. My latest work was about Christmas, commissioned by the Oxford University Press. Evidently, it seems there is a great shortage of carol music for symphony orchestras and I was delighted to have the opportunity to arrange many of our classic carols. I called my arrangement *Carol Fantasia,* which included, 'Little Town of Bethlehem,' 'Hark the Herald Angels Sing,' and 'The Holly and the Ivy.' The Bournemouth Symphony Orchestra played these selections during Christmas 2007 in Bournemouth.

In recent years, I have become very friendly with more of my neighbours, including Sally and David Frost who live just over the road from us. David plays drums, and knows a very good bass guitar player called Richard and we sometimes have 'jam sessions' consisting of piano, bass and drums, which we enjoy immensely. I used to love playing for this type of combination when I was much younger, and it takes me back to the days of my youth. Isn't it strange how seventy years later, you come back, as it were, to the number you "first thought of!"

Another recent friend is the lovely Carmenna Bailey and her husband, Richard, who also live just a few minutes walk away. I feel Carmenna is an extra special lady, who I first met in the field with her bouncy, black dog Lucy. She has a wonderful, kind personality and when she is around, her presence and humour certainly make life worth living.

At one of the 'jam session' evenings here at home, I was playing piano with David's friend Richard playing bass and David the drums. Getting carried away, (not in the true sense of the word!), I played some lovely melodies while still managing to improvise at my tender age! I gave both Richard and David solos and we all extemporized (that's improvising in layman's terms), until the cows came home! We had a lovely 'jazzy' evening with the girls and Peps sitting in the conservatory in the dark, chatting, eating and drinking while we played the night away all feeling as if much younger, especially me!

I love listening to Oscar Peterson, George Shearing and Roy Budd, who died in 1993 of a brain hemorrhage at the age of thirty-seven. Roy began playing the piano at just over two years old! His widow, Sylvia Budd, originally from Paris, came to see me a short while ago because she wanted to talk about her husband's music to the silent movie version of *Phantom of the Opera.* Peps and I have become very good friends with her. Roy could really play wonderful jazz and he was a child prodigy, playing solo piano on BBC Radio at the age of six. He has composed music for sixty films with his best known being the score for the 1971 Michael Caine film *Get Carter.* What a tragic waste that he should die so young.

59

Concert for Princess Diana

Along with many millions around the world, I watched the *Concert for Princess Diana* on 1 July 2007, the day she would have been forty-six years old and nearly the tenth anniversary of her death. Primarily, it was a concert organized by Prince William and Prince Harry as a tribute to their mother and a celebration of her life. It also helped to raise thousands of pounds for a number of charities, including Centrepoint, which is a London-based charity for homeless youngsters.

Held at the new Wembley Stadium in London, sixty-two thousand people attended the concert, which was shown on television in one hundred forty countries and watched on one hundred fifty million screens. We saw a whole host of stars, including Sir Andrew Lloyd Webber who wrote a special music medley, Sarah Brightman, Elton John, Bryan Ferry and Nellie Furtado.

Princess Diana was very keen on all kinds of music and she particularly loved ballet. In this concert, which lasted over six hours, there were mostly 'pop' groups with the crowd clapping and waving their arms about while thoroughly enjoying themselves and why not! Being happy in this way with such incredible togetherness is very good indeed.

In the middle of the concert, there was a ballet sequence by the English National Ballet, which gave a magical performance. Apparently, Princess Diana's favourite ballet was *Swan Lake,* composed by that genius Tchaikovsky whom I have already spoken about at length.

What amazed me was the complete silence while the ballet was performing accompanied by a large orchestra!

For those few magical moments, the whole crowd in that massive stadium appeared mesmerized. At the end of this marvellous performance, there were just a few seconds silence as if the whole audience were holding their breath before incredible applause broke and rippled around the stadium that went on for what seemed a very long time. It was almost as if many in the crowd had never seen a ballet before or perhaps had never even thought about ballet and it was a great moment to see the audience so captivated. I was very surprised at this ovation and it made me feel very happy. If everyone who was watching that big event on TV in so many different countries throughout the world thought the same, I'm even happier.

Princess Diana had a heart of gold; there was something very special about her and her overwhelming presence, which people from all over the world felt. She loved people from all walks of life, rich or poor, and it seemed most people you speak to or know, including Peps and myself, loved Princess Diana. Many demonstrated this by leaving millions upon millions of flowers, candles and gifts at Kensington Gardens after the tragic car accident in Paris took her life. The thousands of tears shed at the time and perhaps still, are for the loss of someone who made such a large impact on everyday people's lives.

Princess Diana had a sparkling personality and everything that goes with it and there are not many of us blessed with such gifts. She was indeed and always will be, for many around the world, an icon!

I composed a piece in memory of Princess Diana not long after she died, which has been broadcast a number of times. I called it *Portrait of Diana* and after this concert, I looked for a copy of that piece and luckily eventually found it. I would like to think the recording and performance of my orchestra on that piece proves she never really changed, although she had gone through very hard times. The sereneness of my tribute to this lovely lady shines through like the brightest of stars she was in her life.

I have recently thought about recording my *Portrait of Diana* composition for all to hear. I spoke to Philip Lane, who said he would certainly include my *Portrait of Diana* in a session to be recorded in London in January 2008 with the Royal Ballet Sinphonia and conducted by Gavin Sutherland. I have reorchestrated this regal piece and by the time my memoirs are published, you'll be able to purchase it on a commercial CD.

My gratitude along with millions of others in the world goes to her two sons, Prince William and Prince Harry, for organizing this very special, successful concert in loving memory of their mother, who will never be forgotten.

Many today believe we don't need a Monarchy and it costs the country too much money. However, it's important to remember the Royal Family really does keep the United Kingdom together and they bring in millions of pounds to this country through tourism. Peps tells me the British don't really appreciate what it means to have a Monarchy and if we lived outside the United Kingdom, we would understand how the Royal Family unites this country with the rest of the world. Also, because of the Royal Family, the United Kingdom is perceived as a force to be reckoned with and other countries that don't have a Royal Family believe we are really rather privileged. Peps says because we take the Royal Family for granted, we don't realize just how precious they are to the well-being of Britain, with the Queen being seen as an important figurehead and the 'Mother' of our country. When the Royal Family visits abroad, there is generally much excitement, with their presence helping other countries feel as if they belong. In December 2007, at the age of 81 years, Queen Elizabeth became the oldest reigning British Monarch and is the third longest reigning Monarch in over twelve hundred years of British history. There is no doubt that Her Majesty has worked tirelessly for her country.

In 2007, an ITV programme was broadcast called *The Queen, 60 years of Marriage* and my arrangement of 'Pomp and Circumstance,' by Elgar was played during the programme which was a lovely surprise for me!

60
Friends and Artists

I have two friends who have a most unusual name. It is Mr. and Mrs. Cakebread! Ann and Philip Cakebread are always around when little things need doing such as feeding the dogs while we are out, or how to work out certain things on the Internet. They live in a very cosy detached bungalow a short distance away and it is so nice to know that they are 'just round the corner!'

Another good friend is Mike Samson (a.k.a. Sam), who teaches at the Priory School in Banstead. He is a very good punster and makes you laugh! He fiddles his way around and plays the fiddle for a local band called the Rampant Roosters, who play at barn dances in local villages, and plays in the second fiddles for the Epsom Symphony Orchestra. He even writes his own melodies, which he usually names after the pubs where he plays.

Sam acted a short while ago in *Fiddler on the Roof* in a small local hall in a village close to Banstead called Woodmansterne. He grew a black beard for this musical and what a wonderful beard it was! In fact, it was the best beard I have ever seen in my life and apparently while he was growing it, his pupils were greatly amused!

I must mention Dr. Rafi, who has been my doctor for many years now. He has so much patience, especially for people like me who think we are more ill than we really are! He also is a really likeable fellow and when I last visited him, he mentioned his son was learning to play the violin. I suggested his son might like to get in touch with me as I hoped my own experiences would help persuade him to stick at it and practise regularly. Good violinists are very rare, as are good doctors.

I'd like to say a few words about a fantastic musician and well-known radio and television presenter, Brian Kay, who used to be the leader in *The King's Singers*. *The King's Singers* is an a cappella choral ensemble, which took its name from King's College Cambridge in 1964 where Brian and two other founding members were choral scholars. Today, it remains one of the world's most popular vocal groups. Brian had two very good programmes on BBC Radio 3, which were axed early in 2006. He has played many of my light classical compositions including *Love of Joy* on the programmes he used to present and he certainly always seemed to promote my music whenever possible. He has a terrific personality and conducts all over the world, including Salzburg, Prague, Venice, New Zealand and China. A nicer man you couldn't possibly wish to meet.

Brian is also in charge of the annual *Vaughan Williams Leith Hill Musical Festivals,* of which I have already spoken, for the local choirs such as Leatherhead, Shere and Dorking and I have often had the pleasure of attending these concerts. It is always a 'shere' delight and what a pleasure it is to see this tall man conducting an orchestra, without a baton and sometimes a 250 or more piece choir singing together on a Saturday night.

In 2007, these choirs sang together in *Handel's Messiah* on a Sunday evening in the Dorking Halls. To conduct these massive works from the great masters needs some doing, but Brian does it so well he makes it look very easy! I have a lot of experience myself conducting choirs (not as large as Brian's mind you!) especially a cappella. It is such a wonderful feeling just using hand movements and eye contact to engage the choir to sing exactly as you want them to, without a baton. It is heavenly for me to conduct a choir especially if you '*re-choir*' it! Brian Kay and his lovely wife, Gillie, are both 'o-Kay' by me! Strange how I feel in a 'punny' mood!

Peps has many friends from Zimbabwe, whom I like very much. However, I especially like her three daughters, Pamela, Nyasha and Beverley, who are such lovely and personable people. Something has got to happen soon for that country which is in a bad state at the time of writing. The mighty Victoria Falls is one of the few wonders of the world and I feel God must give this country something to live for and it is indeed a 'sad occasion' in my book. Please pray for better things for this jewel in muddied waters.

Alan Hartwell, who played with me at the Grand Hotel, and his wife, Eileen, who is an extremely lively lady, live close by in Ashstead, where they have been in the same house for over fifty years. I have known Alan since our college days. We have always got on well and in addition to being a fine teacher, he is a pianist and plays on many wind instruments including saxophones. Age is creeping on us both, but we still partake in many areas of our profession. We are both good punsters, and seem to have the same sense of humour. It seems I've known them both all my life and we have never in all these years had a cross word!

David Ades and his wife, Moira, are a dear couple and you may recall he wrote the article about Joy after she died in the magazine *Journey into Melody*. He has been editor of the Robert Farnon Society magazine, for the last fifty years! This club has members from all over the world and many of them travel long distances to come to the regular meetings. The charm and personality of Moira and David, I cannot easily put into words. Perhaps David could play one of my very emotional compositions from *Heartstrings,* called 'Let's Dream of Tomorrow' to sum it up. Music can often express feelings sometimes better than words.

Maureen, my cousin on the Fox side, lives in Guildford and because she is a great friend of mine, she is not just a cousin but also someone rather special who has always been very keen on listening to my music. Maureen is kind and serene with such a charming personality and on top of all that, very good looking for her age! She has lived on her own for a number of years since her husband, David, died very suddenly, yet she still manages to remain very cheerful.

I must mention another couple of friends, Peter Taylor and Alice, his wife, who came to our wedding from Calafell, Northern Spain. When Peps and I went there for a holiday, the four of us visited a popular restaurant where the owner is an Italian called Giorgio and a famous television chef in Spain. When he heard from Peter and Alice I was 'John Fox the composer and arranger' he got very excited and he treated us like royalty.

Many photographs were taken and many of the customers asked me for an autograph. The four of us enjoyed many companionable hours together, hardly pausing for breath as we talked away the hours! Peter is a courageous man and has gone through a lot of pain and surgery after breaking his thigh-bone when a car knocked him down while he was out walking. He reminds me of Hugh's determination, which I wrote of earlier and Peter wrote a lovely article for the Robert Farnon Society magazine about my marriage to Peps.

Phil Stout works for an 'easy listening' radio station in New York City called *Music Choice,* which plays many of my musical arrangements. He has been a friend of mine for many years and is a member of the RFS. I was amazed when he first told me about the new technology where photos of me conducting an orchestra come up on a television screen when my music is played on the radio, through the television. It also contains information about my life as an arranger and composer. Seeing is believing; or is it believing is seeing? He also told me his station has millions of listeners and is very high on the New York radio ratings coming in at third place.

That is good news, isn't it, for listeners who love good melodies and plenty of strings? When are we going to have such a Radio Station in England? Soon I hope!

I'd like to talk about Alan Bunting who lives in Sterling, Scotland. He worked for the BBC as head sound engineer for BBC Television and Radio in Scotland. Since his retirement some years ago, he works on audio restoration, which in other words means making the old LPs from the twenties up to the sixties sound better (which must be quite a difficult task) and restoring them so they sound as good as the standard of the present CDs. He has worked on some of my old LPs, making them sound so very much better without the 'hissing' and 'scratching' noises.

Although we have never met, Alan and I have had many interesting conversations on the phone. Nevertheless, I refer to him as a friend of mine because we have so much in common and because he tells me he enjoys my style of arranging and composing; he particularly loves making my music sound better on these old LPs and he does just that!

My cousin, once removed, Tony Slaymaker and his wife, Joyce, also live in Banstead in a lovely house called 'Red Gables' and they are both keen followers of my career. Tony and I have wonderful chats over one or two glasses of good wine when he pops in to see us sometimes. At the time my A *Surrey Rhapsody* was recorded at the Angel Studios in London, Tony and I met outside those studios at exactly the same time walking from totally opposite directions! I was late because I had lost my way coupled with the fact the taxi driver didn't seem to know the way either. Isn't that odd? Just a pure coincidence and quite bizarre!

His late father, Tom (my cousin) could play the piano very well. In his teens at parties, everyone would sit round the piano and sing while he would bang so hard on the keys that if he played for a few hours, his fingers would begin to bleed and my mother would have to wash the piano keys after they left. Tony and Joyce also have an apartment in Portugal and spend a lot of time there so we don't see them so often now.

While writing these memoirs, my latest composition, *A Surrey Rhapsody,* was recorded on a CD called the *British Light Music Premieres Vol. 4.* Adam Saunders is also included on the CD, with his overture *Pirates Ahoy!*, which is superb! I'm very impressed by the colourful sleeve of the CD, which is a poster of Bexhill on Sea by Ronald Lanpitt. I'm personally very pleased with my *A Surrey Rhapsody,* as I've tried to capture the different parts of this popular county in England where I was proud to be born.

I have already spoken about Marlin and Alicia Taylor. Marlin runs the easy listening digital radio station in Washington, D.C. called *Escape,* a good title for music to get away from all the hustle and bustle of everyday life. They have both been great friends of mine over many years and Marlin plays quite a number of my musical arrangements every day, including the Gershwin album I wrote in 1972. Americans certainly seem to like listening to this kind of music.

Alicia is a soprano singer and what a voice she has! Some years ago, she sang at the famous Carnegie Hall. Long live Marlin and Alicia!

Now there is a man who lives in New Jersey who also runs an easy listening radio station. He was an invalid in his younger years and he could only get about in a wheelchair. I'm telling you this true story because it proves that music can heal! The young man in question is 33-year-old Ryan James Granito.

When he was very young, he was bedridden and spent most of his time listening to music. He wrote to me a few times telling me he swears it was my music that helped to heal him. He listened to it the whole time and over the years, he became well enough to walk and now enjoys life to the full. What a joy it is to hear a story such as this one, knowing the heart and soul I have put into my music has not only brought so much joy into someone's life, it was also instrumental in his recovery.

I most definitely think beautiful music can help those in discomfort or need, as I'm aware certain faith healers use my gentle music to play in the background whilst patients are being healed. Music does heal, I'm positive of that and if you have the chance to listen to my latest composition, *A Surrey Rhapsody,* you will know it contains some healing music that almost has a 'spiritual' air to it. When I was composing it, I had the Harry Edwards Sanctuary at Burrows Lea in Shere, Surrey in mind, where in the past I have often gone when suffering from headaches or backaches.

During the autumn of 2007, a CD was released called *British Light Music Premieres,* which I have spoken of briefly and *A Surrey Rhapsody* is track number six on the album which includes other British composer's music such as Ernest Tomlinson's suite *Aladdin.*

I'd like to mention a gentleman friend of mine called David Shore OBE, who lived in Banstead and who sadly, recently passed away. He was certainly a gentleman of the highest order. We used to regularly walk round the field at the bottom of my garden with our Border collie dogs and talk about everything including how to set the world right!

David and I both threw Frisbees to see which one of our lovely collies jumped the highest. He was awarded the OBE in recognition of his services to engineering. He will be sorely missed, I am sure, by his family, especially his charming wife, Pam, and friends. David and Pam were very much part of the local community, attending the church service at All Saints, and they were often at the parties or special occasions we held at Coniston.

When his dog died a few years ago, I suggested he buy another collie but he told me that he was too old. David was four years younger than me and I shall never forget those lovely walks and talks we had in all weather together.

Two more friends of mine who live in Paris also spring to mind. They are Brian Allgar and his charming Parisian wife, Françoise. Brian is a cousin of painter Peter Atkin's wife, Pam, and he studied at Oxford University, having quite a lot to do with computer programming in the very early days. However, he is also an extremely keen musician who creates fine compositions at the computer.

One year, Françoise, who enjoys singing, bought Brian a white grand piano for his birthday, which looks striking in their luxury apartment. I am happy to say I have played on that piano on my visits and it is a beauty! The atmosphere in the apartment is stunning and music is a great part of their lives. I have composed a piece called 'Françoise' especially for this charming Parisian lady. It is quite a short piece and can be found on my chamber ensemble CD titled *Interludes.* On Francoise's fiftieth birthday, as a surprise, Brian bought her a lovely white, long-haired dog called Clotis, after one of the ancient Egyptian kings.

I like to mention another friend, Rosemary Tames, whose late husband was the Rev. Kenneth Tames. Rosemary 'puns' a lot and she was a soprano singer. We joke together and she tells me off for not ringing her! Throughout this book, I have mentioned Gerhard Narholz and Heidi from Germany quite a number of times, so that friendship goes without saying.

61

Wishes and Hopes

It seems times change too quickly when you reach a certain age, and I personally dislike the phrases: 'Keep up with the times!'—'You are too old fashioned'—'You have to live in today's world'—'Move On'—'change!...change!...change!...change!' I admit some change is for the better, but at times I believe change is made for the sake of change, without improving people's quality of lives. Look what happened when British Airways decided to change their livery colours. Nobody wanted this change, yet they insisted they knew better than their customers. After spending millions of pounds, a couple of years later the colours were changed back to the Union Jack.

Another recent example is when the Post Office and Royal Mail changed its name to Consignia! Well that didn't last long either, after once again spending millions of pounds (this time taxpayers' money, too!) it went back to its old name. These two examples are change for the sake of change, because both these brands had been around for a long time and probably some young executive wanted to make his or her mark on the world by proving these existing brands belonged in the past. How wrong they were!

Greed drives so much of the world today, with people in our society borrowing more and more money to buy luxury items and goods that many cannot really afford. Sadly, the lure of 'status' drives people to keep buying at whatever cost to themselves. The old songs 'Money is the Root of all Evil' and 'Money! Money! Money!,' in my humble opinion, say it all: 'Money is the *route* to all evil.'

There are so many things money cannot buy such as health, love (yes, The Beatles were right!), peace, grace and natural beauty that is all around us if only we took more time to 'see.' Yet, most of the world seems to pursue ugliness whether it's general behaviour or the pursuit of material wealth. Yes, we squander our lives in work environments where we neither enjoy, respect, or even like our fellow colleagues, yet are hell bent on buying the next bigger and better car or house. Humanity is convinced it needs that large cheque at the end of the month. We only have one life; why sacrifice it? I know it's easy for someone to look back on their life and see wishes and regrets; however, if you can be determined enough, you, too, can follow your dreams and do something you love that brings pleasure not just to you, but maybe to many others, maybe millions of others. My advice is: go for it!

These next sentences are all about my own personal wishes and I list them here because I would like to think in the years to come as readers reach this page, they will be inspired by my wishes and hopes when facing life's difficulties:

Wishes

I wish Joy and I had had that child, who would have been a boy of twenty-six years old by now.

I wish I hadn't been so nasty to my eldest sister Lee, before her sudden death.

I wish an Englishman or woman or both would become a champion tennis player at Wimbledon.

I wish I had travelled the world, instead of relying on television to see it.

I wish I hadn't been a spoiled brat, expecting everyone to do things for me.

I wish the world would become a better place, especially for those who suffer.

I wish Light Easy Listening Music would return to our airways and improve the culture in our country.

I wish the underprivileged countries would bear more fruit.

I wish I hadn't broken so many hearts.

I wish my dogs would live forever—Jamie and Sophie.

I wish Peps' people in Zimbabwe could enjoy leading better lives.

I wish I didn't flair up to those I love.

I wish there weren't so many cars in this world polluting the environment.

I wish the very rich would stop wanting more and more.

I wish I didn't have false teeth.

I wish I had more hair on my head—but then, hair doesn't grow on a busy street.

I wish the hymn 'Jerusalem' was an English national anthem.

My last wish: '*When you wish upon a star, your dreams all come true.*'

Hopes

I hope for peace between all nations in this world of ours.

I hope for better things to come for everyone.

I hope I meet all the ones I love—and there are many—in spirit, in the next world.

I hope I get good royalties this year.

I hope I'm spared a few more years to compose more music.

I hope light classical music will become very popular again, to satisfy those who love it.

I hope the ones that I've hurt will forgive me.

I hope composers in the future are as keen and dedicated as I have been throughout my musical career and work extremely hard to reach their goals.

My last hope: that my music will inspire the talented musicians of tomorrow and give listeners in the future much pleasure and that my music will last forever.

62

Is Light Music Going into Oblivion?

In January 2007, the BBC axed its last Light Music programme. It was Brian Kay's weekly programme on Radio 3, and how sad I feel the BBC and other stations do not believe there is enough demand for this genre of music today. I appreciate that audiences have dwindled over the years, yet there are still many who love and enjoy light melodic music and it's a real pity we can no longer hear this on our radios.

The many fans and followers will become even fewer in years to come if the radio stations do not make this genre available, and I believe commercialism is killing off light music. However, I was thrilled in early summer of 2008, to hear my *Countryside Suite* in four movements, being played on Classic FM in an evening programme called *Full Works*. So not all is lost!

Light music originally developed from the seaside orchestras in the late nineteenth century becoming more popular and widely known after World War I. With the launch of the BBC broadcasting services in the early 1930s and its BBC Light Programme, it is generally accepted light music's heyday was probably from the early thirties until the mid-sixties.

Not so long ago, how pleased I was to learn a traditional seaside orchestra still exists in Scarborough! Also, as I briefly mentioned in an earlier chapter, there are a number of individuals who are working very hard to keep this music alive by promoting its charm, quality and craftsmanship to audiences who might otherwise dismiss it.

How wonderful it would be if we were once more given the choice of listening to this kind of music on our radio stations instead of having to listen to stations that just blast out the same 'sounds' in their efforts to appeal to the mass market. We certainly have no shortage of pop radio stations in the United Kingdom with BBC Radio 3 and Classic FM playing mainly classical music; because this is a subject so close to my heart, I feel deeply about this situation and I know there are many of all ages who share the same views. Melody has always come first, in my humble opinion, and I pray this kind of beautiful music, which is often regarded as 'old fashioned,' will one day come back into fashion.

Recently, there were two BBC Prom Concerts on television from the Albert Hall in London. One was about films with the BBC Concert Orchestra conducted by John Wilson, which included Gavin Sutherland's excellent arrangements of *Carry On* comedy film scores. The second concert featured Britain's foremost musical star, Michael Ball, who is currently in a leading role in the London stage musical *Hairspray*. He sang about the *Music Theatre* with songs from Sir Andrew Lloyd Webber's *Cats, Sunset Boulevard, Phantom of the Opera* and Leonard Bernstein's *West Side Story*. He was fantastic. The whole event was quite thrilling and many thousands of people throughout the world must have heard and seen it. How wonderful it was to see this famous hall with a full house and a standing ovation for the music played that evening.

I feel there must be a demand for light music if those two marvellous concerts came about at the Proms in London of all places. Could it possibly be there are many more fans out there than commercial radio stations lead us to believe? Are they afraid or perhaps too lazy to demand to have this music back in our country again? In my opinion, it is essential this melodic style of music reach our shores once more.

Along with other musical talents, we are trying very hard to keep this type of music heard, but it will take many thousands of listeners and lovers of this music to convince the radio stations how very important it is to them. I can never forget that in the early days, the BBC nurtured my musical talent, for which I am truly proud and forever grateful. It was through the BBC that many countries throughout the world heard my music, but sadly, the BBC no longer believes there is enough of a market for this type of music today.

63

Fond Memories of the Past

Have you ever had a surprise that leaves you completely astounded? In December 2007, after having had our annual flu jab, Peps and I thought we would pop in and have a late lunch at a local pub called The Woolpack in Banstead Village. A few months ago, this pub hardly had any customers at all so when we arrived at about 2:00 p.m., we were very surprised to see the place almost packed to capacity, with a large number of people as happy as sandboys at the end of the large saloon bar enjoying a drink or two. There was a six-piece jazz group preparing to play, which consisted of trumpet, trombone, sax (doubling clarinet), piano, bass and drums.

To my utter astonishment, I recognised Rex Bennett, who I used a lot in the John Fox Orchestra years and years ago. He is a wonderful all-round drummer who is eighty-six years of age and still playing those drums as if he was half that age! Also a great bass player, Mick Durell (you may recall in my earlier chapters, I mentioned his ability to produce flatulence in B-flat at the Grand Hotel!) who must be in his late seventies now, and what a character. The trumpet player, Ronnie Hughes, also played for me in my orchestra on a number of occasions. He was lead trumpet for Jack Parnell (Sunday Night at the London Palladium's musical director) in the 1970s and 1980s. Ronnie is a very busy session player who apparently plays in a local Banstead church on Sundays. Despite the fact these wonderful musicians have been working in the Surrey area since we went our separate ways, I have not laid eyes on any of them for over twenty-five years!

What a lovely afternoon we had going down memory lane, talking about the old times of course and what a great pleasure it was to hear them still playing so brilliantly in their seventies and eighties and I immediately called us 'The Boys of the Old Brigade!' Of course, we are not in any way old because we are still very young at heart and in music. I do believe we might all make centenarians, complete with the Queen's Telegraph (or whatever they call it these days!). Who knows?

64

The Sad Death of Judy

It is with great sadness, my dear sister Judy passed away, just months before I completed my autobiography. In 2001, she suffered from a stroke while living at home on her own. Her neighbour, Edna, noticed something was wrong in the morning when she saw Judy's car hadn't moved, because she knew as regular as clockwork she went out every morning to do a little shopping. Knocking loudly on the door, she couldn't get a reply and called the police who had to break in. They found Judy slumped in her armchair with the television still blaring away.

Joy and I had just put our dogs, Jamie and Sophie, in the car to go for a walk when the phone rang. It was Edna telling us the bad news. By the time we reached Judy's house, the ambulance had arrived and the medics were trying to revive her as they could still hear a faint heartbeat.

Joy went with Judy in the ambulance to Epsom Hospital and I followed in the car with our two dogs still in the back. We waited while doctors and assistants rushed about in the emergency ward. One of the specialists came to see us and said, "I'm afraid I have some bad news; your sister has had a very serious stroke and part of her brain on the left side has been damaged." He also told us she had probably been in that chair all night as he estimated she had had the stroke early evening.

The news completely shook me as I had always thought Judy was as strong as an ox. The doctor also warned us she may not be the same mentally when she came round and would probably have some physical impairment, too. Joy remained at the hospital all day while I took our dogs home and when I returned, Judy had regained consciousness. When she saw me, she immediately said, "Hello Jack."

She had lost most of the use of her legs and she wasn't so bright mentally, but other than that, she was still my same old Judy. As she gradually became better, she was able to get about with the help of crutches; however she never went home again. Judy was in hospital for about a week and then she was transferred to Parkside Nursing Home, which is situated just a short distance from Coniston, where, despite her illness, within a week, she was taking centre stage with the other residents!

We had to sell her house, which she had always been so proud of, and sort out her affairs. As the months passed, she began to deteriorate slowly until finally she could not get about without a wheelchair, while mentally she began to live more and more in a fairytale world. She would talk about going to see Mum and Dad along with many other incidents that happened years before.

We often took our two dogs, Jamie and Sophie, to see her and she would burst into a little ditty—*Have you seen such a good dog Lou? Tell me if you can!*—which we had put together some years before. Judy wrote the words, I put some music to them and we called it simply *Playful Pets*.

Judy celebrated her eighty-seventh birthday in her sixth year at Parkside, and the home had arranged for a keyboard entertainer to be there, while I also played a few of our favourite songs on my old piano, which I had given to the Home. Judy and her fellow residents had a wonderful time laughing, singing and clapping, with Judy still the life and soul of the party.

It was great to witness, particularly as Judy was so special to me. She had not only been a wonderful sister, but also a dear, dear friend, and I know I would not have gotten so far in my music career if it hadn't been for Judy's determination to help establish recognition for my talent in those early years.

On 19 September 2007, Parkside called us with an urgent message that Judy had suffered another stroke. Although barely conscious, Judy immediately began to sing our *Playful Pets* ditty in a very weak voice when she saw me. She was ill for about three days, then one late afternoon I knew her time on this earth was coming to an end. I sat by her side holding her hand, with Peps, who had looked after her and had become so very fond of her, sitting close by, too. As I talked to her about the lovely times we had shared in the 'good old days,' she would raise her eyebrows as she attempted to open her eyes, while mimicking the sound of our song with her left hand.

Finally, I told her how much I loved her and whispering many cherished words in her ear, squeezed her hand tightly for the last time, then Peps and I walked away. When I reached the door, I turned to look back and the nurse said, "Look John, she's waving to you." There she was actually waving goodbye to me with a strong wave using her left hand, as her right arm was paralyzed. I waved back, but this sight completely astounded me because she was so weak. It was as if she knew this was goodbye and she was using every last ounce of her strength to let me know she was on her way to Heaven.

We held my Judy's funeral at Randall's Park Leatherhead at 12.30 p.m. on 2 October 2007. Rev. David Chance read the Order of Service with the entry music a special composition of mine called 'Kiss Away Each Tear,' which seemed so right for this sad occasion. During the time Joy was very ill, I wrote a solo cello piece for her called 'In Memory' and I decided it was very fitting for Judy, too. A gifted cellist called Jonathan Williams played it beautifully, which certainly added something rather special to the service. I stood up and spoke about our childhood days, how close we had always been, and especially how instrumental Judy had been in launching my career.

During the committal as the curtains closed, the whole congregation sang 'Jerusalem' loudly, and to close the service I had chosen a recording of Judy's favourite song, 'Over the Rainbow,' sung by Judy Garland. If you remember, she had changed her name from Lucy to Judy many years previously, after her idol.

After the service, the mourners gathered round to look at the various wreaths and read the messages. It was very touching, especially when several people commented on our wreath with 'Judy' written across it. Then Peps, my old friend Bill and I each held a white dove. First I let mine go, then Peps, followed by Bill. The doves flew off, one in front of the other before circling four or five times round our heads and flying away.

It was a touching sight and I was so glad I had decided to organize it in memory of my amazing experience with Joy, when three white doves appeared at her window. It was indeed a spiritual end to Judy's departure from this world and for myself, I felt I could almost see her waving another goodbye to me just as she did on the day she left us. My sister Judy will always live on in my heart, just as I know she will live on in many other hearts of family and friends who came to know and love her over the years.

65
Carol Fantasia with a Mishap

In November 2007, the Oxford University Press contacted me and asked if I was interested in writing a *Carol Fantasia*. Philip Lane had put my name forward as he remembered I had written a *Christmas Fantasia* many years before, in the late seventies for the BBC. In fact, this *Christmas Fantasia* was once played two years running in a programme just before the Queen's Christmas Day Speech, on BBC Radio 2. It was wonderful to receive this commission and I of course accepted, particularly as there is a great shortage of Christmas music for orchestras.

Oxford University Press gave me about three weeks to write this large work and once they had printed all the parts for orchestra, they sent me a beautifully bound copy of the score containing forty-seven pages. I was rather amused and flattered to see just my surname 'Fox' on the cover and decided they obviously thought I belonged to the famous league of composers who are only referred to by surname, such as Beethoven and Mozart!

This *Carol Fantasia* was played over Christmas by the popular Bournemouth Symphony Orchestra and performed at six different venues along the south coast with the first concert being held on 13 December at the Guildhall in Portsmouth. Gavin Sutherland conducted and played his role as he joked about with the seasonal sing-a-longs, which he does very well. Like many composers, he can be very funny!

It was Ron Goodwin who used to conduct these very happy popular Christmas concerts, until he died a few years ago. I do hope many orchestras will send for my score and the parts to play my *Carol Fantasia,* because I wrote the work not just for professional orchestras, but also amateur and school orchestras. While I was working on it, I thought hard about this type of music that is only played once a year, meaning there isn't generally much time for lots of rehearsals. Bearing this in mind, I made sure it was a score that wasn't too difficult and one which anyone at different levels would enjoy playing.

Peps and I drove to Portsmouth to hear the concert and after the orchestra played my *Carol Fantasia,* Gavin turned to the audience and said, "That's a selection written by my friend John Fox who is an icon and a living legend and I believe he is here in the audience, only I can't see him." A spotlight went round the auditorium, but they couldn't find me, even though we were in the best seats at the front of the circle. In the end, I called out, "Here I am!" It was a packed audience and everyone turned to look at me and clapped very loudly. What a proud moment it was!

This Christmas programme included many popular songs and a piece by Philip Lane called 'The Night before Christmas' with a narrator speaking the words. This piece is a sheer delight and it is available on CD, narrated so well by Stephen Fry, on the Naxos label and recorded in 2006. Philip was there, too, and after the concert we met for drinks along with Gavin and a few other musicians who used to play in my orchestra many years ago, including Andrew Vintner on piano and Harold Fisher on the drums. Those were the days! What an enjoyable and jolly evening we had!

Feeling very happy by the success of the evening, Peps and I set off for the drive home. Not far out of Portsmouth, we came across some road works and I think the road signs had been covered up by the traffic queue, buses, lorries, vans and many cars. Guess what? We took the wrong road. If you have ever taken the wrong road on a motorway, especially late at night, you will know how we were feeling. It was dark and very frightening not knowing where we were going.

After many miles, we saw some signs saying six miles to Southampton! Who on earth wants to go to Southampton when you live in Surrey? It was a nightmare; we both felt a little panicky and our tempers were becoming frayed, too. Peps thought it might be a good idea if she drove, but I insisted on carrying on and we were both praying to see a sign that would at least tell us we were heading in the right direction. After going about seventy miles out of our way, we finally saw a sign for London, which we almost missed, too. It was only because we noticed the signs for the M25 that we saw it at the last moment!

Exhausted, we eventually arrived home in Banstead, well after 2:00 a.m., greeted by our two dogs, Jamie and Sophie, who were very pleased to see us after such a long time. They barked our welcome loud and clear, which probably woke the whole neighbourhood! What an ordeal! But we did enjoy *Carol Fantasia* very much and judging by the applause from the audience they did, too. I would like to think it will be performed at Christmas all over the world for many years to come.

66

Peps, the Zimbabwean Crisis and the Archbishop of Canterbury

Two of Perpetua's granddaughters, Bronte, who is twelve years old, and Tarenda, who is eleven, flew over from Sydney, Australia, to spend Christmas 2007 and the New Year with us. We had a great time together because they are such fun-loving, intelligent children who brought much laughter and merriment into our house. They played endlessly with our dogs, Sophie and Jamie, while Bronte even typed at tremendous speed, the last couple of chapters in this autobiography of mine. Now, isn't that something?

They were particularly fascinated with the fact I was a real composer and before they returned to Australia, I wrote the words and music to a little song called 'Bronte and Tarenda' in their honour. A local very talented singer, called Milly Saunders, sang the words with great tenderness, while I accompanied her on the piano and my good friend, David Frost, kindly recorded it on his own equipment. He brought it over to Coniston for me, so the girls could take the song back home on a tape and tell everyone a famous composer in England had written it for them!

A few days before the girls left for their home in Sydney, David drove us to the Angel Recording Studios in Islington to attend a recording session of the Royal Ballet Sinfonia playing my recent composition, 'Portrait of Diana.' Gavin Sutherland conducted this piece and the magical sounds that came floating through the studios completely overwhelmed both Bronte and Tarenda.

On the way back to Banstead, David took a special route home to show the girls the highlights of London's famous floodlit landmarks including the London Eye and Trafalgar Square. When the time came for Bronte and Tarenda to go home, how terribly sad we were when we had to say our goodbyes, hugging, kissing and crying all at once. For a long while afterwards, we missed their happy presence in the house very much. I shall never forget how special those two months spent with Bronte and Tarenda were, and how very fond we both became of them. I am in my eighties now, so perhaps I may never see them again in this world, but they certainly left a lasting impression on me.

Although what comes next has very little to do with my musical career, I feel it's important to include it because it might help the world to remember what troubles the underprivileged countries are going through. My wife, Peps, recently returned to her home country in Zimbabwe and she saw first-hand what is happening there.

As soon as the plane touched down at Harare, the first big change struck her. The tarmac was deserted apart from one airplane belonging to the South African airline Com Air and when she was last there in 2002, the airport was a beehive of activity with many tourists on their way to popular destinations such as Victoria Falls and Wange Safari. The airport building was completely deserted, apart from the passengers on her flight.

The roads were full of potholes and quiet as most petrol stations were closed because the country is short of petrol. Apparently, every day the electricity and water supply is cut off during the evenings. There were large groups of unemployed young people hanging about or walking about the city, trying to exchange money for U.S. dollars or English pounds. Schools are not functioning because the teachers are on strike and many have been beaten, because they are blamed for encouraging people to vote for the opposition.

Banks are open but the currency has devalued so much that if you are lucky enough to see a loaf of bread for sale, it would cost over a million Zimbabwean dollars. The phone lines have been down for months while in some areas there isn't even a mobile phone signal.

There is hardly any food to eat apart from sweet potatoes, with most of the shelves in the supermarkets empty and clothes shops open, but with little custom. There is no milk, bread, flour or potatoes. It's hard to imagine that such fundamental foodstuffs are unavailable. During her stay, Peps saw one person with a loaf of bread, which he was trying to hide behind his jacket. There is only maize available with vegetables from private gardens. Sometimes there is flour, although this too can only be bought through word of mouth. People are lucky to have one main meal a day and supper is a luxury.

Water from the tap has to be boiled and tea isn't available unless you cross the border to South Africa and then it's this brown liquid without milk or sugar. One weekend, Peps arranged for the whole family to meet at her sister's house when she saw potatoes for the one and only time during her visit. Her son-in-law had bought them and they were very, very expensive. Peps' brother, Edward, who flew to the United Kingdom for our wedding, is better off because he is self-sufficient. He has a vegetable patch and he uses open fires and lamps fuelled by solar power. Nevertheless, he is danger living in the rural areas and his family advised him to join them in Harare for a while.

Peps' journey to Zimbabwe was to sort out her large property, which is situated in a suburb close to Harare, because her daughter, Nyasha, and her husband, Gutsi, who have been looking after it, are leaving to work in South Africa near Cape Town where they can live more comfortably and buy food for the family. Beverley, her youngest charming daughter, also made the journey back to Cape Town University to complete her degree very soon after Nyasha left. We are both looking forward so much to the time when she returns to stay here as we have missed her very much. When Peps left her country, she was very sad thinking of her family and what they may have to face in the future.

I have great admiration for Peps and think she was very brave to travel on her own to Zimbabwe at such political and troubled times. I was very sorry I wasn't able to go with her; however, we both agreed it was too politically unstable. It was a great worry for me while she was over there, especially when we couldn't even speak over the telephone because the lines weren't working. While she was away, I suffered from a sciatic nerve in my back and down my right leg and could hardly walk, although I obviously didn't suffer in the same way Peps did while she was in her home country.

The whole world knows Mugabe bullied the country into allowing him to win the presidential run-off on 27 June 2008, particularly since Morgan Tsvangirai, the candidate of the Movement for Democratic Change (MDC), withdrew suddenly, after violent intimidation and even death of his supporters. It seems the whole world will do nothing about this desperately sad situation, because it is divided by political, economic, or military agendas. The world is just standing by waiting for the first move from the nearby African states, which themselves appear to be doing nothing to bring this terrible chapter to a close. How I hope and pray for all Zimbabweans' and Peps' sake this regime will bring about a peaceful situation soon.

Just recently, Banstead had a visit by the Archbishop of Canterbury who listened to a choir service one Sunday evening at All Saints Banstead with a congregation from the five different local churches. Our very old church was packed to bursting point and the Archbishop took a wonderful sermon from the Old Testament. After the service, there were refreshments served in the 1906 church hall where the Archbishop went on a walkabout and chatted to everyone, including Perpetua and me. It certainly was another unforgettable experience!

This reminded me that for some time now, I have had the urge to write the music to accompany some of the beautiful words from *Song of Solomon,* in the Old Testament. It would require something rather special and a lot of thought to work out the best way of composing it. I would want to use a very good soprano and tenor singer for the solos and the duets, together with a chamber ensemble and possibly a choir. I hope to begin working on it very soon, so remember to watch out for it!

67

Notes of South Africa

Little did I know that soon after Pepsi returned from Zimbabwe, I would be making a trip of a lifetime with her to South Africa. Approximately eighteen months ago, Gerhard had asked me if I would consider writing some music about South Africa for the Sonoton Library. Over the months, this has constantly been on my mind but I had not done anything about it.

Pepsi's daughter, Beverley, was due to graduate in Social Psychology at Cape Town University in early December 2008 and desperately wanted Pepsi and I to attend. This became increasingly important when it was clear Beverley could not return in the immediate future to this country for a holiday because of the tightening of immigration laws in the United Kingdom. For some weeks, we discussed our options and ultimately Pepsi decided she would go, but not without me! Of course, I have travelled extensively over the years, but these days do not enjoy flying long distances and certainly didn't see myself coping with an eleven-hour flight to South Africa.

Equally, after I was so unwell when Pepsi visited Zimbabwe, she was determined not to leave me behind! We spent a lot of time discussing the pros and cons with friends and family, as I agonised over the decision because I really did feel quite frightened about making such a long journey.

Finally, I decided to take the chance. Encouraged by the thought the trip would help me compose the music Gerhard wanted me to write, I overcame my reservations. We took a first-class evening flight to Cape Town with British Airways, which meant we had beds and could sleep on the overnight flight. The day of the graduation ceremony was beautifully sunny and hot, with well over 300 students waiting to receive their 'cap and gowns.' Most of the students were black with a few white and some from places such as China and Japan. There were students from all walks of life, with ages ranging from early twenties to fifties. I was thrilled to learn there were even a couple of students collecting Degrees in Music.

I felt the atmosphere was different to anything I had ever encountered in the United Kingdom. I think this is because we see it as rather commonplace, whereas in Africa it does mean something rather special and will really make a difference to the individual's life.

We were both very proud of Beverley, knowing how hard she had worked at her studies to achieve high marks for her degree. At the end of the ceremony, Nelson Mandela's wife, Gracia Machel, who is the Chancellor of the University, made a speech full of hope and inspiration. As a child born into poverty who was determined to become educated, she spoke how she hoped the graduated youth of today would help make South Africa a better country. A brass band closed the ceremony with students and visitors mingling as we enjoyed a sumptuous buffet on the university grounds.

On the evening of Beverley's graduation, we took her out to Stellenbosch for a celebration meal. Stellenbosch is the second-oldest European settlement after Cape Town in South Africa. Being the centre of the South African wine industry, it is famous for its vineyards and is often known as the 'city of oaks' because of the large number of oak trees planted by its Dutch founders.

We found a restaurant where seven or eight of us could sit at a round table and the place we found also had a grand piano in it! During the evening, no pianist appeared so encouraged by my family, I obliged by tinkling those ivories! The restaurant wasn't particularly busy but suddenly several people appeared from out of nowhere to listen to my playing. The atmosphere of the place seemed to transform completely and everyone rewarded me with loud applause when I finished my piece.

During our stay, I noticed that quite a number of places, mainly hotels, had grand pianos, but sadly, there didn't appear to be anyone to play them. Of course, my friends and relations often ask me to play if we visit a place where there is no resident pianist. I am always rather touched and very happy to oblige. Unfortunately, modern keyboards appear to have taken over the piano and by pressing different knobs here and there, some people believe they are musically clever but I have only known a very few who actually are very clever with keyboards. Even so, this type of musical talent cannot be compared to playing the piano, which I have mentioned before when talking about my experience with the rock star Ted Nugent.

We stayed at Nyasha and Gutsi (Masimba) Mutsai's elegant home situated in a classy residential area called Somerset West, outside of Cape Town. Approached through automatic gates, it is a white house with a veranda and is full of large rooms looking out onto a pretty garden and swimming pool surrounded by trees.

Gutsi took us by car to many wonderful places including the Cape Point where the Indian Ocean merges with the Atlantic Ocean. What a magnificent sight! The Indian Ocean is very rough, making much of the coastline rocky with lots of coves, although there are some parts of the coastline with lovely beaches and calm seas. Travelling by car in remote places, we hardly saw another vehicle and one day we drove so high up into the mountains, we were above the clouds with mist all around us.

One evening, Gutsi took us to another high mountain so we could marvel at the thousands of twinkling lights of Cape Town and beyond to Table Mountain. It was breathtaking. It is truly difficult to put into words how different it is from England's scenery and coastline. All I can say is, I knew instantly I had never seen anything like it before. It certainly has inspired me musically and from the moment I landed in this wonderful country, I felt the music 'locked' in my mind and I knew instantly there would be nothing 'English' about my South African compositions. My only sad thought is that there is so much security about with properties surrounded by high walls and fences, which is a constant reminder of the violence and poverty in the country.

We went by boat to Roben Island, or Penguin Island as it is sometimes known, where Nelson Mandela was held prisoner for twenty-five years. What a depressing place! Just four miles off the coast of Cape Town, it is rather flat and there appears to be very little vegetation. It once joined the mainland, but at the end of the last ice age, the sea levels flooded the land making it into a small island. During the mid-nineteenth century to the 1930s, it was used as leper colony and animal quarantine station before becoming a maximum security prison, mainly for political prisoners of apartheid, in 1959.

For the last five days of our trip, we flew to Johannesburg and stayed in the very comfortable Garden Court Hotel in Santon City. One day, we were taken on a trip by a South African gentleman in his seventies who was employed by the hotel as a guide. He took us on a tour about thirty miles outside the city into the wild. During the journey, he chatted away, telling us lots of interesting local information including the fact he was once a soldier and fought outside his country. We travelled along little made-up roads only just wide enough for a small car and at one point even left the car to mingle with some of the wildlife.

When we were about 20 miles from Johannesburg, we saw some lion cubs under a tree and our guide said it was okay to approach them, as the lionesses were not about. On reflection, it might have been better to question this. But our guide assured us he knew the best and safest places to see wildlife, so we happily approached the cubs. It really was very exciting! We stood very still and the cubs came tumbling over and even tried to climb up my black walking stick! Pepsi and I managed to touch them, marvelling at their very soft coats. I also managed to stroke a giraffe and zebra, as the guide gave us special food to entice the animals to us. It was some kind of bread and when the giraffe smelt the grain, he leaned down to take it. Immediately, I noticed giraffes eat underneath their tongues. How fascinating is that?

Back in the car, our guide took us deeper into the countryside where we saw five prides of lions, tigers, leopards and hyenas. For me, it was a totally amazing experience and one I shall never forget. We enjoyed Johannesburg but didn't like it quite as much as Cape Town as we felt the atmosphere was very different. It doesn't have the calmer, friendlier feeling of Cape Town and this is probably because there is quite a lot of crime and poverty. The streets were clean but I noticed there were quite a few youths hanging about on street corners, obviously out of work with nothing to do.

Another unforgettable experience was a visit to an enormous gambling 'den' just outside of Johannesburg called Monte Casino. A friend took us and as I have never been in a gambling place before it was quite a revelation! Most amazing of all, it was like a mini-town under this great big enclosed dome that had a blue sky with clouds flitting across it, and at night, the blue sky changed into twinkling stars! It was so convincing that if I hadn't known it was a false sky, I really would have believed it was the real thing! The place was made up of traditional buildings, apparently built by Italians, but which reminded me a little of nineteenth century London during Charles Dickens' era.

Some of the buildings were very large with enormous roulette and gambling tables. Also, I have never seen so many people putting their money into brightly lit gambling machines that seemed to be everywhere!

The return flight home took about ten hours and we were quite comfortable on our beds, but unfortunately, we made the mistake of choosing to go upstairs. On the upper deck, the plane's engines were very loud and our journey home wasn't quite as enjoyable as our outward journey. Nevertheless, how very glad I am that I overcame my initial fears and made this trip. It really was an amazing and colourful experience and I have all the wonderful images of scenery, sights, sounds and wild animals in my head. Now I just can't wait before I take my manuscript, paper, pencil and rubber out once more and begin composing music about this extraordinary voyage to South Africa!

68

Grand Finale

Well this brings me to the end of my story. I do hope my music will continue to bring pleasure to many of you for years to come, and the world will add it to the many favourite lists of composers, arrangers and conductors. During my musical life, there have been great advances in technology, which have changed the way music has been brought to mass audiences. My work belongs to that era where my classical and light compositions, songs and arrangements have given ordinary people who are not 'learned' in music the means to enjoy music at different levels.

It is very difficult to put in words just how sublime music has made my life. I am deeply spiritual and believe strongly in a greater good or 'God.' Not a God who judges us through our misdeeds or sins, but a God who blesses those who have nurtured their talents and used them to make the world a better place.

I am proud my music has so moved audiences they have stood up and applauded me. I am proud the sheer emotion of my music has often reduced audiences to tears. I am proud I have also made them laugh and I am very proud I have laboured night and day to bring hours of pleasure to millions around the world because I have enjoyed every second.

More than anything else, I am proud my music has touched so many people's lives. I was born with a gift and I have lived and breathed that gift every day of my life. There is a famous line in the

1940s movie *Now Voyager* between Bette Davis and Paul Henreid, 'We have the stars; let's not ask for the moon.' Well I believe I have been lucky enough to have had both, and it is a humbling experience indeed to understand this aspect of my life.

Yes, I have my regrets. Everything in life comes at a cost, but ultimately the benefits have far outweighed that cost. My life in music has helped me understand that in the great scheme of things, we are all quite insignificant, but a few, and only a chosen few, are given the means to enlighten other people's lives through art in whatever form that takes.

It matters not that one composer or musician is perhaps more famous than another; it only matters we have played our part and shared our talents, so in the midst of a world beset with poverty, war, cruelty and greed, we can bring humanity to a place where we are surrounded by harmony, beauty and grace.

It is believed that since the beginning of time, music has played a role in the development of man and music is believed to have been around for over 50,000 years. How lucky I feel to be part of the very core of man's existence.

I think this next quote from almost 1,200 years ago says it all, "Without music no discipline can be perfect, nothing can exist without it. For the world itself is composed of the harmony of sounds, and heaven itself moves according to the motion of this harmony." (Hrabanus Maurus, ca. 856).

Why did I write this book? Well for many reasons, including the fact it documents an episode in the important era in the history of music and it also includes a well-chronicled piece of social history. Mostly I wrote it because I want to share my experiences, both good and not so good, with the budding composers and musicians of tomorrow.

I want to share my life so that one day in the future, musicians might chance upon my book and be inspired by my story, which, if you remember, nearly didn't happen as I was almost packed off to a lunatic asylum simply because my passion for music was misunderstood. This is how close the line is in life between greatness and madness. My message to you all is believe in yourselves, trust your intuition and let your music and other forms of art take you to the place where God intended.

So for the very last time, *"If music be the food of love and man—play on—play on—play on—play on—John—forever"!*

John celebrates his 85th birthday at the Ritz Hotel—of all places in the heart of London!

Lightning Source UK Ltd.
Milton Keynes UK
20 April 2010
153066UK00002B/2/P